We're Moving Where?

The life of a
MILITARY
★W★I★F★E★

Jeanette Russell

Jeanette (Shetler) Russell

Published by

GENERAL STORE
GSPH PUBLISHING HOUSE

499 O'Brien Rd., Box 415, Renfrew, Ontario, Canada K7V 4A6
Telephone (613) 432-7697 or 1-800-465-6072

ISBN 1-894263-87-1
Printed and bound in Canada

Design, layout and printing by
Custom Printers of Renfrew Ltd.

©General Store Publishing House
Renfrew, Ontario, Canada

National Library of Canada Cataloguing in Publication

Russell, Jeanette Shetler, 1941-
    We're moving where? : the life of a military wife /
    Jeanette (Shetler) Russell.

ISBN 1-894263-87-1

    1. Russell, Jeanette Shetler, 1941- 2. Air force spouses—Canada—
       Biography.
    3. Canada. Canadian Armed Forces—Military life.
I. Title.

U773.R89 2003   358.4'0092   C2003-905869-7

Table of Contents

Dedication	**4**
Notes from Friends	**5**
Introduction	**7**
Chapter One	**11**
Chapter Two	**13**
Chapter Three	**21**
Chapter Four	**23**
Chapter Five	**36**
Chapter Six	**44**
Chapter Seven	**48**
Chapter Eight	**52**
Chapter Nine	**56**
Chapter Ten	**61**
Chapter Eleven	**64**
Chapter Twelve	**75**
Chapter Thirteen	**85**
Chapter Fourteen	**88**
Chapter Fifteen	**98**
Chapter Sixteen	**113**
Chapter Seventeen	**117**
Chapter Eighteen	**121**
Chapter Nineteen	**123**
Chapter Twenty	**131**
Chapter Twenty-One	**143**
Chapter Twenty-Two	**149**
Chapter Twenty-Three	**158**
Chapter Twenty-Four	**163**
Chapter Twenty-Five	**167**
Chapter Twenty-Six	**177**
Chapter Twenty-Seven	**181**
Chapter Twenty-Eight	**183**
Chapter Twenty-Nine	**185**
About the Author	**188**
Photo Album	**189**

DEDICATION

This book is dedicated to the two journalists in my family:
my father, Harold Adam Shetler; and my father-in-law, David Beatty Russell.
If every parent carried some of the qualities these two men possessed,
what a wonderful world we would live in.

NOTES FROM FRIENDS

While in Europe, I had the good fortune of seeing the Bayeux Tapestries. The unforgettable work of art was embroidered on a very long narrow cloth and depicts Crusaders doing battle with the enemy. They are shown lying prostrate, in pieces, or bleeding. Their women are also featured on the tapestry, trying to put their men together or roaming the battlefield looking for their remains.

Fortunately for Jeanette Russell and me, our role as wives of our now-retired crusaders was not so horrendous. In fact, it was a great life. We were in the Air Force during a time of relative peace. Our men seemed to spend all their energies waiting for the big bad Russians to come over the North Pole, or stomp over Europe, in order to bomb us to smithereens.

In the days before Paul Hellyer's brainwave of amalgamating the Army, Navy, and Air Force into the Armed Forces, our husbands were gentlemen of the Air Force, as Winston Churchill so aptly put it in one of his speeches. Because they were in communications, postings were not necessarily to bases with airplanes. There were several lines of defence across Canada with radar and listening devices in operation waiting for the attack.

In most cases, we were able to accompany our men to their postings. This allowed us to experience life in the far north, as well as central and southern Canada. We were also fortunate enough to live and travel in Europe. In Jeanette's case, she experienced life in the U.S.A. as well. Our children attended many different types of schools, depending on which province or country we happened to be in at the time. Therefore, we now have adult children who are well adjusted and successful in all they do, and who have friends around the world. It may be interesting to some that none of our children joined the military. I wonder what that means?

To know Jeanette Russell is to laugh and enjoy life. I am smiling now as I think of our escapades in Greece. If one is to travel somewhere, who better than with a tall, slim, gorgeous redhead with an infectious laugh? No matter where we have gone or what we have done in our years of knowing each other, the memories spark many a smile and, more likely, guffaws. She sees the humorous side of every situation and, what is even better, she can put it down on paper and get the reader to visualize the happenings.

Take it from me, this book is as interesting as sitting across the table from her, sharing a glass of wine, as she talks about her experiences. Well, almost!

Viviane Lafraniere

Little Current, Ontario

I have known the author of this book for seventeen years. I have been connected to the military life, having two brothers who served a total of sixty-four years with the Canadian Armed Forces.

I truly never realized the sacrifices that military families made when their spouses left for tours and extended time in faraway places, like Alert.

Knowing Jeanette Russell has brought to light the strength, understanding, and total commitment a military wife must endure to keep the family unit feeling stable, contented, and secure.

Reading this book through her eyes will leave you with a smile on your face, a longing for travel, but most of all, a vision of hope that the military will once again regain the respect that she and her husband Dave came to know.

Eva Janveau

Mattawa, Ontario

INTRODUCTION

Is it a compulsion to write about one's personal life? I think so! You write about what you know, and what do I know better than my own life!

I've lived more than half a century. (Where has the time gone?) A mere flash in front of my eyes. If I should be so lucky as to survive another quarter of a century that would be great, but rather than tempt fate, I thought that I should reflect on the past and jot down my memories and their echoes. For you see, I've had a wonderful life.

I wrote this book at the urging of my late father-in-law, a journalist who saw fodder for a story in my letters home. Wherever we happened to be living at the time—Canada, Europe, or the United States—he was always kept up-to-date on our rambles.

That is how my book began. But as I continued to read and hear hurtful allegations about the Canadian military, I thought that my life's story could undo some of those tales and show other people a time when dignity and honour were the prerequisites for a happy life in the Canadian Forces.

The story about my marriage to a career military man has little about the pressures, heartaches, skullduggery, and disappointments that many military families endured thirty years ago, and which some continue to endure to this day. You see, I was an exception to the rule. I enjoyed this life. I felt privileged in my role as a military wife, and if I live to be one hundred years old, those years will have been the best.

Military life, however, was a challenge, although I didn't enter it naively. My brother had been in the Air Force, and I knew what to expect from the tales I heard as a youngster. I had to make things work. I had to dig in and hold a strong line so Dave could go forward with his life and career. I also wasn't blind to the hardships some families encountered, nor to the unequal structure, rules, and regulations that are so much a part of the military.

No doubt it was more difficult for wives of personnel in the Infantry and Navy, and also the wives of pilots, to cope with everyday life. Their men would be at sea or in the field or on flight missions for long periods, and the families were left home alone, sometimes for months on end. (It was said that if the Navy wanted you to have a wife, it would have issued you one.) But because my husband's trade was in communications, I didn't endure these hardships. He was "home" most of the time.

Moving and frequent postings were tough for many families. We were lucky during our career (we only moved four times), but many of our friends spent only two or three years in an area. No time to put down roots. They left behind their friends, their doctor, their dentist, their church, and their school, and had to start all over again. This did pose hardships, and not just personal. The military didn't cover all of the expenses for moving, such as new curtains and curtain rods, telephone and hydro hookups, new wallpaper, paint—necessities that are taken for granted.

As an NCO (non-commissioned officer), you sometimes lived from payday to payday, and if the wife had no job outside the home, it was hard to cope and sometimes almost impossible to survive. We never felt this hardship as I always had work. However, while the extra salary came in handy, I worked because I wanted to. And, once my kids were in school, I couldn't wait to get a job. I wasn't a coffee-and-soap-opera type of gal.

I opposed many rules and guidelines during Dave's career and often voiced my opinion, usually to no avail. I opposed the fact that I wasn't allowed to canvass for any political party and had to remain neutral. I opposed the requirement that personnel belong to a mess, an opportunity for the men to drink beer for ten cents. And I opposed the annual military fitness tests, but no encouragement to live a healthy lifestyle.

The system was rarely spouse-friendly, and being a woman, my views were not always looked upon as positive interjections. But this determination I had and still have for equal rights did not deter me from being a proud military wife and a goodwill ambassador for my country.

Dave's career as a non-commissioned officer and our corresponding life had more ups than downs, but for many that wasn't the case. To have been the family of an officer appeared to be untroubled, simply because the rank provided extra prestige—better living quarters, higher salary, and many other advantages. For example, I could never understand why there was such a variance in travel expenses between the officers and the men. After all, they ate in the same restaurants and travelled on the same planes. However, Dave could only afford a hamburger while his senior counterpart could enjoy a steak. I remember my best friend telling me that we wouldn't be able to socialize as much after her husband received his commission as an officer. After all was said, we didn't socialize at all. A class distinction certainly existed, and officers were definitely the upper class. But that's the way it was, and that's the way it continues to be. I refused to bow to class distinction and, over the years, reminded others that my husband was in the military, not me.

In 1964, Dave applied for a commission in the Infantry. The Army required young officers in the electronics field and men they knew who would climb the ladder quickly. Although the Air Force was his lifelong dream, this opportunity afforded him a clear advancement and, of course, more money. We were somewhat apprehensive about changing from the Air Force to the Army, but we made the decision to go for it. Unfortunately, this change didn't transpire. Dave's evaluation read: "We the Board have determined that Sgt. Russell is too old to start a new career in a new environment. Commissioning is denied." Dave was twenty-six.

From that day forward, he declined to apply for another commission and was determined to reach the pinnacle in his field as a non-commissioned officer.

I busied myself and refused to become overwhelmed by stories I heard. There were times when I felt inferior, lonely, unappreciated and irritated, but I moved on. Military wives are not the only wives who experience marital problems. There are many civilian families that are not fortunate enough to have a protective military umbrella above their heads.

I never felt betrayed by my husband or by the military. I wish everyone felt the same way, and I pray for those who have to face such adversities. Everything is changing—the world has become a much angrier and volatile place than it was thirty years ago, and the life a military family has today will most certainly be different from mine.

When I started to think about writing this book, I sometimes pondered about not being a celebrity. Who would want to read about my life? As a writer, I must leave it to the reader to decide whose life story can be judged as interesting as any others, but I think every person is a star in his/her own right—with or without Hollywood hype.

I sometimes think that my involvement in the military began at birth. Memories are what you make of them, but a mystery remains when I think back to 1945 and an air raid siren. The Sydney Steel Mill on Cape Breton Island was a potential target for German submarines during World War II, and precautionary measures were taken for everyone's safety. I remember being frightened. I didn't like the dark and hiding behind those blackout curtains.

That mist unfolded only when I grew older. I was six years old and had fallen ill with red measles. My mother pulled down the bedroom shades. I was horrified and became hysterical. She sat beside me on my bed and told me not to be afraid. She said, "There will be no sirens this time. There isn't any war now."

"Mommy, what is war?"

"Well, Jeanette, sometimes people want everything, even other people's countries, so we ask our military to protect us."

"Mommy, what does military mean?"

"Well, Jeanette, the military is a group of men and women who serve our country in time of crisis and need. These men and women wear uniforms, like Daddy does sometimes. You remember Daddy's uniform, don't you? Well, when there was a war on a couple of years ago, he helped to keep us safe. His military was called the Cape Breton Militia."

"Mommy, when I grow up, can I belong to the military? I want to protect you, and Pat, and Daddy forever."

As a child, the military was already playing a part in my life. Was the seed of curiosity planted? Was the surface of my curiosity being scratched? Unbeknownst to me, my military journey was just beginning.

During the same time period, in Bay Roberts, Newfoundland, David Howard Russell had already decided that, when he grew up, he would become a soldier. He loved to sit on his father's knee and listen to him read stories from the newspaper about the brave young men in their uniforms. Sometimes the stories were sad and made him cry, but other times they made him smile.

Were the two of us destined to meet and live the military life together? It certainly looks that way.

CHAPTER ONE

Wives, although sometimes lost in the shuffle of military life, are as important to the military as the enlisted member. Would I fade away in loneliness and despair, or would I become a mere cog in a spinning wheel? No, I didn't think so. My father's strength, determination, and strong will began to flow through every fibre of my being. I began to realize I had the fortitude, and perhaps a small bit of needed ego, to survive.

Recently, news about the military has screamed scandal. Sexual harassment, hazing, and overuse of authority seem to be the buzzwords. Or we read about the aftereffects of the Gulf War. Agent Orange or post-traumatic stress disorder appear to strike many ex-military personnel.

But what about the bright side of life in the military? Didn't anyone in the Canadian Forces enjoy at least *some* of that life?

Well, I did and so did my husband, Dave, and our two children, Glenn and Alan. For more than three decades, my children and I followed Dave to postings in Canada, the Netherlands, and the United States, before retiring in North Bay, Ontario.

I revelled in the constant moving around, making new friends, working at different jobs, and getting into and out of scrapes. Combine that with my inborn sense of humour and red hair, and you have the ingredients for a pot of military stew. I stirred that pot many times over, and of course, family and friends got mixed in with the other ingredients, too.

Does one believe in fate and destiny? How could it be that I would meet a man whose life was so intertwined with my own upbringing? Was this divine intervention?

Dave was a non-commissioned officer in the Royal Canadian Air Force in Quebec, who upon his transfer to Sydney, Cape Breton Island, ran head-on into me at a local dance. I played hard to get, first turning down Dave's request to take me home, then jaunting about Europe for four months, before finally deciding to marry him in 1962.

Dave always knew he was military-bound. In 1955, he won the Strathcona Trust Award for outstanding cadet. Three years later, on October 12, 1958, he joined the Royal Canadian Air Force. Basic training took place at St-Jean, Quebec, followed by studies at the Radar and Communication School in Clinton, Ontario. He arrived in Clinton the day before Christmas. A care package from home awaited him—homemade fruitcake, canned mussels, and Newfoundland candy. It helped.

Following graduation, Dave's first posting landed him on a radar site in northern Quebec. Known as the Pinetree Line, construction of the military site began as a joint Canadian (RCAF) and American (USAF) project in the early 1950s. These radar stations were constructed and strategically located to counter the Soviet air threat against North America. They were fully manual early warning or aircraft control systems, and RCAF Station Parent, Quebec, was one of the sites.

The station was built around a lake nestled about two miles from the town of Parent, a small lumber town located approximately three hundred miles north of Montreal. Although extremely isolated, the station had every amenity one could dream of, and more. The recreation centre featured a swimming pool, bowling alley, gymnasium, and restaurants. The theatre comprised about two hundred seats and played the latest releases. An arena housed a hockey rink and curling club. People flocked to the ski hill in snowy weather, the ball fields and lake in sunshine. What more could a single fellow want for a solitude posting?

The popular hotel in town, the Commercial, had a tradition. The first time anyone stepped over the threshold, they had to kiss a moosehead that hung from the rafters. A gargle of straight whiskey followed. The head had naturally mummified. The smell was not odourless.

It is said that in Parent, you can pick a bucket of gargantuan blueberries in twenty minutes . . . that is, if the mosquitoes don't fly away with them first. Mosquitoes that resemble small hummingbirds.

A transfer to Sydney in those days meant bachelorhood would certainly be jeopardized. Sydney maintained the reputation that no single Air Force fella ever left Cape Breton Island unhitched.

When Dave was informed of his new posting, he was apprehensive and prayed that the bachelor's nightmare would not come true. However, little did he know that Cape Breton girls were totally irresistible.

He arrived in October of 1960 and guess who he met?

CHAPTER TWO

During my teenage years, recreational activities centred on the dance halls, and to prove our expertise with the new rock and roll craze, my girlfriends and I would cruise them looking for the sharp dancers. We were always on the prowl for a new guy in town. The YMCA on Friday night and the Venetian Gardens on Saturday night were favourite places. On weekends we travelled between the two famous Sydney landmarks, dancing up a storm.

One Saturday night, Dave and his friends arrived at the Venetian Gardens. The Gardens had been built in the 1930s as a dance hall on the waterside in downtown Sydney. An outside balcony let you view the ships and boats as they cruised up and down the waterway, while the orchestra performed from a balcony inside and above the front entrance. How we loved that era of the Big Bands. The music sounded as if it been played by the masters themselves, Glenn Miller and Jimmy Dorsey. When "In the Mood" rang out, no one was left standing, not even the wallflowers.

On dance nights, the bright overhead lights were recessed behind small, star-shaped holes in the ceiling. The dancers whirled and twirled about as if beneath a starry sky. At the end of the dance floor and separated from it by a brass railing was a small platform with some tables and chairs, an area offering dancers a spot to take a break, to sip a soft drink, and to watch the dancers. Dance styles differed according to each individual's abilities, and it was so easy to spot the seasoned dancers—they simply didn't watch their feet.

The guys, many with ducktail haircuts, long sideburns and red nylon bomber jackets, stood together on one side of the hall and eyeballed all the chicks. The girls also made comparisons. One could say that there were stag lines organized by gender.

You could almost hear the whispers.

"Gee, hope that fella with the slicked down hair doesn't come over and ask me to dance. I'm crossing fingers and toes that the guy next to him does. Please, Lord, hear my prayer."

In Dave's words, he spotted a tall, skinny redhead in the fifth row. It appeared obvious to him that this gal was anxiously waiting her turn to dance. Even today he exaggerates how they chose which girls to dance with, but I'm getting ahead of myself.

When the first line emptied, the second row of girls moved to the forefront, then the third, and so on. When the fifth row (my row) finally became the front row, a long-limbed slender guy asked me to dance. Years later he commented that anyone who had the patience to move up slow-moving lines without getting discouraged merited being asked to dance.

But what he failed to say was that the tall, patient, and skinny redhead looked fabulous that night. She wore a powder-blue angora sweater and matching skirt and heels—no saddle shoes or bobby socks on this gal.

From the fifth row, I, too, noticed this tall, skinny guy with cropped hair making his way over to me. I still remember the words of the song being played—"Do Ya, Do Ya, Do Ya Wanna Dance?"

I believe Dave was totally smitten the moment he put his arms around me, and I felt a bit of a flutter, myself. Even in the darkened hall, he had good features. Perhaps his nose could have been a touch smaller and his cheekbones a touch lower, but for all intents and purposes, this tall skinny guy looked pretty darn good. I liked him. And after a few dances, he asked to take me home.

Our group of girls had a pact. No one would go home alone at the end of the dance, and we would check with each other before the end of the evening drew near.

I told Dave that I'd give him my answer at midnight.

"Midnight! Who in the hell does she think she is?" He didn't say that, but I could sure read his mind.

At the stroke of midnight, like Cinderella, I waited for him. I was excited that he had chosen me. However, while I stood by the front door, out he went with another girl on his arm with nary a sideward glance. How dare he! It became quite obvious that Valentino Dave wasn't used to being put on hold. I got the message—real fast. Months went by before I saw him again.

Occasionally the Air Force station had a dance at the recreation centre, and Cape Breton girls never passed up the opportunity to attend. I'd see this big-nosed stranger once in awhile, but unfortunately he was never alone. He always had a competitor sticking to him like glue, and I truly believe he had totally forgotten me.

The pool at the recreation centre also became a meeting place, which Dave and his friends frequented on a regular basis, showing off their swimming prowess. As Cape Breton girls knew all the haunts for the single guys, one afternoon my girlfriend, Mabel Spencer, and I drove my car to the pool. We were good swimmers and looked more than acceptable in a bathing suit. Our mission . . . to impress! The pool was jam-packed. I, meanwhile, loved to high dive. I slowly climbed the ladder and scanned the area for Dave. I found him sitting beside a girl with blond hair. I couldn't help but notice her skimpy bathing suit as they dangled their feet in the shallow end.

I wanted to create some rumpus so I jumped a couple of times on the diving board. The sound could be heard throughout the pool area. I leaped into the air and plunged downwards, executing a swan dive any professional diver would have been proud of.

However, my brand new, candy-apple red bathing suit had two rubber falsies tucked into the bodice, and as I surfaced, I noticed something bobbing on top of the water. My God, it was one of my breasts. My heart raced. I reached up and grabbed it. I tucked it back into my suit where it belonged. Panicked, I looked about to see if anyone had noticed. If they had, I couldn't tell. Perhaps they might have felt as embarrassed as I did.

Dave continued to frolic in the shallow end with the blond. It appeared he hadn't even seen my swan dive. Another chance meeting foiled.

I mistakenly put my swimsuit in Mabel's bag, and when she got home, her mother put both suits on the radiator to dry. My rubber breast fell to the carpet. Her father, an extremely stoic man, began to laugh hysterically. He watched as his cat frolicked with my breast, tossing it again and again into the air.

Not too long after my bathing-suit caper, I saw Dave at the Venetian Gardens. After making my way through the row elimination and reaching the forefront, I heard, "Do Ya, Do Ya, Do Ya Wanna Dance?"

"Yes, yes, I wanna dance."

This time when he asked to take me home, I didn't play coy. Maybe he liked red bathing suits after all. And, when I looked at him closer, his nose wasn't really that big. I liked his cheekbones, too.

I received my first present on February 10, my birthday. The doorbell rang and there he stood—so tall, so good-looking. He had to stoop to get in under the doorframe. Dave then handed me a box of Pot of Gold chocolates, the first of many birthday presents to come.

In June of that year, my mother and I sailed to Europe to visit my brother Pat and his family, stationed with the RCAF in Marville, France. We planned to stay four months. However, before I left Sydney, Dave gave me an extra-special present. A pearl ring that would keep my finger warm for the real thing yet to come.

As Mom and I sailed from Montreal aboard the SS *Homeric* for LeHavre, France, I found it hard to focus on this wonderful adventure that lay ahead of me. My thoughts were of Dave. Would he go to the Venetian Gardens without me?

The moment we stepped aboard the huge cruise ship, the captain and his staff greeted us. A string quartet was also playing on the deck. Why did I suddenly get a vision of the *Titanic*?

Mom and I could hardly grasp the size of the ship . . . a floating resort with circular staircases. In the lounges and restaurants, the scent of fresh flowers titillated our nostrils. And the activities! We wondered how we were going to fit everything in—swimming, shuffleboard, movies, nightclubs, and ten meals per day. We were mesmerized. Today a cruise is so commonplace that almost anyone can afford to indulge. But in 1961, taking a transatlantic cruise was a luxury usually only the wealthy could afford. We weren't rich, but it was a once-in-a-lifetime dream for my mother. And who better to accompany her, but her daughter.

Dances were held every night aboard ship, and though we were in tourist class, the first-class passengers would join us in the ballroom. A passenger by the name of Fitzgerald—I've since forgotten his first name—met me at every turn. Tall, with black hair, he wore horn-rimmed glasses, and his black bushy moustache curled at each end. I didn't like a moustache. I didn't like him.

My mother always maintained that looks were only skin deep and that beauty was in the eye of the beholder. But this beholder thought this guy needed major restoration.

He pestered me every day aboard ship for a date, and he wouldn't take no for an answer. I guess you could say he stalked me. Wherever I looked, he lurked behind a corner or post and gawked at me through his thick coke-bottle lenses.

One night, I spotted him in one of the clubs. I raced out onto the deck where I knew I could get lost in the crowd. A few minutes passed when I heard the steward say, "Good evening, Sir. So nice to see you again. Lovely evening, isn't it? You should be dancing. After all, you must take advantage of the starlit night, especially on the ocean. You know we'll be docking in the morning.

"If I could make a suggestion, why don't you ask that good-looking girl over there behind the post to dance?"

Someone tapped me on the shoulder. When I turned around, it was Mr. Moustache.

I gave in and danced on that starlit evening, while Mr. Moustache related a little of his family history. He was John F. Kennedy's first cousin. Perhaps my mother's words had been true. Looks are only skin deep.

We arrived at LeHavre the next day, and I could hardly wait to tell my brother Pat about Dave. I referred to him as the prize I had left behind in Sydney. But my mother interrupted and said, "Perhaps your sister left behind a bigger prize on the ship."

Without ever having seen his picture, Pat knew exactly what Dave looked like, down to his big nose, high cheekbones, full lips, and large navy-blue eyes. I assured him that when all features were aligned, he was actually quite handsome.

We travelled extensively throughout Europe that summer. My top priority in every country I visited was to find a shop that sold postcards. Being on the other side of the world wouldn't stop me from maintaining daily contact with my suitor back home.

Perhaps Dave had given out lots of pearl rings in the past? I wanted to make sure that my pearl ring would be replaced as promised.

Dave got no respect for his private mail at the station post office. After the clerks read the postcards, they took the stamps. How fortunate that the cards he received from me were not love letters, although I badly wanted them to be just that.

For our final week in Europe, my mother and I visited London and Ireland. In London, we stayed at the Park Court Hotel on Hyde Park, a hotel that housed young men and women who attended a nearby university. There I met Brenda Wilson, and we became friends. Although from northern England, Brenda had become very knowledgeable about London and the surrounding countryside. Who could ask for a better tour guide? In her company, we visited places tourists might have never seen. We travelled throughout the city on the Underground. We strolled through famous Hyde Park, where in the eighteenth and nineteenth centuries, royalty rode, military reviews were held, and duels were fought. We stopped and listened at Speakers' Corner, the meeting place of soapbox orators. And we rowed a boat on Serpentine Lake. Out-of-the-way British pubs became favourite destinations.

On one of my shopping expeditions I fell in love with a winter-white cashmere coat framed with a matching fox collar. The store didn't have my size, but for a small deposit, the owner of the shop would order another. She assured me that the coat would be shipped to Canada.

How did I know I would wear it on my honeymoon?

After living out of suitcases for four months, October arrived, and I couldn't wait to get home. There I was, a young girl from Cape Breton Island experiencing the opportunity of a lifetime, yet I was pining away. I missed Dave and Canada.

I convinced my mother to let me fly back home, rather than return by ship. I didn't want to spend seven days on the ocean when I could be home the next day. My mother wasn't thrilled with the idea, but only because I had been seasick on the trip to Europe did she agree. I flew Air France from Paris to Montreal, and my mother continued her journey as planned.

The overseas flight was a long one, but how would I know that this would only be the first of many such flights during my lifetime? Anxious and excited about seeing Dave again, I memorized what to say to him when we met.

Decked out in a white, custom-made, knit suit purchased in Rome, I felt like a million bucks. (My poor mother had hoped this would be the case, because she had certainly piled the lire high on the counter at the designer's boutique.) Besides my new suit, I sported a new Paris hairstyle called "the flip"—high on top and curled behind the ears. I figured I looked pretty darn good.

We landed in Montreal and shortly thereafter I hopped aboard another plane that would take me to Sydney and my Newfoundlander.

As we taxied up the runway in Sydney, I saw Dave. He towered above the crowd. Were those flowers he held? Brushing past the passengers and the stewardess, I was the first to reach the plane's door when it opened. I almost fell down the steps, before racing through the airport terminal and into his arms. My heart pounded. I had forgotten everything I had memorized. But, it didn't matter. The delight on my face said it all. I picked up the roses that had fallen to the ground.

A week later, when my mother arrived home in a taxi at eight o'clock in the morning, her eyes opened wide. Dave's car sat in the driveway. We often wondered if she ever paid the cab driver, for I'm positive that when he saw her glazed eyes and frothing mouth he didn't care whether he received his fare. He just wanted to get the hell out of there before the fireworks were ignited.

Much to my mother's astonishment, I was alone in bed, and I laughed at her huge sigh of relief when I said that Dave had loaned me his car the day before. Belatedly, I tried to tell her that Dave had jumped out the window, but she didn't accept it.

I had been home two weeks when Dave proposed. A very cool-looking diamond replaced the pearl ring that had kept my finger warm for the summer.

But Dave made a grave error.

"I had a choice between two diamonds. I chose this one because I thought the other one was too big and too gaudy."

Excuse me. Newfoundlanders may think big diamonds are gaudy, but Cape Breton girls do not.

"Well Dave, let's you and I go and see this gaudy diamond."

Twenty minutes later, I walked out of that jewellery store with a dreadfully big and gaudy diamond on the third finger of my left hand. It has remained there to this day.

We set a date: January 20, 1962. Why January? Why not? I have always wanted to be different. My girlfriends were June brides, so I would be a January bride. And besides, my new winter-white cashmere coat with the white fox collar would fit perfectly into my going away ensemble.

We had no relatives living in Sydney, but that didn't stop our wedding day from being perfect. More than one hundred people attended, but while the day was filled with a special joy, there was sadness, too. My father would not be there to proudly escort me down the aisle. He had died from a ruptured appendix in June 1957.

Never again would I hear my dad whisper funny comments in my ear. Nor would I ever hear him tell me how proud he was that I had chosen such a wonderful man. I realized on my wedding day that now that another man had come into my life, Dad's affection would be but a cherished memory.

Never once in my sixteen years had he raised a hand in discipline.

Memories are such wonderful echoes.

I prayed that Dave, as a father, would have the same qualities.

Everyone looked wonderful on that cold sunny day. My wedding gown was three-quarter length and in white peau de soie. A scooped neckline and long sleeves made it elegant, yet simple. The bodice and lower portion of the skirt sparkled with tiny pearls and sequins. My shoulder-length veil cascaded from a tiara and fell loosely around my shoulders. A dainty pearl necklace and earrings—gifts from my new husband—completed my ensemble. This time it didn't matter that the pearls were not big and gaudy.

My bouquet comprised white gardenias, white baby's breath, and white satin ribbons accented with a touch of greenery. The day was sunny, but cold, and what a task the florist had to make the bouquet. Every time the frigid temperature came in contact with the gardenias, the flowers turned yellow. Five times the bouquet had to be created before it arrived perfectly white in an insulated container.

But still, there was a panorama of colour! My maid of honour wore a mid-length peau de soie gown in the latest shade of shocking pink. She carried a bouquet of pink-, white-, and blush-coloured roses. My mother shone in a turquoise velvet dress with long sleeves and a pillbox hat to match. Dave's mother felt wonderful in a gold silk dress with matching accessories.

My father's best friend, Dr. G. G. Campbell, escorted me down the aisle. A Nova Scotia historian and author, he was also the principal of Sydney Academy. The previous week, he had walked his own daughter down the aisle at her wedding. He revelled in the fact that he had made local history . . . giving away two daughters in one week.

Reverend John Clarke performed the ceremony at the Military Chapel of RCAF Sydney. Our wedding was the first to be performed in the new non-denominational chapel.

Dave and his attendants wore Air Force blues. Dave's best man, ironically, had been my childhood friend. Walter (Lefty) Pretty and Dave met when they went through basic training together in Clinton, Ontario.

So the "curse" did come true. David Howard Russell didn't leave the island a single guy after all. Neither did his friends.

Dave and me on our wedding day, January 20, 1962

I had planned to wear my new coat from England on that special day. A money order for the final payment had been sent to my friend Brenda, and she shipped my winter-white coat with the white fox collar. When it arrived, I could hardly believe my eyes. Inside lay a black and grey coat with a matching black fox collar. I rushed to phone the shop in London. The owner informed me that the coat Brenda had picked up was white.

I broke with tradition and tossed my garter, not my bouquet. I had promised my father's mother that I would give her my wedding flowers when Dave and I honeymooned in Montreal, where she lived.

Our wedding night aboard the train did not go as planned. Somehow our reservations got mixed up and instead of the compartment with flowers and champagne, our bridal suite turned out to be an upper and lower berth. Dave on top . . . me on the bottom. My negligee that I had so carefully packed would have to wait until we reached the hotel in Montreal. Fortunately, I had tucked a pair of flannelette pyjamas—always an old standby for cold winter nights in Sydney—in my suitcase, just in case.

Dave and I thought we were so quiet, yet, two days later when we arrived in Montreal, the porter winked and said to Dave, "You sure did a lot of sleepwalking, young fella! Congratulations."

At my grandparents' home in Mount Royal, I presented my grandmother with my wedding bouquet . . . yellow gardenias.

My grandmother replaced my father in word and deed when I saw her joy as she cradled the flowers in her arms, flowers she wished her son could have placed in mine.

My grandparents were enchanted with Dave and pleased with my choice of a soul mate. Almost immediately my grandfather escorted Dave to his bedroom and very secretly opened a "medicine" bottle he had stored in his dresser drawer, and they shared a shot of Irish whiskey. My grandfather, who loved a "snort," concealed his whiskey in a variety of medicine bottles, hidden from my grandmother. Whether or not he really fooled her was questionable.

So, now I was a military wife. Did I look like one, if in fact there is such a look? My role would be to learn to live under the umbrella of the military, our protector and provider of our livelihood. Nineteen-sixty-two was the beginning of our thirty-six-year career in the Canadian Armed Forces, where Dave's career took us to Europe and the U.S. and exposed us to other cultures and nationalities from around the world.

CHAPTER THREE

How appropriate that our first son was due to arrive on Canada Day.

While someone told me that I would forget the pain (hah!), I'll always remember the controversy I created the day I went into the hospital to give birth to Glenn David Adam Russell. Maybe I can't be blamed too much for what happened, since my beloved son made his entrance into the world nine days late, on July 10, 1962, sparing me some comments.

Pregnant was a not a word commonly used in the sixties. You were either in the family way or expecting. Heaven forbid nine months didn't pass from the very day you married before that small bundle from heaven arrived.

I suppose I wasn't unique in that I had a gargantuan craving for strawberries during those nine months, yet to find fresh strawberries in February and March was almost impossible. Dave somehow managed to satisfy my desire and I constantly gorged. Everyone feared my baby might be born marked with a strawberry.

The state of pregnancy did not thrill me. I never babysat a great deal and, to be honest, I didn't care much for little kids, and I knew absolutely nothing about babies. I wondered what kind of mother would I be? Was I too young to have a baby? But as the days and weeks passed, maternal instincts began to surface. I talked constantly to everyone about my pregnancy figuring if I talked enough, God would not allow any problems. I read somewhere that if you talked directly to a baby growing inside of you, his brain becomes more alert much faster . . . than what? That's what the experts said in 1962. Who were these experts? "They," that's who they were. Most days I had laryngitis I talked so much. This baby would have to be born gifted. He had no choice.

The nurses on the fifth floor of City Hospital earned every penny of their salary that day. I also imagine they questioned the science of human and animal emotional behaviour, for I screeched from the very moment I arrived until the moment Glenn was born. Didn't everybody? The nurses couldn't convince me otherwise. I had them scurrying everywhere, fetching cold cloths, massaging my back, opening and closing the blinds. Heaven forbid a nurse would leave my side. The terror went on for two and a half days.

In the room next to me a Portuguese woman silently awaited the birth of her second child. The nurses said, "You can't hear a sound coming from her. She's as silent as a lamb."

"Hey, I know a lamb is young and innocent, but so am I. I'm only screaming because it hurts. Besides, she can't speak English, so no wonder she's silent."

What a silly thing for me to say. A scream is a scream, no matter what language it's shrieked in. But hadn't I read somewhere that some European people merely wail. Maybe my neighbour did that silently. Perhaps they couldn't even hear her.

The nursing staff changed shifts at 3 p.m. The head nurse on the maternity floor decided to get even. She told one of her colleagues that she needed a urine sample from a patient that couldn't speak English.

So, there I lay, redheaded, fair skinned, freckled, huge as a barrel, and hollering my head off at every twinge. I have no doubt that I do not look Portuguese. It was obvious that the nurse who entered my room was somewhat slow witted.

"H - e - l - l - o! My-name-is-Sue. I-need-to-take-a-sample-of-your-urine. Do-you-see-this-little-bottle? Well, I-want-you-to-pee-pee-in-it!"

This being my first time in a hospital, needless to say I was somewhat perplexed. Between every spasm I wondered, does this happen often? What is wrong with this nurse? Could she be retarded?

Get me out of here. I'll have my baby at home.

I peered up at her.

"Pardon me?" I asked.

Oblivious to what I had just said—in English—she continued in her slow-witted way. "I-need-you-to-void-in-this-little-bottle. Can-you-do-that-for-me?"

This is too much. I am very confused. What exactly is her problem?

Sweating profusely, I tried to focus on her.

"I don't understand. Do you want me to piss in that bottle, or what? You are getting on my nerves."

Her eyes became as wide as saucers.

"My God, you speak English. They told me you were Portuguese!"

Glenn David Adam weighed in at seven pounds, seven and a half ounces.

"Is that a mark on his nose?" I asked the doctor.

"Yes, Jeanette. A skin blemish known as a strawberry."

CHAPTER FOUR

John F. Kennedy became a household name in 1962, when he insisted that Fidel Castro remove from Cuba nuclear weapons that had been provided by the Russians. News of the Cuban Missile Crisis and the Bay of Pigs proved a harrowing and scary crisis. People worldwide were scurrying about building fallout shelters and stocking up on food, water, flashlights, and batteries. I recall reading hurriedly published booklets on what to do in the event of a nuclear explosion. This world-shaking emergency went on for nine days, and during this time, one reflected on how precious life really was and how quickly it could be snatched away.

For nine days, Glenn and I stayed home alone. As I recall, my civilian friends didn't panic. Life went ahead as normal for them. But my husband was away. He didn't call. I didn't know whether he was even in Canada. Then the weapons were removed from Cuba and a sigh of relief shuddered around the world. I'm certain the earth would have shifted had the expression of human relief been capable of doing just that. This crisis was my first real taste of military life.

When news of President Kennedy's assassination was broadcast on November 22, 1963, military personnel were once again on guard. Dave received word that he was to attend a course at Chanute Air Force Base in Illinois. The particulars of this course and the impending transfer were unknown. Designated top secret, it involved nuclear devices, including the Bomarc missile.

In January 1964, Glenn and I joined Dave at Chanute Air Force Base, and we rented a small trailer in the nearby town of Rantoule. During the hours Dave spent at school, Glenn and I became friendly with some of the U.S. military wives and their families in the trailer park. This was my first experience as a military wife, and I noted a definite difference between these military wives and the married girlfriends I had left behind in Sydney. Even though these new acquaintances were from a different country, I bonded with them. Was it the independence of these women I respected? Were they a singular type of person? A different breed? I simply didn't know.

In June we received our transfer to RCAF Station North Bay. Saddled with suitcases and boxes, we boarded a Greyhound bus and made the trip from Chicago to Toronto. Why a bus? Don't think I didn't ask.

Discrimination? Rank? Enlisted men versus officers? Oh, yeah!

Dave's boss travelled by train. Why couldn't we? Why a bus?

"Jeanette, that's the way it is."

"Dave! I beg your pardon, but it simply isn't right. It's not fair."

We arrived in Toronto the next day. That day and night riding on a bus with a small child will be etched in my mind forever. However, faced with an exhausted child and exhausted parents, the military finally granted us the privilege to travel the rest of the way to North Bay by train.

North Bay. My God, it sounded so cold! My aunt had lived there in the 1940s, and reports I received from her were scary—cold in the spring, cold in the summer, cold in the fall, and freezing in the winter. I looked at Dave. He snoozed with Glenn in his arms. The train wobbled over the tracks. I consoled myself.

Hey you! This posting can't be all that bad. It's not as if we're venturing into never-never land. So, what's up with weather anyway? Why do people always concern themselves with that? I snuggled closer to Dave. *Besides, I have you to keep me warm at night. We're young and adventuresome. The military umbrella will protect us from the mist.*

It seemed as if we rode the train for days. We never saw a car, person, or light from our compartment window. Finally lights could be seen in the distance. We passed a sign. "Welcome to North Bay. Population 25,000." We had arrived!

When any military person arrived at a new posting, whether you were single or married, a sponsor awaited your arrival. You never felt alone. Your sponsor made you feel like family. That's the way the military was. They gave you shelter.

Our sponsors, Terry and Sandra Schisler, were there at our beck and call. They had already arranged accommodations for us at a North Bay landmark called the Empire Hotel. We dined in their home many times during the month we waited to move into our apartment. Sandra introduced me to other military wives and their families while Dave was at work. She and I soon became friends.

We rented a two-bedroom apartment in a new building. We purchased our first car. Soon we were involved in the military community, with making friends a priority. But I remembered conversations I had had with military wives in Illinois.

Our next door neighbour in Rantoule received word of their new posting to Colorado. I asked her whether she planned a return to Rantoule some day to visit friends she had made. She told me that seldom did she ever return to a former posting. What would be the point? Her friends would have been transferred somewhere else as well.

Did military wives only get to meet military wives?

The snowflakes fell in big white icy clusters, like in a fairytale, the night our second son, Alan Douglas, arrived on December 8, 1964. The temperature was thirty degrees below zero and the wind cut through us like a thousand razor blades. I had a better delivery this time, and in all probability it may have been because I hadn't thawed out. Glenn was two and a half, and with a new baby, our days were filled with bottles and diapers. The nights were endless and often sleepless.

Dave babysat the night I visited a friend for the evening. Her husband had been a member of the Military Police. Not only did the Military Police protect the interests of those people residing on the station, making it safe for members of the Forces and their families, but they also protected the interests of the young single men who lived in the barracks. Free condoms were issued.

My friend had a stockpile of condoms in her bathroom. She asked whether I needed any. After all, they were useful tools and probably wouldn't go to waste. Besides, they were free. Anything free was a godsend in those days.

When I left her home that night, a large box—twelve dozen to be exact—accompanied me. Dignity flew out the window. While I drove home with my newfound treasure, my vigilance about obeying traffic signs became more acute. I didn't want to be stopped by a city police officer. The large circular box sat on the seat next to me. How could I explain what it contained?

When I arrived home, everyone was sleeping. I never had a chance to tell Dave about our riches. I laid the box on top of the freezer in the kitchen and went to bed.

All that week, we had been packing boxes for our move to a larger home. The kitchen resembled a warehouse, and the landlady had prospective tenants coming the following day.

I woke up early to the sound of Glenn playing in the kitchen. Only two and a half years old, any new object or toy would set him at ease for quite some time. It became obvious by the sounds of glee we heard that Glenn had indeed been occupied.

I may have been sleepy-eyed before I approached the kitchen, but my eyes opened wide when I saw what had caused Glenn's joy. For there on the freezer and trailing to the floor, up and over boxes, were twelve dozen condoms, out of their protective coffins. The boxes lined up exactly as Glenn imagined a choo-choo train would be.

Oh my God! Dave and I took one look and immediately burst out laughing at the sight of the plastic locomotives covering the kitchen floor.

"Where did these 'choo-choos' come from?" Dave asked. He couldn't restrain his laughter.

"I'll explain later," I snickered.

You never saw two people scramble and clamber like we did that morning trying to find all the pieces. Glenn, of course, wasn't amused that we packed up his railroad station. A short time later the doorbell rang. The tight-lipped landlady stood there with an older couple wanting to see the apartment. We were out of breath and red-faced. I know my face felt as if it were on fire.

On their way out, the gentleman turned to Dave and with hand extended said, "I believe this must belong to you."

His hand held a tightly rolled condom.

Our second move occurred when an irresistible home and landlord became available. In the short time we had lived in North Bay, I had made a point of becoming acquainted with the local populace. Our friends would not only be military. I wanted to be able to come back to a community and know its people. I refused to become a military wife that only got to know other military wives.

This philosophy paid off. We have retired in North Bay and still enjoy the warmth and companionship of many longtime friends. Actually it was because of the friends we made that year in 1964 that we decided to move back to North Bay.

The test of real friendship is simple. A real friend is a person who can put your interests ahead of hers and really care what happens to you. A real friend doesn't boast about his own accomplishments, but sincerely asks after yours. When you fail or suffer a blow, your real friend is sympathetic, concerned, and ready to back you all the way. When you succeed she's happy for you and takes pleasure in your happiness. Real friends are spiritual mates.

Donna and Ken Warren have been allies, confidants, chums, playmates, and supporters. We consider them family, and I shall never forget my first encounter with Donna.

Dave and I had been living in North Bay for almost a year. We lived on the top floor of a duplex in an older subdivision. The owners of the neighbouring homes were of the same vintage. In our twenties, we figured anyone over thirty-five was middle-aged.

A similar duplex next door had been for rent. Lucky for us that a young couple with a small daughter moved in. We were elated. Finally, neighbours our age.

I decided to welcome them to the neighbourhood. Even though I realized they'd be up to their necks unpacking boxes, I couldn't wait to meet them. I remember I had put a cake in the oven. The timer said I had forty-five minutes for a visit.

I ran down my back steps, crossed the driveway, and knocked on their door. Donna answered.

"Hi. I'm your neighbour, Jeanette. Welcome to Kingsway Avenue! By the way, do you have a clock? I just put a cake in the oven, and I want to make sure it doesn't burn."

"A clock?" Donna looked puzzled. "Well, we have one somewhere, but as you can see, we're not unpacked yet."

Donna later told me that I was one strange woman. The meeting had been timed, and to make matters worse, the cake in the oven wasn't for her.

Although I did not make a good first impression, we did become friends, and we have unforgettable memories of the days we lived on Kingsway Avenue.

Ken worked for Bell Canada and made a good salary, while Dave, a corporal at the time, didn't bring home half of Ken's pay. They drove a brand new Plymouth. We drove a secondhand Chevy.

As I said earlier, in military life, a class distinction presented itself between the officers and the lower ranks. They were definitely the upper class. The family of an officer appeared to be much more untroubled, simply because the rank provided extra prestige, better living quarters, higher salary, and other advantages. That's the way it was, and unfortunately, that's the way it continues to be.

Not so with Dave and Ken! They respected each other. The civilian versus the airman got along like two peas in a pod.

Dave and Ken were true Toronto Argonaut football fans. When the games were not televised, the car radio picked them up clearly. They would sit for hours in the driveway listening to those games. Can you imagine today's young fathers thinking that was fun? Now, Grey Cup parties are planned a year in advance.

December 12, 1965, is etched in my memory. Early Sunday morning, I noticed something odd when I looked out my kitchen window. Ken waved at me from their kitchen window, opposite, and I waved back. I couldn't help but notice a heap of suds rising from the sink. It appeared he had been washing clothes, or perhaps dishes. I wasn't quite certain.

The phone rang.

"Jeanette, it's me, Ken. Can you please come over right away? I think Donna's going to have this baby any minute. I've already phoned our doctor, but he believes her contractions are false. But, they don't sound false to me. I have no idea what to do!"

I didn't even take time to dress. I threw a coat over my housecoat, stepped into a pair of boots, and practically flew down the backstairs. Donna lay curled in a fetal position. She cried and writhed in pain. In between a grunt and a contraction, she told me that she had consumed an entire bottle of castor oil. She wanted to ensure her baby would be born before Christmas Day. She had company coming for the holidays.

I was no moral support for either Donna or Ken. I resembled a caged panther. I paced up and down the hallway, not knowing what to do. Visions of my own labours whirled through my head. I felt the phantom pains.

If my landlady had not been in church that morning, help would no doubt have been on its way. But, it was only ten-thirty, and Orida wouldn't be home till after eleven o'clock.

Orida Cuksts was born and raised in Latvia, a country taken over by the Communists during the Second World War. She and her family escaped the country and spent the duration of the war in Germany. After the war, they sought refuge in England, where Orida studied nursing. She also practised midwifery.

Minutes seemed like hours. Ken and I paced back and forth from the bedroom to the front window as we waited for Orida to show up. Finally a car arrived. We were so relieved.

"Orida! Orida! Over here!" I waved frantically. "Donna's having her baby. Please hurry."

Immediately, Orida's professionalism took over. She calmed Donna down all the while she timed the contractions.

"Ken, it's time. Help me get Donna to the car," Orida commanded.

Everything happened very quickly. In a matter of minutes, Ken pulled out of the driveway. Orida and an unruffled Donna were in the back seat, where someone had put a blanket over Donna's shoulders, covering her nightgown.

An hour later my phone rang. Ken was jubilant.

"It's a healthy baby boy. Donna's doing great!"

I still giggle when I think about Ken that December day. He washed dishes, over and over again. He must have suffered dishpan hands. For years I wondered about the symptoms of compulsive disorders.

After the doctor had reassured him that Donna's pains were the result of castor oil and not true contractions, Ken had needed another distraction. A sink full of dirty dishes offered that release. And who knows, had he not called me that morning, maybe his dishpan hands would have handled something softer than a china plate.

They named their baby Cris.

Donna and Ken are now retired and continue to live in North Bay. They are the proud grandparents of four grandchildren.

In 1967, the Forces unified. Every military person, whether they had joined the Royal Canadian Navy, the Canadian Army, or the Royal Canadian Air Force, was now integrated into the Canadian Forces, but with the designation of Sea Element, Land Element, and Air Element. According to the volume of troops, Canadian military establishments throughout Canada and Europe became known as either Canadian Forces Stations or Canadian Forces Bases. RCAF Station North Bay, which had a large military establishment, had now been changed to Canadian Forces Base North Bay.

Glenn started kindergarten, we moved once again, and this time to housing on the base. It was cheaper.

We loved our three-bedroom PMQ (personnel married quarters), and we soon learned to adapt to our own little community. The base resembled a small city with its own schools, churches, hospitals, fire station, and police force. Dave didn't work on the base, but at the Bomarc Missile Site, located ten miles away.

Two incidents known either as Dull Sword or Broken Arrow were recorded in Bomarc history for Canada. The Bomarc missiles were located at two sites from 1963–72: 446 Squadron, North Bay, Ontario, and 447 Squadron, Lamacaza, Quebec.

The year was 1970. Dave had been on duty all evening at IMSOC (Interceptor Missile Squadron Operation Centre). IMSOC regulated all of the equipment for launching and controlling the Bomarc missile. There were twenty-eight shelters on the site, and each shelter contained a missile. As an IMSOC technician, Dave was accountable for the safe mechanism and function of the sono sentry, located in the missile shelter. The sentry, a part of a motion-detection system, reported any movement within the shelter whether it was a person or a fire.

Although the shelters were inspected on a twenty-four-hour basis by various teams, only the technicians could check the system via the doors. The door would be opened slowly, inch by inch. The technician then stepped into the shelter. With little movement, the technician scanned the area to ensure everything was in order. Anything other than a soft step could trigger the sono sentry alarm.

The missile contained two different fuels: solid fuel for the booster and liquid fuel for the ramjets. The hydrogen-type fuel was colourless, odourless, and flammable and could incapacitate a person immediately when breathed.

One evening during a compulsory inspection, Dave opened the shelter door, and before he stepped inside, he noticed liquid on the floor in front of the missile. Because of the imminent danger involved, he immediately ran to the side of the silo and pulled the fire alarm. The silo was promptly taken out of service.

All safety procedures were put in motion, and the danger of a mammoth explosion or the loss of a life was eliminated.

Dave's action produced a Broken Arrow, a military term indicating the possibility of a nuclear accident.

Investigation revealed that the liquid on the floor was PJ4. Had a spark ignited, an explosion could have wiped out the phalanx of rockets and any personnel nearby.

Once a year the crew at the Bomarc Site went to Eglin Air Force Base Auxiliary Field 9 (Hulbert Field) in Fort Walton, Florida, to test-fire the missiles (with deactivated warheads). To prepare the missile for firing required a combination of craftsmanship and hard work, and to see the missile take off stirred excitement for the personnel who worked on it.

The Bomarc remained an untried weapon of dubious effectiveness, designed to meet a hypothetical bombing threat that never materialized.

Dave remained in this job from 1964 until the missile site disbanded in September 1972. The missiles returned to the U.S., where they originated, and eventually were used as high-altitude target drones. But one Bomarc missile remained in North Bay. It has since been erected at the entrance to the city.

Dave, no doubt, played a role in Canadian defence history.

The Blue Spruce, a nightclub located near the Bomarc base, became known as Shelter 29. Although Dave didn't frequent the Bomarc's watering hole on a regular basis, this particular TGIF (Thank God It's Friday) turned into an exception. Dave decided to have a going-away party for a crew member, so he called me at work to say that he would be home late and not to wait up.

I worked with Northern and Central Gas and during my coffee break that morning, my colleagues and I discussed the latest news item on the front page of the *North Bay*

Nugget. In Sturgeon Falls, a stripper known as Fuzzy Bear had been charged with gross indecency. An undercover cop had attended the nightclub after receiving a report about a stripper who had performed an immoral and lewd act during her debut performance. Her court date was pending.

Our bedroom window looked over a sea of houses beyond our backyard. The day was scorching, the evening, humid. Windows were open, and the PMQs were so close together that even the faintest whisper could be heard in the still night air.

Dave arrived home around one in the morning and climbed into bed next to me. He had a strong smell of alcohol on his breath. He tried to be quiet and not bounce the bed, but I was already awake.

"I suppose you went to see Fuzzy Bear," I said sleepily.

Dave bolted up in bed.

"How did you know that?" He sounded somewhat surprised.

Well, little did he know that I really didn't know that . . . but now I did.

"You what? You did what? She was there?" I screeched, wide awake.

Even though Dave tried to explain, I wouldn't listen. I couldn't believe he would do such a thing. Look at a stripper! My God, he had the best stripper at home.

Dave must have thought the truth would set him free.

He squirmed, knowing I wasn't impressed. He went on to tell me how he had been hoodwinked into going up on the stage. He had been in the bathroom when Fuzzy Bear had asked for volunteers to join her on stage.

As Dave headed back to his table, he couldn't figure out why his presence was being applauded. Everyone in the room was chanting, "Dave! Dave! Dave! You volunteered. Go on, get up on that stage."

He said he had no choice.

Well, he did go up on that stage, and he did lie down next to Fuzzy Bear on a pink fur rug. I didn't quite get all the details of what happened, but apparently he was quite a hit. He had the audience in stitches. In fact, Fuzzy Bear asked him to join the troupe on tour.

Had the trap not been laid, I wonder whether I would ever have known. A trap even I didn't know who it would catch.

Our neighbours got quite an earful that warm, humid night. It became very obvious to them that something was amiss at the Russell household.

The next morning the phone rang.

"Can I please speak to the Pink Panther?"

Dave was known by that name for quite some time. I wasn't impressed.

I suppose Dave wasn't the only virtuous member of the human species to get into the odd confrontation. The following incidents happened to me, but I'm sure many military wives would have similar ones.

Many people attempted to intimidate me during our military career. I never stood by and put the thoughts on hold. I spoke out, always. During my secretarial years, there were people I detested with whom I worked and all because of the sexual advances, sly comments, touching and whispers, all given by men. I refused to be bullied or browbeaten. At times I had to become the aggressor. It's a better way to live and enjoy life.

I appreciate and am thankful that I experienced no bullying during my childhood. Raised with a strong sense of independence, I learned early on that everyone is equal, whether rich, poor, black, white, Protestant or Catholic; no one is better than another.

Invited to a formal dinner and dance at the Sergeants' Mess, I debated whether or not to wear my new backless mini dress, but opted for a two-piece pant outfit instead. I didn't want to be dressed inappropriately for this grand occasion. Maybe the dress with no bra would be too risqué.

My cream palazzo pants were long and full. The matching turtleneck with long sleeves was buttoned down the back. The top stopped at my midriff. A small area of my waist was exposed.

The military had receiving lines for almost all informal or formal functions. Practically everyone stood at attention in the line, even some of the officers' wives. For reasons unknown to me, many of these wives considered themselves to be one rank above their husband.

Dave and I had completed the formal how-do-you-do's when the base warrant officer approached me. I remember hearing his heels click together. Again he stood at attention. Then he stared at me.

"Mrs. Russell. I don't think you are appropriately attired for this mess. We do have a dress code, and your dress is unsuitable. I'd like you to go home and change."

"Excuse me," I said. "You want me to do what?"

I couldn't believe what I heard. *How dare he say that to me and with such insolence? Who in the hell did he think he was?*

Dave had gone to the bar and didn't hear what had happened. I believe Dave's absence gave this so-called male false courage.

"Excuse me, Sir, but what did you say?"

"Like I said, Madam, your dress is not proper attire for this evening, and you are creating quite a stir amongst the men. I would like you to leave."

"How dare you say that to me? Who in the hell do you think you are, anyway? Well, let me tell you one thing, Warrant Officer, I don't like the way you're dressed either. I especially don't like the way your ugly waxed handlebar moustache absorbs your drink and drips to your tie. Maybe you're the one who should go home and change. Please . . . go and dominate someone else!" Fire stung my nostrils at this point.

I glanced around the room. The backless, sheer, mini dress I had thought improper to wear that evening appeared to be a style favoured by most of the women in attendance. There wasn't a bra strap in sight.

And there I was, dressed in heavy fabric, covered from head to toe, except for a small section at my waist. I wondered whether this so-called gentleman had been disappointed that I even wore a bra.

I turned to the base warrant officer and pointed to the women who wore the backless/braless dresses.

"If I go, so do they! And one more thing, Sir. Did it take much training to become an ignoramus?"

He turned a few shades of red, stammered and sputtered something, but strode off. This cretin then proceeded to ogle me most of the night. His pig-headed obstinacy did not intimidate me. He harassed the wrong gal that night.

An authoritative approach means something to me only if it is to give approval, not to appear godlike. Everyone in those days feared the base warrant officer. As second only to the commanding officer, he had power.

On yet another unforgettable evening, we were again at the Sergeants' Mess. My mother had been visiting from Sydney and accompanied us to a dinner dance. We sat at a long narrow table with other friends. Our servers were young male waiters.

One young man in particular I remember. He looked to be no more than sixteen years old, too young to be in a bar, let alone working in one. He waited on our table and as the night wore on, we kibitzed back and forth, especially my mother, as she became somewhat tipsy.

"What a fine young man you are, and so good looking."

My mother complimented him and tipped generously each time he served us. Little did we realize that he didn't appreciate the attention. He ran to tell daddy.

His daddy, a chief warrant officer, came over to our table.

"Madam, you are privileged to be a guest in our mess. Some rules of decorum must be followed, however. Will you kindly refrain from embarrassing my son. If you fail to do what I've asked, you'll have to leave."

My mother was mortified.

I couldn't believe what I heard. Before Dave could respond, I bolted from my chair and went nose to nose with this creep.

"Who in the hell do you think you're talking to in this manner? You'd better apologize to my mother, or I'll file so many charges against you for harassment that you'll forget you even have a son. How dare you speak to her in that tone of voice? If you had half a brain in your head, you'd realize my mother had been complimenting your son, not intimidating him.

"Besides, I must ask if your son is old enough to be working here. Has the Liquor Control Board been notified of his age? I'd also suggest he learn that when you work in a bar, your skin must be thick. That's what bartending is all about.

"My mother is seventy years old and has no intention of seducing him!"

Everyone in the club by this time could hear what had happened, and many of them were yelling at this overbearing dictator, demanding he apologize to my mother.

He did apologize and so did his son.

Glenn and Alan became independent during the years we resided at the base in North Bay. It was a safe haven for children, everything being so close at hand. They walked everywhere—to school, to the pool, to the hockey rink, and to the ball field. Our days and nights were spent either at the rink or the ball fields. They learned to play with other children and acquired the rules of sportsmanship that would take them through life.

When children grow up their innocence is so pure. Their trust, their unquestioning belief, makes you, as a parent, a better person. The layers of social deceit have not yet formed, and they call things as they see them. Their joy is complete, and they can get rid of unhappiness so easily, crying one minute and laughing the next. However, one day this trust was broken.

Glenn came home from school with a note signed by the school nurse indicating that students would be given polio shots and any other needles they hadn't yet received, as required by the Board of Health. I sent the note back saying that Glenn would be exempt. His inoculations were up to date.

That afternoon I heard a mournful wail at the front door. I opened it to find Glenn, holding his arm. He sobbed. Tears ran streaming down his little face.

"You told me I didn't need any needles. You lied to me. The nurse gave two hundred of them."

Glenn ran past me and upstairs to his room. He slammed his door shut. I spoke of trust earlier, now his had been broken.

Furious at the school nurse, I ran to the phone.

After she reviewed the consent forms, she realized her mistake. "I'm so sorry! The needles were given to Glenn Russell, but not the right Glenn Russell."

What are the odds of having two Glenn Russells in the same classroom? Both names spelled identically—two Ns, two Ss, and two Ls.

But, only one—the wrong one—received needles. An unreal situation! As it turned out, Glenn recovered from his discomfort after a couple of days, and the nurse did not lose her job. An honest mistake that could have ended in tragedy. The school board and principal assured me that this type of error would never reoccur.

Glenn is now forty-one. Not once in all that time since has he come across another person with the same name as his.

As an NCO, you sometimes lived from payday to payday. If the wife had no job outside the home, there could be lean times.

In the 1960s, I played by the rules for parenting. We raised our children for the first five formative years and focused on the bible according to Dr. Spock. Only when the child reached school age was it acceptable for the mother to have an outside interest. How times have changed. Today it is not unusal to find fathers at home raising children.

How vividly I remember my first job at the *North Bay Nugget* and the paycheque that came two weeks later. When I deposited the cheque into my bank account, how proud I felt. This was the first time in five years that I had been able to help my husband financially.

When the Bomarc site closed in 1972, a transfer became inevitable. We were lucky to have stayed in North Bay since 1964. Eight years in a posting was almost unheard of. Many of our friends had two or more postings during this time.

Every spring we sat on pins and needles. Would we be transferred this year? Where would it be? Everyone due to leave recited this little poem: Spring has sprung, the grass has riz, I wonder where my posting is.

In April 1972 we learned that our new adventure would take place in Moosonee, Ontario.

"Where in the name of God is that?" I asked.

We knew about these isolated northern postings and prayed that our number would never come up for them. When I learned that the CN Railway went no further than Cochrane, Ontario, I knew we were in big trouble.

For the time being, I tried to postpone the thought. I became like Scarlett O'Hara in the movie *Gone With the Wind*: "I'll think about it in the morning!" Morning came too soon.

This transfer almost made me lose my faith in the Canadian military. Was this a punishment posting? I asked Dave. I guess I hoped the military had forgotten about us.

How could I leave the town, our friends, and my job? Would my friends forget me? How could we continue to stay in close contact with no physical nearness? Would my boys be emotionally scarred when they had to say goodbye to friends, kids whom they had known all their young lives?

Military brats is a term used even today for children brought up in the Forces. It has to be tough going to be a military kid, to leave friends behind and start fresh, sometimes in a different part of the world.

Had we been able to look into the future, we might not have felt so bad.

In 1979, Alan wrote an essay for a high school project on the Year of the Child. His topic: Advantages of Being in an Air Force Family. Here is an excerpt of that essay.

> Many people believe that being a member of a service family holds many disadvantages in that they think it would be difficult to adapt to a new society, school and friends.
>
> During the years I travelled with my family, I feel that I have become more socially adjusted. I have a keen awareness of world affairs and have been able, because of my different homesteads, to acquire lasting friendships in such countries as the Philippines, the United States of America, Europe, and closer to home, Moosonee, Ontario. I have enjoyed expanding my knowledge and walking through the pages of history. I thank my parents for their understanding and perseverance in my developing years.

Dave and I realized then that perhaps our two military brats were not that hard done by after all. This awakening certainly erased any guilt feelings Dave and I might have had when we had no other choice but to move from place to place.

The posting to Moosonee lasted two years. I pondered whether or not I should only make acquaintances and not friendships this time. Perhaps my U.S. counterparts were right not to make close friends in the civilian sector. It may have been easier for them to pack up and not look back.

But I understood fully that as an Air Force wife, I had to get with the picture. I had to adapt physically and emotionally to constant change and being on the move.

Dave went on ahead to make arrangements for our living quarters, while I stayed behind to pack and to ensure that our PMQ was clean enough to withstand the white-glove inspection. Anyone who lived in base housing feared the dreaded housing officer. I called him the Grim Reaper.

The Grim Reaper actually donned a white glove. I followed him with bated breath as he walked slowly from room to room. Everything had to be immaculate, or else. The refrigerator and stove had to look brand new, the floors polished to a shine. The glove brushed over the tops of window ledges and doorframes. In the basement, the gloved hand passed over pipes, the furnace, and into corners of the cement floor.

I often wondered what the consequences would have been had I not passed the test. Solitary confinement perhaps? I failed to understand why the housing officer was never a female? When it came time for his transfer, who inspected his PMQ? Where were our civil rights when we needed them the most?

The dreaded trip to the scrubland of Moosonee was just around the corner.

CHAPTER FIVE

On September 1, 1972, Dave arrived back in North Bay and gathered up his family. Kicking and screaming, we boarded the Polar Bear Express in Cochrane and headed off to never-never land. We heard an accordion and were surprised to see a polar bear playing it. Upon closer inspection, I noticed a bottle sticking out from his pocket with a label that read, "Newfie Screech."

As we neared Moosonee, the trees became terribly sparse. My spirits sank further. How would I be able to trim my Christmas tree if there was none available? I could see tumbleweed flying by the tracks and no cows, pigs, or horses on the few farms that we passed. Where were the animals? I turned to Dave.

"If you think I'm getting off this train, you're nuts!"

Finally, after six hours aboard that hot, crowded, and rattling railway car, we arrived. I could see the welcome committee through the steamy window—a handful of native Canadians and a van with Military Police written on the side. But what really caught my eye was the long, narrow, unpaved road that ran straight ahead . . . three miles to CFS Moosonee.

After a few minutes my heart rate steadied, and I managed to collect myself. I knew I had no other choice. I made my exit—depressed, full of tears and anger, and ready to blow up at anyone who looked at me the wrong way. The kids clung to me and stared wide-eyed at the many native people.

I wanted so badly to go back to North Bay, but that wouldn't happen. There was only one place to go and I was there. I had to make the best of it. I surrendered. I gathered up our luggage and climbed down the train steps. We all scrambled into the van and bounced up that dreary-looking road.

"Welcome to CFS Moosonee." After we passed the sign and drove through the gate, my eyes skimmed about, fast and furious. The buildings were freshly painted, and flowers appeared everywhere. They hung from lampposts and were colourfully arranged in window boxes. I noticed an absence of vehicles. (There was none permitted other than for the commanding officer, the fire department, and the military police.) In mostly every driveway sat a motorcycle and a snow machine.

We passed the recreation centre, the social hub of any base with its indoor pool, gymnasium, bowling alley, and restaurants. The school, churches, fire hall, medical centre, and arena were all within walking distance for the residents.

The van came to a halt on Polar Drive, the street that housed our double-wide trailer. We walked down a long wooden boardwalk and stepped into a screened-in porch attached to the front of the trailer. We kept our freezer in that porch. The two years we lived there, we only plugged it in during infrequent hot summer days.

I must admit I was surprised. The trailers were tastefully furnished, and the interior looked quite delightful. With a few personal touches, I could live with it. Can you imagine that? What a waste of a good sulk!

Within a matter of days—hours for the kids—we had all adjusted. Glenn and Alan found the swimming pool and made friends immediately. Alan settled into Grade 3 and Glenn into Grade 5 in a school that offered classes from kindergarten to Grade 8. Glenn's best friend was also named Glenn, but thank heavens this time the last name differed.

Although the station had no full-time doctor, we considered ourselves fortunate to have the services of a medic, a registered nurse, and a dentist. Dentists do have medical training, after all, so Captain Bill MacInnis, the station's dentist, was approached, often daily, for opinions on conditions other than tooth decay. A volleyball injury gave me reason to sit in his chair once. My hand was X-rayed, and the finger straightened with a tongue depressor, then wrapped in tape, before I was sent on my way.

Moose Factory, the town across the river from Moosonee, had a large hospital to which the station had access. In the summer months, a hospital boat was used to transport sick people, and in winter, a large, enclosed snow machine crossed the ice.

During the freeze-up and breakup of the Moose River, a military doctor was assigned to the station. For approximately six weeks he worked night and day. Mind you, the women would have preferred a female physician, but in our situation, one couldn't be fussy. Some of the women, including myself, hated that yearly physical examination. We wondered just how many women the doctor had attended to in the past. We needed that feeling of reassurance. However, once we dispelled the myth that there was no gender classification in the military, we set ourselves at ease. Of course he attended to the female race. He must have!

The semi-isolation encompassed everyone. We were all in this together. No one really wanted to be there, but we were determined to make the best of it. Why live any other way? A special bonding took place among everyone. We made friends, not just acquaintances. We had to if we were to keep our sanity.

I was hired as secretary to Commanding Officer John Kilby. With my newly acquired security clearance required for the job, I began to feel as if I were in the military as well as my husband. I, too, have secrets I must carry to my grave. And, the great thing about working in Moosonee was that it made the monotony less painful. Shopping malls, libraries, supermarkets, and theatres became nothing but a distant memory.

John Kilby's wife, Perry, became my best friend. She was John's right arm and without her engaging personality and untiring energy, days and nights in our small community would have been distressing for many. Not only was she a great cook, Perry was a terrific organizer. She and I were always putting our heads together to try and generate ideas to help those wives who had nothing to do during the day. We began a new venture.

The Thrift Shop was located in a small corner at the rec centre and was run during the day by the stay-at-home wives. Not only did our popular shop sell clothing and various items on a consignment basis, but we also bought and sold native crafts made by the local Cree Indians. We placed many orders for the Indian parka known as the *koolatuk*, Indian snow boots called *mukluks*, and beaded jewellery.

On weekends, Perry and I looked forward to calling on the crafters in their homes. Deerskin was the leather of choice, and we marvelled at their expertise with a needle and thread. To see first hand the natives create art with beadwork on items they designed made you understand why they are so skilled at carrying on this traditional craft. It truly represents one aspect of the richness of their culture.

We developed a lucrative business and created employment and income for the Cree artists and artisans. Some of our profits also helped to subsidize station sports activities for military children. We purchased equipment for the ball field, and during sporting competitions, we provided sandwiches and juice for the kids.

One Saturday at the arena, Perry and I watched as some of the native children from the nearby village struggled to stand up on the ice with skates either too small or too large. Some skated with no laces. From that day on, the native children were issued proper equipment. This mutual sharing of cultures not only provided entertainment, it created an understanding and respect for each other.

Unlike most military stations, all families, regardless of rank, mingled. I suppose we all were in this together—isolation I mean. It would be a lonely two years if members of the forces were not conjoined. Although Dave was a sergeant, our friends were privates, corporals, majors and colonels, and vice versa. We had dinner parties and all ranks socialized together.

Dawn and Jerry McSherry were quite the entertaining couple. We became good friends. Jerry was the SWO (station warrant officer), and Dawn, forever on the move, had bundles of energy. Without her organizational skills, many functions wouldn't have occurred. Her motto: "I'm at your beck and call if you need anything at all."

Dawn somehow managed to acquire all the latest movie releases. I remember it was a Wednesday evening when she called Dave to ask if he could run a brand-new release that had been favourably critiqued. Dave was the projectionist for the Warrant Officers' Mess.

Cabaret, starring Liza Minnelli and Joel Grey, attracted a standing room only crowd at the mess. Those people fortunate enough to get a seat relaxed with hot buttery popcorn perched between their legs. In the front row sat two Catholic priests from the nearby parish in downtown Moosonee.

Dave went to the back of the room, put the film into the projector, and turned it on. The prelude film included scenes for upcoming productions that everyone would be interested in. Then the movie began.

Two scantily clad women jumping for joy raced across a stage and into the arms of a less than scantily clad male. He proceeded to handcuff each of them and tie them to a bed. Yes, it was a pornographic movie. Everyone rushed to shield the eyes of the priests.

Dawn never lived that one down. From that day forward, she screened all movies.

Dawn passed away a few years ago, but I'll never forget her. She more than contributed to the many fun times everyone had in Moosonee.

I purchased six long gowns in those two years. Formal parties could be planned in an instant. The commanding officer was smart. He knew that in order to maintain a high morale for his troops, he had to entertain them, and what better way to do that than to keep the spouses happy. When the wives were happy, so were his troops. Every holiday, diplomatic birthday, or promotion was recognized.

Before he joined the service, the station cook earned the title of gourmet chef from his home province of Quebec. He could concoct the most exotic recipes, everything with its own succulent sauce. He refused to set the table with salt and pepper. Meals he prepared required nothing extra, he maintained. There was no such thing as a ketchup bottle.

Generally at a formal dinner there would be a head table usually occupied by the CO and his wife and various guests. Perry knew that for her taste and mine, the meal would require a small dash of salt, so she carried a salt shaker in her purse at all times. She would pass the shaker from her table to my table. Everyone took advantage, before an empty salt shaker returned to the head table.

The dinners began with military decorum and dignity; they were structured, traditional, and formal. But as the wine flowed and the night went on, buns, grapes, and anything else light enough to fly through the air bounced off an unsuspecting diner, irrespective of rank. Bands were flown in from the south to provide entertainment. Our parties were the talk of the station for weeks to come.

In the past, I never had a great skill at balancing a chequebook, let alone understanding a financial statement, or even following a budget. As time progressed, however, I've learned a few strategies for record keeping.

I am reminded, time and time again by my dutiful husband, that I must plan in the event of an emergency. However, his words always seem to go amiss for me. It's not that I don't pay attention, but you know how it is when you're bored from hearing the same thing over and over. Words tend to go in one ear and out the other. But, I suppose having twenty-five cents left in your wallet when you're still on holidays could be classified as an emergency.

Once a week the Buffalo or Hercules aircraft landed in Moosonee. The Hercules transport plane carried necessary military supplies to the isolated community. We all shopped at the

Canex (Canadian Exchange), and every Wednesday a fresh supply of meat, produce, milk, and bread arrived. Everyone ate well on Wednesdays.

As the aircraft went back empty, sometimes the wives were able to take advantage of free flights aboard these planes. The flight was always one way, so we had to return by the Polar Bear Express. But that made no difference. We got to know the polar bear fairly well. He even shared his screech.

Living in isolation and doing our shopping at the one store in town, The Hudson Bay Company, North Bay became our sanctuary. There was no need to travel any further south. And for those of us who had the opportunity to go on these flights, we often carried lists from many that couldn't escape.

On one excursion to North Bay, I had exactly twenty-five cents left in my wallet for my return trip. I had not even bought my train ticket yet. I didn't panic. I had a purse full of Canadian Tire money, and when I found a buyer, my problem would be solved. Fortunately, I knew exactly where to go.

Dave's sister, Betty, and her husband, Colonel Gordon Davis, were stationed in North Bay. Gord loved to shop at Canadian Tire, and that week the specials were phenomenal. I don't think they actually were, but I was determined to convince him of that. It took a lot of strategy.

Money exchanged hands and with my newly acquired loot, I breathed a sigh of relief. Dave would never have to know.

I looked quite the sight when I boarded the Polar Bear Express, well laden down. Suitcases were packed with clothes I had purchased. Garbage bags were filled with fresh bread, household plants, homemade pickles, and fresh fruit. But, the most recognizable thing about me that day was the bicycle tire slung across my shoulder. I had no room left. I had no choice but to put the tire over my empty head. It was for our commanding officer, and whatever the CO wanted you to do, you obeyed.

On yet another of my escapades to North Bay, I had been there about a week when Dave called to say that he and the kids would join me. An emergency flight was due to arrive in Moosonee later that day to transport a critically ill person to hospital in North Bay. Three vacant seats were available. Even Dave could get cabin fever.

Everyone boarded the Buffalo aircraft for the three-hour flight. The weather stayed clear until halfway through the trip, when a horrendous thunderstorm with lightning crackling all around erupted. The plane bounced like a yo-yo, hopping, swaying, and grinding through the storm. Even though Dave had flown dozens of times, he was more than a little concerned. The storm frightened him. The lady with the gallbladder problem was worse off than she'd been in Moosonee. She was so ill that she didn't give a hoot whether she lived or died. The plane could have crashed for all she cared. Glenn and Alan had their heads in the barf bag the whole time.

Betty and I waited near the runway at CFB North Bay. The control tower informed us of what was happening up there.

"The aircraft is having a difficult time with turbulent weather, but the pilots have everything under control. Everything should be okay."

Betty and I looked at one another and asked, "Should?"

My God, my entire family was aboard that plane. I couldn't stop shaking.

The night was pitch black but when lightning hit, the entire sky lit up like a rock concert. Thunder bellowed and crashed. Rain flooded the runway. It felt horrifying to be so helpless, unable to do anything but pray. Finally we heard the dual motors and spied the plane struggling through the sky. Were we holding our breath? Absolutely!

The plane circled overhead, again and again. Finally it approached the runway and landed ever so smoothly.

The door of the plane opened faster than it ever had in the past. Down the steps ran the passengers and the pilots. Even the lady on the stretcher got up and decided she wasn't that sick after all. In unison they looked up at the heavens, fell to their knees, and kissed the ground they stood on.

"Wow!" we heard them say. "We made it."

The last night of 1973 will remain in my memory forever, for the residents of CFS Moosonee celebrated New Year's Eve on January 5, 1974. Of course we all blamed the commanding officer for his decision.

The commanding officer received a message from Headquarters in Ottawa announcing that all scheduled New Year's Eve celebrations on military bases should be cancelled out of respect for the recent death of Lester B. Pearson, our former prime minister. A tough decision for the CO to make, but he had no choice. There would be no party.

The hired band had been about to board a Hercules aircraft at RCAF Trenton. They were not happy campers when they received news of the cancellation, but soon recovered when they were told the northern party would occur the following week.

The women looked aghast at one another. Many of us had gone to North Bay to Christmas shop and to find that unique outfit for the last special shindig of our tour.

Let me tell you, it wasn't easy to shop *haute couture* in Moosonee. Designer clothes were not top priority for the Hudson Bay store. It took a lot of contriving to find something suitable for any gala or not so gala affair. Catalogue orders were our lifeline.

We stood around mumbling amongst ourselves and pondered what to do the night of December 31. We were determined to ring in the New Year somehow and in some way. The women found a solution. We elected to begin a snowball.

A snowball? Well, according to *Webster's Dictionary*, it means to increase rapidly, like a rolling a ball of snow, but in Moosonee it meant a rolling party. The Russells began the snowball at approximately eight o'clock the evening of December 31, 1973.

Our next-door neighbours came over for a drink and a snack. Soon after, we rolled to neighbours across the street for a drink and a snack. We rolled from door to door, gathering every adult along our way. Our objective was to reach the home of our "chef" before midnight. The delicate morsels of gourmet food had already been prepared for the cancelled New Year's Eve dinner. It would not go to waste. The chef had transported it to his home earlier in the day.

That evening, duty became a word we failed to recollect. We avoided all contact with the commanding officer and his colleagues. They were not included in our snowball.

Around eleven that evening, thirty-five inebriated and famished ex-patriots rang the doorbell at the home of the gourmet chef. The only piece of furniture left in his living room was a pool table, which had enough room for a few plates and some cutlery. Never had I seen such a feast. We gorged on lobster, shrimp, crab legs, roast beef, and every salad imaginable. Chocolate-covered ants were optional. For a split second I thought about what the officers might be eating and felt guilty about consuming their share. But, we joyfully licked our fingertips. No salt or pepper had been required.

The fire chief, a member of the entourage, was determined that we put some spark into the evening. He suggested we put on our coats and follow him. He guided us to a clearing where all the Christmas trees from our living rooms were piled high. He lit a match, sending a huge orange fireball into the starlit sky. We formed a circle, held hands, and swayed while we sang "Auld Lang Syne." What a teary occasion!

The wind came up and sparks flew everywhere. The fire chief wanted us to leave the area so that he and his crew could contain the fire. I suppose he didn't want the whole town to burn down. Although we couldn't tell him our destination, he said that he'd find us somehow, even if he had to peek into windows. We assured him that his wife would have excellent care. She came with us.

We slowly made the trek homeward, sad that the night was almost over. We passed by the padre's home. We heard someone holler.

"Hey! Where have you guys been? Please come and join us. Come help us celebrate."

We looked at one another with smiles on our faces. The padre? Having a party? What kind of party? A church service for the late prime minister? But, we all knew the padre better. Hymns were not the songs of choice that evening.

We stomped in the door and were welcomed graciously by the smiling padre. We were stuffed, sooty and exhausted, but managed to find the strength to party on. The rejected officers were elated. They saluted us as we walked over the threshold. That party had to be the best. Dave and I reminisce sometimes.

At one point in the evening, the doorbell rang. Who was at the pushing end but the fire chief, covered in soot from head to toe, an empty flask in his hand.

"Happy New Year, Padre! Is my better half here? Lord in heaven, Padre, I must have walked a thousand miles. For God's sake and my sake, Padre, I need a drink!"

When our bonfire finally died a couple of hours after we had moved on, the fire chief tried to find the troupe and knocked on practically every door on the station. Fire Chief Leon Buehl knew us all too well. I believe he heard my laughter as he passed by the padre's domain. It appeared to him that good times were happening, and he abandoned the thought that it might have been a revival meeting. As he edged closer, he said to himself, "Yep, that's Jeanette's laugh."

Four o'clock in the morning, the commanding officer looked for the recreation specialist. Unnoticed, Bob and his wife had given us all the slip and gone home. The CO had not yet wished them a Happy New Year. Whether or not it was four in the morning or four in the afternoon, when the CO wanted to do something, it got done.

The party went en masse to the home of the rec spec. No one locked doors at CFS Moosonee. We walked straight through their front door and into the bedroom.

Bob and Denise Buckley were fast asleep. When we bellowed "Auld Lang Syne," Denise practically jumped out of her skin. She squinted at us from her pillow, then gave her head a shake. I knew she couldn't believe what her eyes saw.

Denise turned to Bob and poked him. "Bob, Bob—wake up! It's the CO."

Bob opened one eye, a rather bloodshot one, bolted straight up in the bed and saluted.

"Happy New Year, SIR!"

The commanding officer returned the salute.

A few seconds later the recreation specialist passed out.

We all went home and fell into bed.

Only in Moosonee could this have happened!

CHAPTER SIX

Would I be crowned Carnival Queen? I think it only fair that something positive should occur after surviving the scrubland of Moosonee.

The carnival presented the opportunity for everyone to demonstrate their prowess in various sporting activities, drinking activities and eating activities, to name a few. It didn't matter how old you were, your rank or serial number; in February 1974, competition was fierce among the officers, warrant officers, sergeants, and enlisted personnel. Everyone had scads of fun.

Carnival Queen, Moosonee, Ontario, February 1974

February was winter carnival month at military bases throughout the country, and in some parts of the country, like Moosonee, it helped to distract us from the long, cold winter.

The carnival lasted one week, beginning with the traditional torchlight parade. The adults carried torches, and the children carried candles and sparklers. What a gorgeous sight it was. With a military band leading the way, we marched throughout the station, up and down every street.

Like the pope giving his blessing, the padre was in his element on that opening night. The gleam in his eyes made us wonder if he might have an edge over us. After all, he was closer than most to the man upstairs. But, his collar was off all that week.

During the daytime, families got involved in sporting events and other activities geared to specific age groups. Amongst the adults, competition was intense, and every advantage was taken for a chance to win. Strategy was planned far in advance, and tips were shared with friends. There were skating races, hockey games, volleyball matches, swim meets, basketball games, snowshoe races, snowmobile races, and even nail-driving contests. Evenings primarily were reserved for adult activities, like beer-drinking contests, spaghetti-eating contests, beer-drinking contests, and beer-drinking contests. I was the anchor for my team. Does that tell you anything?

Each mess created their own theme—Western, Flapper, the 1950s, Space Age—you name it. The mess represented that era throughout the week in their dress, skits, talent contests, and even the design and making of ice sculptures. A panel of judges tallied the results of each event, and at the end of the carnival, the mess with the most points was declared the winner.

The same rules applied to the contest for Carnival Queen. In February 1974, the members of the Warrant Officers' Mess voted me in as princess, while Perry Kilby was voted princess for the Officers' Mess. We represented our messes during all carnival events and became ambassadors and spokeswomen.

The CO told everyone that he was in a no-win situation. His wife was princess for the Officers' Mess and his secretary was princess for the Warrant Officers' Mess, and as boss, he had to consider the others. Who should get his support? What a dilemma! At the end of the carnival, he needed to ensure that his wife still managed his home and his secretary still typed his correspondence.

Finally the day came to tally the votes. The Warrant Officers' Mess came out on top, and, yes, I was crowned Carnival Queen. Finally, after thirty-one years, I was Queen for a Day. I knew it would happen some day.

The night of my victory, I had two costumes to wear. During the skit for our mess, I wore a skimpy animal-print costume and swung by a rope over the stage as I whooped my Tarzan cry. I was Jane and the rec spec was Tarzan. He crouched below hiding in a vine plant as I flew overhead.

The plan was simple. Bob was supposed to grab the rope, and we would sail together through the air from one end of the stage to the other. His only piece of clothing was a loincloth. After a couple of hits and misses, I swooped down and connected.

Tarzan yelled in terror.

"No, Jane, No! The vine, Jane, the vine. Grab the vine!"

"No, Jane, that's not the vine. Ouch! Ouch! My loincloth! My loincloth! Where's my loincloth?"

We finally made contact and the two of us swung across the stage, red-faced and cackling. After the curtain closed, Tarzan walked over to the end of the stage and picked up his loincloth. Thank goodness he wore a small bathing suit.

My second costume that night was a backless evening gown, with a halter top, and black and white stripes running diagonally from the neckline to the scalloped hem. Combined with a new hairdo, I looked pretty darn good, even if I say so myself. Crowned by the Mayor of Moosonee and presented with the traditional Carnival Queen's tiara and bouquet of flowers, I beamed. The arctic fox stole placed round my shoulders made me feel squeamish. Every time I looked down, the wee face of that fox peered back. At the end of my reign, which lasted for the evening, I had to give it back, thank goodness. I still have that dress, and every once in a while, I take it from the closet and remember that wonderful night. Only in Moosonee.

The only time members of the Forces were permitted to grow a beard was at carnival time. (I believe the Navy is excluded from this rule.) At the beginning of the year, the razors were put aside, and the race for stubble began. The Beard Competition was judged on closing night.

Now was my opportunity! I was selected to shave off the commanding officer's beard.

The CO sat on a chair in the middle of the auditorium. I had a ten-inch straight razor in my hand. Everyone cheered, clapped, and stomped their feet.

"Do it, do it, shape him up a little, Jeanette. It's your chance to get even."

So, I took the razor and held it in front of his eyes.

"Am I not the best secretary you have ever had in your entire career? I want an answer right now."

"Yes, yes, you are the best."

"Am I not the best-looking secretary you have ever had in your entire career."

"Yes, yes, you are the very best."

The crowd was in a frenzied pitch. "Do it, Jeanette, do it!"

Then I bent down and whispered in his ear.

"And now, Boss, between you and me, Dave and I want a posting that one only dreams about."

He nodded his head, and with a steady hand, I began to lather him up, following which I stropped the razor on a leather belt and dramatically took a hair from his head to test the blade's cut.

The audience went wild.

In June of that year, Dave received his next posting. We were elated—AFCENT (Allied Forces Central Europe Headquarters) in Holland! What an opportunity awaited us!

Although we had had a fabulous time in Moosonee, two years in semi-isolation was more than sufficient. It always surprised me when some people actually requested an extension. But still I doubted if we'd ever have so much fun somewhere else.

After all, only in Moosonee could you go to a Chinese restaurant and order egg rolls, merely to be told they only had one left; be dressed in a ball gown waiting on the side of a gravel road for the bus to pick you up; stand in line one hour before the grocery store opened to get the best choice; ride your snow machine through the bush to the base cabin, and very carefully at that, when it was weighted down with moose steaks and wine; wear pantyhose over your head to fend off trillions of black flies; find the most beautiful of all dresses in Moose Factory; hop on your motorcycle and spend a Sunday afternoon at the train station watching the tourists disembark from the Polar Bear Express; and overhear an American tourist turn to her husband and say, "Dear, I didn't realize the Canadian Indian had red hair."

But the crowning moment that will remain forever fixed in our minds is celebrating the New Year on January 5, 1974—five days after the fact.

We left at the end of June with many mixed feelings, and before we boarded the Polar Bear Express for the last time, we took a good look around.

"See you guys! Hey, it was great, wasn't it?"

I couldn't believe I had once thought it would be impossible to make such wonderful friendships.

CHAPTER SEVEN

Finally, after serving our country for twelve years, along came a posting one only dreams about. For the next three years, we were to walk streets of a country with a history centuries older than Canada's, live in a foreign land, learn a new language, and discover, first hand, a culture much different from ours.

On August 3, 1974, we arrived at CFB Trenton in time to hop aboard the flight that would take us to the Old World. The fire chief, Leon Buehl, from our memorable New Year's Eve in Moosonee, and his wife, Kay, were there to see us off and wish us well. His eyebrows and eyelashes were still singed from the historic bonfire.

The overseas flight was an experience in terms of length and anticipation. Even though I had logged many hours in the sky, I still had a fear of flying. I have always preferred to have one foot on the ground.

Yet, for some strange reason, I feel safe aboard a military aircraft. I have a great deal of faith in the trades that make up the military. Everyone is trained to become experts in their field. You never hear of a crisis happening aboard aircraft that prime ministers, kings, queens, or presidents fly on. I believe it's because of the skill, knowledge, and desire for perfection that Air Force personnel bring to their jobs.

Safe and sound we landed in Lahr, West Germany, one of our European bases. Exhausted from the long trip, we recovered at the Europahoff, a military hotel. We spent the next few days getting acquainted with the Old World.

We found no difficulty adjusting our taste buds to the flavours of Europe. Where the vendors on the streets of New York sell hot dogs, the vendors on the streets of Germany offer bratwurst served with hot mustard and thin slices of rye bread, and depending upon your taste, a touch of sauerkraut on the side. I drool at the very thought of them.

We walked for miles around the quaint little town of Lahr. It was like stepping through the pages of an illustrated fairytale. Had we seen a troll or gnome that would have cinched it! The church bells chimed, the cobblestone streets glistened in the sun, mothers and babies chatted and cooed in an unknown language, and stately men in their lederhosen proudly displayed their poodles.

We didn't see any Chevs, Olds, or Fords on the streets. Everywhere we looked were Fiats, Citroëns, Morgans, Volkswagens, Mercedes, and Porsches. But where were the German shepherds and Dobermans? All we could see were French poodles in every size and colour. This posting would definitely be an exercise for the mind.

On our third day in West Germany we climbed aboard a Cosmo aircraft in Lahr and a couple of hours later arrived at Beek, The Netherlands. As we flew, we looked down in awe at the many windmills that dotted this flat land.

Did you know that flowers are a Dutchman's joy? They grace their homes and balconies, and hang from lampposts. They punctuate shopping streets with kaleidoscopic colour, and every occasion, from afternoon visits to birthdays, calls for a bouquet of these beauties.

Brunssum would become our hometown. A small, picturesque town, as are most of the cities and towns in Holland, it is located in the province of Limburg and bordered on what was then West Germany. Many of the homes are semi-detached and made of brick, while parks and beautiful old buildings dating from the seventeenth century with step-roofed gables lean over the canals, which seem to wander everywhere.

We spent a month living in a small hotel on the main street. The hotel, or family pension as they are called in Holland, was owned and operated by a family known as Leanders. Originally it had been their private home, but after World War II, they converted it into a hotel. Money was scarce, sometimes non-existent, and a living had to be made.

Three or four families could be accommodated, and like many older homes in Holland, it had a long, narrow staircase leading to the bedrooms and the one shared bathroom. The bedrooms were sparsely furnished, but what intrigued me most were the feather duvets that covered every bed. This was our first introduction to the duvet. Today, the bedspread has become a thing of the past in most Canadian homes—almost everyone prefers a duvet for comfort and warmth—but in 1974, they were a novelty.

Later that evening we watched television and a sombre Richard Nixon tell the world he was resigning as President of the United States following the incriminating outcome of the Watergate Hotel break-in. Dutch subtitles were shown at the bottom of the screen. A majority of the programming was in English.

The next morning, we had our first taste of a continental Dutch breakfast. On the table sprawled freshly baked bread and rolls, boiled eggs, all varieties of cheese, cold meats, and jams. Glenn and Alan were flabbergasted at the warm milk served. Milk in Holland was purchased from grocery shelves, not the cooler. It reminded us of canned evaporated milk. It was great when you baked with it, but you really couldn't develop a taste for it as a beverage.

After breakfast, Mrs. Leanders wanted to know what our tastes were. What did we like to eat? She had never cooked for Canadians before and had never been to Canada. Were our taste buds the same as her other guests? She didn't think so, especially after the kids nearly threw up when they tasted the warm milk.

Each day we prepared a menu, and she'd walk to the local markets to buy the vegetables, meat, or fish. She also made bread and pastries each morning. Although the preparation was different from what we were used to, she was an excellent cook. Meals at the hotel will never be forgotten.

Finally, our belongings arrived from Canada and the home we chose was ready for its Canadian tenants. Can you believe that the first meal in our new residence was beans and wieners? They tasted scrumptious.

We rented a two-storey, semi-detached, brick home owned by Joe and Annie Beumer. The Beumers owned a furniture store in Brunssum and were also the landlords for several other Canadian families living in the area. We became good friends, and our families still correspond.

We lived a stone's throw from the sidewalk, and that first year we learned many a Dutch song from the drunks as they staggered home from the local pubs. We also got to know our next-door neighbours, Theo and Ellie Jeurinsen, who also had two sons. Neither of us could speak the other's language, but that didn't stop us from becoming great friends. Heineken beer has a way of loosening up the tongue. Soon we all spoke the same language, whatever that was.

Theo and Ellie introduced us to many Dutch customs and traditions. We were invited to confirmations, anniversaries, and birthdays, and became known by their family and friends as "that cute Canadese couple."

We purchased most of our groceries at the local supermarket, but we bought seafood and vegetables at the farmers' market in the town square. On Saturday mornings, the farmers came to market laden with fresh fish, vegetables, cheeses, and every flower imaginable. Saturday markets became a tradition and raw herring a staple breakfast item for the Newfoundlander I married. I still get squeamish when I remember him holding that smelly fish above his mouth.

The market was a social gathering place for the Canadian families living in and about the area. We caught up on all the gossip. We'd then lunch at the nearby U.S. base and shop in their Exchange. The remainder of the afternoon we reserved for discovery trips.

Albert Heinz was one of a chain of Dutch supermarkets and my favourite. It was a business very similar to those found in Canada, but with one exception. All meat and vegetables were packaged in very small containers. No such thing as hamburger, T-bone steak, Butterball turkey, or rump roast. Meat and poultry were cut into small portions with not a smidgen of fat visible.

You see, the Dutch shopped every day, purchasing their meat, fish, cheese, milk and bread—just like Mrs. Leanders. It wasn't necessary for the stores to package anything in large quantities, as freezers were not a priority there.

Until I chose to shop like the Dutch, I was embarrassed when I got to the check-out counter with my cart stacked high. Everyone stared in disbelief.

However, I soon became accustomed to buying chicken already deboned and meat containing no fat. The fresh bread, especially that stuffed full of raisins, was heavenly. I purchased fresh flowers each day, and freesia filled every room of my home.

I even began to look European. I purchased my clothing in the Dutch stores and applied my makeup and coiffured my hair European-style. My family loved my new sophisticated look.

Once or twice a month we made the trip to shop at the U.S. Commissary at SHAPE, Belgium. SHAPE (Supreme Headquarters Allied Power Europe) is located in Brussels; General Alexander Haig, later advisor to President Ronald Reagan, was the Supreme Allied Commander for Europe at that time and his headquarters was located there.

Had we not been able to frequent the U.S. Commissary, we certainly would have adapted completely to the Dutch culinary lifestyle, but the smell of a T-bone sizzling on a barbecue was still fresh in our minds.

When we made the trek to the commissary, one would swear we were stocking up for a famine. T-bones, turkeys, roast beef, and every name-brand pickle, soup, salad dressing, or vegetable that was ever put in a bottle, jar or can, we purchased.

When we crossed the border at Liège in Belgium, the guards would peer into our car and ask whether we had anything to declare. Our answer was always the same.

"No, Sir, nothing to declare."

The back end of our car practically scraped the ground.

We were a small contingent of Canadians stationed at Allied Forces Central Europe, an international base. Our fellow Canadians stationed at Lahr and Baden Solingen in West Germany had privileges they sometimes took for granted. We had no Canadian schools, hospitals, doctors, dentists, or clergy. We came under the umbrella of an international community and shared the above. We were under the care of a British doctor, an American dentist, and a British hospital in Germany. Our kids attended an international school. We had no Canadian options.

I know that at one time I compared the different military units in terms of fairness, and I believe I envied the U.S. military wife. She seemed to have everything, while I had nothing. The U.S. military appeared to treat her as if she had never left her homeland. Whether she lived in Japan, Saudi Arabia or Holland, practically everything was provided for her and her family's comfort.

On the other hand, the Canadian wives had privileges the British wives only dreamed of. Salaries for the Americans, Canadians, and Germans far surpassed those the British military received. To shop on the economy was expensive, and my British counterpart definitely had limitations. The British Forces shopping facility called NAAFI, a shopping centre stocking virtually all foodstuffs and cheaper than outside shops because of customs concessions allowed under NATO agreements, was available to all international forces. We never shopped at the NAAFI store because everything was still expensive. Unfortunately for the British forces, the U.S. facilities were only open to the Americans and Canadians.

I guess we think the grass is greener on the other side. In most cases, it's not. A military wife is a military wife—some countries take better care of you, some do not.

CHAPTER EIGHT

I'm naked and I'm scared to death. I'm freezing cold and I have to make a decision as to whether or not I'm going to go out that door. A school comprising four nationalities? Will this be worth it?

It's the end of August 1974, and I have been hired by the Dutch government to take over the duties of the executive secretary for the director of AFCENT International School. This is a job of a lifetime, and when you've been a secretary for as long as I have, this is a job you dream about.

Before my hiring by the school could be finalized, the Dutch government required that I have a physical examination. Even though I had endured the yearly physical by my own doctor, the records could not be transferred. I had no choice—no medical, no job.

The NATO civilian personnel officer set up an appointment with a local Dutch doctor. I prayed that the doctor would be female, but no such luck. His office was located in his home, and from what I could see when I walked through the front door, it consisted of a small reception area and one other room. There were no patients. A few chairs lined up against the wall, but not many. My doctor's office practically had standing room only. Oh my, I didn't have a good feeling about this.

The receptionist escorted me into his office. He sat behind a large desk and greeted me with the traditional handshake. He spoke excellent English, which put me at ease for the moment. He asked questions about my medical history, then told me to prepare myself for his examination. He pointed to a door and said I could disrobe in there. The phrase, "to prepare myself" didn't sit well with me.

Hesitantly and nervously, I got up from the chair. My legs quivered. I walked towards the door. It squeaked when I opened it. Inside was no larger than a closet. I began to take off my clothes and hang them on the hook behind the door. I scanned the small area for a robe or sheet—something to cover myself with. Couldn't see anything—not a smidgen of material anywhere.

What was I to do? I sure as hell wasn't going out of that change room without my clothes on. My mind raced fast and furious. I must have stayed paralysed for over fifteen minutes. Then I heard the doctor say, "Madam, I'm ready for you now. I do have other patients I must see today."

I stuck my head out the door, "Excuse me, Doctor, but do you have a robe or something I can wear to cover myself with? Also, do I take everything off, or only a part?"

"A-a-h-h? . . . Well! . . . Yes! . . . Please remove all your clothing, Madam. And, no I'm afraid we don't provide a cover-up. Just disrobe fully please."

Pervert!

I'm scared to death, I'm freezing cold, and I have to make a decision as to whether or not I'm going to go out that door.

I have no other choice, I guess. I somehow must get the energy to go out that door and face him. I can't believe I'm naked as a jaybird and this pervert is sitting at his desk waiting for me to reappear.

Sure, I've been raised to be modest, but all modesty is now going to go out the window. I can't believe this is happening to me. Oh, my, I'm very bewildered. What do I do? I can feel my heart pounding in my chest. I know I can't remain here forever. I have to make a move. Think, Jeanette, think!

Okay, I'm calm. I won't be embarrassed. I'll swallow my pride and make my move. I have no option. Maybe I should tell him that I didn't want the job in the first place? Maybe I should tell him I think he's deranged? What the hell do I tell him?

I took a couple of deep breaths and tried to convince myself that I'd be okay.

Oh, what the heck, I'll probably never see him again anyway, and I'm sure he has seen his share of naked women.

So, out the door I go, with one hand across my chest and the other covering . . . well, you know what. Walking somewhat bowlegged, I tiptoed across the room. I avoided all eye contact. He obviously could see my embarrassment.

"You Americans are much too modest," he grinned.

"I beg your pardon, Doctor, but I'm not an American. I'm Canadian."

"Well then," he said, "you Canadians are much too modest. Please stand tall with arms by your side. I will measure your height."

My heart raced, and I'm sure my blood pressure hit the roof. But, I did as he said. I stood straight, shoulders against the wall, legs close together. I prayed that the only place he'd put the ruler would be on top of my head. At this point it didn't matter much that I was absolutely freezing. Modesty had become a shy and unobtrusive grammar school noun.

Following this medical tactic, it was up on the examining table, where I lay, naked as the day I was born. The only piece of cloth touching me was his tie. I thought to myself as I looked up at the ceiling, *This job better be the best I've ever had and sure as hell worth all of this degradation.*

Later I learned that Dutch women always wear a slip to their doctor's office. This provides their cover-up. Everyone but me thought this exploit had been very courageous, but also found it extremely hilarious.

"Excuse me, Doctor, but do you happen to have a sheet, a piece of cloth, or some damn thing in the form of material?"

Seeing that perplexed and startled look upon his face will remain in my memory forever.

Glenn and Alan attended AFCENT International School, which comprised four nationalities: Canadian, German, British, and American. It offered kindergarten to Grade 12 for 1,500 students.

Co-operation was the key to running a successful international school, and the interaction of students from various countries provided a unique opportunity to learn from one another.

A principal or headmaster led each section, and every nationality had its own curriculum. The Canadian curriculum was based on Ontario's and taught only up to Grade 8. After that, it was American. We were somewhat apprehensive over Glenn's re-entry into the Canadian school system when he returned to Canada, when he'd be entering Grade 10, but as it turned out, he had no problems whatsoever.

There were times when the four nations came together academically as well as athletically.

Glenn and Alan got involved in all sports that first year. They both joined football, hockey, tennis, baseball, skiing and swimming, so for Dave and me, it became a constant trek to the rink, court, field, and pool. I chuckle now remembering when the school decided to have students in the workshop training and home economics classes switch. Although Dave said, "No kid of mine is getting off the football field and putting on an apron," it did transpire, and Glenn learned how to make muffins—European style.

Unfortunately Glenn's athletic career was put on hold for two years while he waited for leg fractures to heal. His mishaps on the slopes halted participation in many sports, but more on that later.

Alan made two good friends at AFCENT—John Argue and Richard Sheppard. John was Canadian and his father, Paul, a fighter pilot in the Canadian Air Force. Richard was American and his father, Dick, also a fighter pilot, but in the U.S. Air Force.

Alan and John were in the same class and played on the hockey and baseball teams. They were two of three Canadians who played hockey for the Geleen Smoke Eaters. Patrick Halfpenny was the other player. The Smoke Eaters were a Dutch hockey team, and they recruited Canadians to join. The arena was unique: one end of the building was open to the elements. The kids played hockey, and the cows and sheep from the nearby countryside were spectators.

Although John was a constant visitor in our home during our tour in Holland, we never got to know his parents, Paul and Sheila. However, since our return to Canada, we have become genuine friends. The day I opened my boutique in 1990, Sheila was my first customer. When she handed me a cheque for an item she had purchased, I recognized her name immediately. Ironic, isn't it, to develop a true friendship after all those years had elapsed.

Paul retired with the rank of general from the Canadian Forces. He and Sheila now reside in the town of Gravenhurst. They have four children. John has followed in his dad's footsteps and is a fighter pilot for the Canadian Air Force.

We are also good friends with Dick and Elizabeth Sheppard, and our families have had many great times together. Dick hails from Chicago and Elizabeth from Texas. Dave and Dick coached the little league baseball team at AFCENT where Alan and Richard played. They had a great team that year in 1977 and went on to represent AFCENT at the European Little League Championships held in Lahr, West Germany. Alan pitched and Richard played shortstop. The AFCENT team put up a valiant fight, but a team from the U.S. military base at Torrejon, Spain, went on to win and represent Europe at the World's Little League Championships in Williamsport, Pennsylvania. Thailand won the championship that year.

During the Vietnam War, Dick flew missions with a night-fighter squadron known as the River Rats. Many of his friends were killed during this war. Elizabeth once told me the only solace that had maintained her sanity and kept her calm was the fact that her husband flew his assignments at night. Because of the dark, he wouldn't make an easy target for the enemy. One night as he piloted the fastest plane made, he followed a light, but that light kept getting farther and farther away from him until, finally, it was no bigger than a star. Both he and I believe in spaceships.

Dick and Elizabeth have retired from the U.S. Air Force and are now the proud owners of a resort in Tennessee. Richard followed in his dad's footsteps and is a jet pilot for the U.S. Air Force.

In retrospect, had it not been for the Canadian military, these three families would never have met and become lasting friends.

It was wonderful to see the children at this school intermingle and share traditions. The experience planted a sense of awareness in Glenn and Alan, an awareness they might not have received in a Canadian public school. They learned first hand through international teachings that no matter what their race or colour, nationality or religion, kids are kids and they thrive on knowledge. I believe both of our children benefited in terms of being guided through this European experience to become responsible adults.

This interaction also afforded Glenn and Alan the opportunity to make friends of all nationalities, from around the world. And, like everything else, contact lessens over the years. But no matter what, memories do prevail.

CHAPTER NINE

My boss, Herr Rudolf Bewer, an educator from Berlin, was a true German gentleman and a person anyone would be proud and privileged to know. Herr Bewer's assistant, Paul Papineau from Providence, Rhode Island, the comptroller, Harry Kickken, a native of Holland, and a redhead from Cape Breton completed the administrative team. Herr Bewer, ever so proud of his international team, often stated that he had the best job in the world.

Even today when I think of Herr Bewer, I recall two particular stories.

Towards the end of World War II when the Nazis were losing control of their so-called world, the desperate German navy recruited young boys, taking them from their homes and schools. These young men were trained for maybe one week then had a gun put into their hands. With cast-off uniforms, some torn at the knees, they were loaded aboard German ships and sent out to sea. Herr Bewer was one. He was fifteen years old.

Herr Bewer shot down German planes, because he couldn't identify a British plane from a German plane. His nightmares never ceased.

After World War II, he was accepted for graduate studies at Yale University. Rudolf Bewer's English was reasonable, but sometimes understanding the origins of words and how they were placed was a difficult process. When he filled out his application, the name and address had not posed a problem, but when he came to the single word, "Sex," he stopped to ponder. He didn't want to appear uneducated by asking what it meant, so he wrote, "Yes. But only once. And that was in Munich."

Herr Bewer never lived that comment down.

My job involved a lot of travelling. Because I was also secretary to the board of directors, I accompanied the director and his staff to various European countries where meetings on educational matters were held. I travelled to Heidelberg, Cologne, Frankfurt, and London.

When I attended these conventions and seminars, my role was to take the minutes of meetings verbatim. That was quite a challenge. Everyone had a different accent. The only person I understood completely was the Canadian principal, Mr. Saunders.

Many of the wives accompanied their husbands to these meetings. During the day while I slaved away taking minutes, they were given tours of the cities. I was somewhat envious, but hey, I had a job. I wasn't there to sightsee. Besides, the evenings were the most fun anyway. The host country wined and dined us. Conversations were intriguing. I appreciated the opportunity to meet educators from Europe and the United States.

I believe that because I was Canadian, many of the people at the convention wanted to talk with me. No one seemed to know much about Canada. They knew what was happening in the United States, but not in Canada. Because of that, I had to bone up on my own country. Before these meetings, I'd get out the Canadian history books and study. Dave would keep me up-to-date on current events via the military headquarters. When I attended school, the focus had been on ancient civilizations and European history; Canadian history didn't enter into the picture. To this day, I can't figure that one out.

Being the secretary at Glenn and Alan's school wasn't always a treat for them. Heaven forbid they did anything wrong! Nevertheless, it afforded them extra benefits and opportunities that another student might not have been able to receive. I suppose it was a mixed blessing for them.

At lunch hour, Herr Bewer set aside one half hour for Alan. Three times a week they ate lunch together in his office. They traded coins. Alan loved to tell everyone that he was having lunch with the "Brass." Herr Bewer made a point of educating Alan during these lunch hours, and Alan learned first hand about the Nazi regime during World War II and the era that followed. Alan still has Nazi coins used during that time.

We travelled the countryside and explored every nook and cranny from the top corner of Holland to the bottom.

Three of Holland's greatest cities are only an hour apart: Amsterdam, Rotterdam, and The Hague. Our first trip was to Amsterdam.

With our newly purchased moss-green 1974 European Chrysler, we blended in with the terrain. It rained a lot in Holland, and the tree trunks were covered in velvety clusters of moss.

We checked into a family pension recommended by the Amsterdam Tourist Bureau that was located in the heart of the city and close to Dam Square. The entire block comprised pensions, called canal houses. Each one was connected, and they were distinguished by awnings and signs in different colours.

Prinsengracht 263, the canal house where Anne Frank and seven other Jews holed up for more than two years after the Nazis occupied the Netherlands, was at the end of this street. It has been turned into a museum, and what's been preserved is unfathomable human cruelty under glass.

As we know, the fugitives were betrayed and their story was preserved through Anne's famous diary, which her father, Otto, later found and published, years after her death in a concentration camp. Mr. Frank was the only one of the eight who did survive. Anne Frank succumbed to typhus and deprivation in March 1945 at Bergen-Belsen, three weeks before the camp was liberated.

Our pension was owned by two university students and definitely had a hippie decor. Posters of Jim Morrison and Janis Joplin lined the walls. We climbed the narrow staircase to our bedrooms and found two large beds covered with feather duvets. They looked so cozy I could hardly wait to lie under them. I began to wonder whether the duvet was becoming an aphrodisiac for me in Holland.

The next morning we began our walk through the pages of history.

Amsterdam . . . a living monument to Holland's Golden Age. Almost the entire city rests on a foundation of piles driven through peat and sand to a firm substratum of clay.

During World War II, the German army occupied Amsterdam for five years. The people suffered great hardship and the port was badly damaged, but it has since been rebuilt and improved. Elegant houses line the city's canals, and ancient bridges arch over the waterways.

Armed with our guidebook, we mapped out our route. First on the agenda was a tour of the canals. Canals divide the city into ninety islands linked by about 400 bridges.

Canal boats are glass-covered with the roof kept open on sunny days. We cruised up and down the waterways and learned stories behind the houses that lined the canal banks. Every home was laden with blossoms, and simply by counting the number of steps to a front door, you could ascertain the wealth of the landowner. The more steps, the wealthier the landowner. Also, the less likelihood the family could be flooded out in the event of the sea reclaiming the land once again.

I pitied the poor family having only two steps. I often said that if I were in their wooden shoes, I'd definitely ensure that the third step was a canoe.

In all of the movies we shot that day, a head appeared in every frame. The kids and I blamed Dave for his inability to take advantage of his height. Why couldn't he have shot above the head of a bald voyageur that appeared to be obliterating the scenery he wanted to film?

We also visited Holland's famous museums: the Rijksmuseum and the Van Gogh.

The Rijksmuseum has about 800 works, one of the largest collections of Dutch and Flemish paintings in the world. I actually touched the frame of Rembrandt's *Night Watch*, the prize of the Rijksmuseum, with its own special room. I learned that it had actually been misnamed. A cleaning revealed, under layers of grime, a scene depicted in broad daylight.

We also learned on this tour that Van Gogh, the self-taught genius, sold only one canvas before his suicide in 1890.

I had to pinch myself a number of times for this opportunity. A Newfoundlander and a Cape Bretoner exposed to all this culture? Who would have known? And made possible only because of our association with the Canadian Forces. I still marvel at the experience.

We always knew that Amsterdam had been famous for polishing and cutting diamonds, so it was only natural that the diamond factory would be next on our list. We were escorted into a large room and seated on chairs in front of a large glass counter. Across the counter stood the jeweller, a small man with a shiny bald head and a monocle in one eye. I couldn't figure out how it remained there so steadily. He didn't even blink.

Once we were inside, an armed guard appeared and stood in front of the door. He may have been a policeman, as there were two handguns strapped to his belt. He pulled the door shut, and three bars with locks automatically sealed the door. Everyone glanced at one another. I'm sure we thought the same thing.

If a thief is among us today, don't take what doesn't belong to you.

The jeweller took out trays of diamonds and placed them on the glass counter. We could try on the pieces if we wished. Personally, I loved the larger diamond rings. When I tried them on, I sneaked a glance at Dave. History repeated itself.

"Mercy, mercy!" I chuckled as I admired the huge clear diamond on my finger. "But I think this one is much too big and gaudy. What do you think, Dave?"

Suddenly out of the blue, the jeweller blew a whistle. We practically hit the ceiling. I guess our tour was finished.

The jeweller put all the diamonds back in the trays, one by one. With the monocle still in his eye, he inspected and counted each diamond. Only when he nodded did the guard open the door.

The tour group was disappointed that samples were not given out.

Rotterdam, the Phoenix City. Levelled by the German Luftwaffe during World War II, the city has grown into a miracle of modern architecture and city planning. Its harbour is the largest in the world. Never had I seen so many cruise ships and tankers in one place.

Outside of Rotterdam is a town called Kinderkijk. We photographed nineteen windmills and all in one click of the lens. We climbed to the top of one, and as far as the eye could see was flat. It was hard to fathom that this land had once been part of the sea.

The Hague, capital of Holland, was our next stop. This city was even statelier than Amsterdam. History tells us that during World War II, Queen Juliana lived safely in Ottawa, and in 1943, she gave birth to Princess Margriet at Ottawa Civic Hospital. So that the child could be born on Dutch territory, Canada declared the delivery rooms a part of the Netherlands.

Two years later, the Canadian Army liberated Holland from the Germans. For all the kindness shown to the Queen and her family by the Canadian government during this volatile time, the Dutch people expressed their gratitude by sending more than 100,000 tulip bulbs to the then dowdy Ottawa. Queen Juliana sent an additional 20,500, requesting that 3,000 of the bulbs be planted around the hospital where her daughter was born. Gifts of bulbs have continued to come each year, so that now more than three million tulips bloom in Ottawa each May. Parliament Hill is ablaze in colour from the thousands of cup-shaped flowers.

My good friend, Bep Van Beek, a colleague from the AFCENT School, was born and raised in The Hague and was a teenager during the war. She told me many stories about her life when the Nazis took control of Holland. They actually ate tulip bulbs, and her family had no possessions to call their own as everything was taken from them. Their lives were made hell. They had no identity. They were a conquered people. They lived in constant fear. Every other day, her father rode a bicycle with no tires thirty miles to the countryside to fetch potatoes and vegetables for their table. The Germans had taken every scrap of rubber they could find, even if it was on a small, simple bike. They took everything that would enable them to keep their military machine going.

Bep's family hid her brother in their basement for years so that the Nazis wouldn't send him to fight for the Third Reich. Every time Bep related a tale, a tear trickled from her eye. Her fondest memory, though, was the day the Canadian Army liberated Holland. The Dutch people—men, women, children and even animals—lined the streets of The Hague, as our soldiers marched into the city. Everyone, soldiers included, cheered and cried. She will never forget that unmistakable glorious taste of chocolate—a gift from the passing Canadian soldiers—and one she had been deprived of for so many years.

When I recall a story such as hers, I swell with pride at being a military wife from a country whose military contributed to Holland's liberation.

Our weekend came too quickly to an end, and we headed back to Amsterdam and our hotel. I was exhausted and had wonderful visions of dreaming away under the cozy duvet covering my feather bed.

However, the next morning, I woke up scratching like a dog full of fleas. Every part of my body itched.

There were large red welts all over me—on my face and all the way down to my toes. But I was the only one of the Russells who itched. I couldn't figure out why, but I knew bed bugs had to be the nasty culprit. Maybe the family had set up house in my feather duvet, but I wondered why these little creatures attacked only me. Maybe these bugs were sexually driven in that glorious duvet. Is it possible they could have been attracted to red hair? I continue to scratch at the memory.

Later that day, back home in Brunssum, I disinfected myself before I dared enter my house. I peeled off my clothes at the back step and tossed them in the trash. I smelled of Lysol for weeks. Ask me if I like a bug? I dare you!

CHAPTER TEN

The Canadian celebration of Christmas proved entirely different from the Dutch way of celebrating the birth of Christ.

Around eleven o'clock on December 23, 1974, the silence of the evening was broken by the sounds of singing. It appeared to be coming from the sidewalk below our bedroom window. Dave was fast asleep, but in the next room, Glenn woke up and rushed into our room. He shook his father awake.

"Dad, wake up. There's a bunch of people outside singing."

"Glenn, go back to bed! It's only some drunks coming back from the bars."

"But Dad, they're singing in English!"

I had been out that evening visiting friends. When I walked up the hill, I noticed a gathering. I heard singing. When I got closer, I realized these people were pretty rowdy and they swayed directly in front of my house.

"There she is! You weren't at home after all. Merry Christmas, Jeanette."

There had to be at least thirty people.

"We've been singing below your window for practically an hour now. Has Dave passed out or what? Or is he even home?"

So reminiscent of Moosonee, this inebriated, yet festive, group had been gathering Canadian friends the entire evening. Living on the other side of Brunssum, we were last on their list.

"Get ready. We're headed for the general's house to wish him a merry Christmas."

I glanced around the neighbourhood and could see the shuffling of curtains and the peeping of eyes from all windows. How would I explain it in the morning? I suppose the melodies could sound familiar to my neighbours, but could they understand the English lyrics?

Thirty people marched behind me through our front door, all armed with a variety of instruments, including an accordion, a washboard, spoons, castanets, and song sheets for everyone. Surprisingly enough, this military troupe sounded pretty darn good. Dave quickly dressed and came downstairs, rubbing the sleep from his eyes. Both Glenn and Alan peeked at the group through the rungs of the staircase, hoping to join in.

The troupe was parched and hungry after singing carols for the past hour under our window. I rustled up some cheese and crackers and opened up chips and pretzels. I then led the way to the wine cellar.

With song sheets in hand, we sang every carol in the book. I can still hear my friend Eileen Halfpenny: "Do you hear what I hear, do you see what I see?" Every time there was a lull she would break out and sing that famous Christmas carol. The more wine she drank, the louder she sang.

The four-star general and his wife had no idea we had planned an invasion. It was two o'clock in the morning when we pulled up in front of their house and lined up in perfect parade formation on the front lawn. Accompanied by a variety of musical instruments, our Christmas choir sang the carols we had rehearsed. Once again I could see eyes peering from all neighbouring windows. Finally, two sleepy Canadians opened their front door. The general saluted.

"Merry Christmas, everyone. Welcome to our home. Come on in and party."

We raided both the liquor cabinet and the refrigerator. We wondered whether the general's wife had been forewarned of our plan to invade, for a pot of clam chowder bubbled on the stove and a Butterball turkey posed on a platter waiting to be devoured.

We sat around the piano and harmonized as best we could, but by this time we didn't have much energy left. We were full to the brim.

"Do you hear what I hear, do you see what I see?" She was still at it!

As the sun appeared on the horizon, we bade everyone adieu and wished one another the merriest and happiest Christmas ever. Our first Christmas in Holland will never be forgotten.

The following day, Dave and I trotted out to the trash cans and stacked them high with empty wine bottles. We sheepishly glanced around.

Those crazy Canucks!

We assumed that everyone with our religious views celebrated the birth of Christ in the same way. Don't we take out the manger, put Baby Jesus in the cradle, trim the Christmas tree, go to Midnight Mass—whether you be Protestant or Catholic—and patiently wait for Santa Claus to come down the chimney?

At the crack of dawn, don't the kids wake up (that is if they slept at all), race us down the stairs and, as a family, gather around the tree? Don't we all sit in our pyjamas before the colourfully wrapped presents with the pretty bows sparkling under the twinkling lights and take turns opening them? Doesn't everyone shake a box and try to guess what's inside, and then, with much fun, ooh and aah over each gift as it is revealed?

Doesn't everyone gorge on Christmas turkey and plum pudding? And, by eight o'clock in the evening, isn't everything quiet as we all head for bed, too exhausted to think anymore?

Our celebration of Christmas proved entirely different from the Dutch way. Santa Claus does not come down the chimney on Christmas Eve laden with gifts. Turkey and plum pudding are not served on Christmas Day. Instead, Santa Claus is Sinterklaas and Zwarte Pieten (Black Peter) has replaced Santa's elves.

Sinterklaas is the white-bearded patron saint of children who arrives from Spain in mid-November. He's accompanied by a host of mischievous servants quite unlike Santa's helpful elves. On December 5, families give each other anonymous and creatively wrapped gifts accompanied by poems written by Sinterklaas about the recipient. But if the children in the family have been bad, they receive only a lump of coal.

On Christmas Eve, wooden shoes are put outside the front door and in the morning are found filled with candies and fruits. The remainder of Christmas Day is observed strictly as a religious holiday eulogizing the birth of Christ.

Just before Christmas, the AFCENT School invited Sinterklaas and Black Peter to meet Santa Claus, his elves, and his reindeer. The young international students had little knowledge about these North American symbols of Christmas, but were excited just the same.

However, the Americans were not. Some members of the U.S. staff took offence to the idea of slavery being praised in connection with the birth of Christ. They argued that Black Peter was a slave to Sinterklaas, not a helper like the elves were to Santa Claus. Meetings took place to try to convince the American contingent that Black Peter was not a slave, but a colleague and friend to Sinterklaas. It made no difference to the American faculty and staff. There would be no interaction among the nations. All students were disappointed.

Tradition was bypassed in this instance.

CHAPTER ELEVEN

The romance of Italy—the Vatican and its treasures, the people, the wine, and the countryside. These we expected, but did you know about the three-minute warning for exiting a train? Dave thought he knew. We caused havoc aboard.

On June 11, 1975, during our second summer in Europe, four families (sixteen people in all) left Brunssum for an Italian holiday. We caused a stir on the autobahn as we travelled slowly behind each other. (If you are familiar with autobahns you know that if there is a speed limit to abide by, no one pays attention. You go as fast as you want to and hope that the cop cars get lost in your dust.) The European travellers behind us were not impressed, even though we had proudly displayed Canadian flags on our trailers. The German drivers kept flashing their lights at us. Oh, yes, you learn very quickly what that means. When you see a BMW or a Mercedes travelling the autobahn at 200 kilometres an hour, you swerve to the right and let it pass. Nationality means nothing on the autobahn.

Our first overnight stop landed us at the U.S. base of Ramstein in West Germany. We craved pizza, and it was recommended that we try a pizza palace in the nearby town of Anweiller.

We gave sixteen different pizza orders to a waiter who spoke only German.

About the only similarity a German pizza has to its North American counterpart is the crust. After that, it's a whole new ballgame. German sausage replaces pepperoni, fresh tomatoes replace pizza sauce, peas replace green pepper, and Limburger cheese replaces mozzarella.

We were not impressed. Our waiter gestured for us to come up to a table close to the pizza ovens where different types of meats, cheeses, and vegetables were displayed. We were then able to point out the ingredients we wanted put on our pizzas.

None of us was enthusiastic about sampling the finished product.

By the time the waiter finally got our orders straight, he must have mopped his forehead a thousand times. We had created havoc.

The evening turned out to be the first of many nights of confusion.

Our next stop was Garmish, a town on the Austrian border. The U.S. military had purchased land in the town where they built a recreational facility for their troops. Military families vacationed there at hotels named after Dwight D. Eisenhower, Franklin Roosevelt, and Harry Truman and shopped at commissaries and restaurants featuring American products and food. The U.S. military ensured that a foreign land took on the appearance and traits of home. Their troops and families could eat, drink, and play as if they had never left the States.

During these years, McDonald's and Burger King had no franchises in Europe. So it was a real treat to enjoy a home-style hamburger when we lunched at the U.S. facilities. Hamburgers and hot dogs were not available in German or Dutch restaurants.

Garmish was more popular during the winter months than it was in June, as the town is situated in a valley surrounded by snow-covered mountains. Most of the houses were built an alpine style out of wood, unlike the brick that comprised many of the homes in Europe. Every window had a flower box, with geraniums seeming to be the flower of choice. Women dressed in the traditional bib and apron, men and small boys in lederhosen and knee socks. Everyone hiked the many trails that bordered the town. Young and old alike carried walking sticks.

Of particular interest to me, and I'm sure to anyone who visits Germany, is Oberammergau. Nestled in the Bavarian Alps, Oberammergau is a delightful place that has managed not to succumb to commercial excess. Its historical character shines through with its alpine cottages, colourful gardens, prosperous farmsteads, and stately homes adorned with ornamental paintings. It is also home to a long and honourable tradition of craftsmanship, especially woodcarving.

Houses are decorated with magnificent carved scenes depicting a panorama of scenes, many of them religious. The buildings surrounding the town orphanage, which is ideally named after Hansel and Gretel, are all carved with scenes from the fairytale. With the many workshops and schools, this artistic abundance is almost as much a part of Oberrammergau's fame as the Passion Play itself.

The Passion Spielhaus is the most famous site in the town. As the story goes, in 1633, the Black Plague snatched away most of the inhabitants of the little mountain village. The parish fathers, driven to desperation, prayed to God that if the plague vanished and their village was freed from the appalling sickness, the townspeople would stage a performance of the Passion of Christ every ten years. From that moment, the village was spared from the Black Death. Attracting pilgrims and playgoers from far and wide, it became a recurring event.

The theatre is used for one day every ten years. More than 1,100 people are in the cast, all born in Oberammergau. The play is performed in any weather and on an open stage. There are years when the sun is shining and years when rain or snow will fall, but nevertheless, the play goes on.

The enactment is always performed on Easter Sunday. Young men are groomed all their lives for this opportunity, and it is everyone's wish to become The Chosen One. The year 2000 was the most recent year this play was performed.

We made a point to visit sites that were notable in terms of beauty and historical value. However, there was one location we regretted visiting. What we saw was unspeakable and deplorable and left us shattered for days. Even though years have passed since we were in Dachau, I periodically think back and remember, always with tears in my eyes.

Dachau is situated six miles north of Munich and has become notorious for the concentration camp located there during Hitler's reign of terror. The huge extermination and labour camp has become a shrine to the memory of those who died there. And the pictures displayed on the camp's library walls are etched in my memory forever.

I have a fear of death, a fear of the unknown. But what about the men, women, and children who were sacrificed to the barbarity of the Nazis? Did they want to die? It's my guess that they waited for that peaceful moment to happen.

The Dachau concentration camp was opened on March 22, 1933, in a former gunpowder factory. The first prisoners were Third Reich opponents and other "undesirables"— Communists, social democrats, homosexuals, gypsies, Jehovah's Witnesses, and clergymen. Many of them were suspected of plotting to overthrow Hitler, who had just been elected chancellor.

According to a U.S. 7th Army report, there were 221,930 people interred at Dachau between 1933 and 1945. Three weeks before liberation, another 7,000 prisoners arrived, many of them women.

However, with the victorious advances of the Allied troops in the spring of 1945, more and more concentration camps were being evacuated by the SS, and prisoners were being transferred to camps in territories still under Nazi control. On these week-long marches, thousands of prisoners, many too weak to walk, lost their lives because of sickness, starvation, beatings, and torture. Those who could no longer walk were shot by SS guards. The survivors—many of them Catholic priests—became guinea pigs for Nazi medical experiments in an attempt to find a cure for malaria. As the priests were not required to labour, it was thought that they would not be missed if they died.

In fact, the majority of prisoners who died at Dachau were Catholic. It was Nazi policy to send the Jews first to ghettos and then to extermination camps in Poland. It was not until the final days of the war that Jews were transferred to camps in Germany. Between June and November 1944, reports indicate that approximately 30,000 Jews were gassed at Dachau in a chamber disguised as a shower room.

As we made our way through the gates, we looked up and saw emblazoned on the gate, *Arbeit Macht Frei* (Work Shall Set You Free). Then, in the square, was a sculpture of skeletons hanging from a barbed-wire fence, with the hands designed to look like the barbs.

While we walked around the grounds, there was an eerie silence. No birds sang, and everyone spoke only in whispers, if at all. In the courtyard, now paved with cobblestones, we walked over the graves of thousands of unknown people. We then entered one of the many wooden barracks, each of which had housed more than 1,500 people. Bunks were stacked five high and had no mattresses and no blankets. Only a few had straw. In the corner stood a small wood stove, which often had remained unlit due to a lack of fuel.

Our tour group was introduced to a gentleman by the name of Martin Zaidenstadt, a Polish Jew who had survived Dachau and who had returned to the camp every day since 1947 to talk with the tourists.

We asked him why the townspeople of Dachau hadn't done something to help these people. He replied that, presumably, when the prisoners were brought to work in the factories, the people had tried to help. In fact, the townspeople resent being made to feel guilty about something over which they had no control.

Did they not see the smoke and smell the stench?

The local population learned a lesson in self-worth when, after liberation, the British and U.S. troops gathered them up and made them parade through the camp. They were forced to view the horror. They were forced to view the rotting corpses, the foulness of which could be smelled a mile away.

The chaplain of the 42nd Rainbow Division, which was in charge of Dachau's liberation, was a Jew, Rabbi Eli Bohnen. And the commanding officer, Major General Harry J. Collins, made sure that the Jewish survivors would be cared for properly. He evicted some homeowners in the town of Dachau to provide some of the survivors with private housing (some of the homeowners, however, were allowed to stay in their attics, but had to leave behind all household effects for the use of the new tenants). A few of the Jewish survivors even settled permanently in Dachau after the war.

> Dachau, 1933–1945, will stand for all time as one of history's most gruesome symbols of inhumanity. There our troops found sights, sounds, and stenches horrible beyond belief, cruelties so enormous as to be incomprehensible to the normal mind. Dachau and death were synonymous.
>
> —Colonel William W. Quinn, 7th U.S. Army

Our brand new European Chrysler had hot flashes every time we hit a long incline. No garage could determine the problem and fix it, which concerned us, as an overheating car would be tricky to cross the mountains with into Innsbruck and later ascend the Brenner Pass into Italy.

As we began to climb, lights started to flash and smoke poured from under the hood. We could go no further and pulled over to the side of the road. We waved to the military cavalcade. Storm ahead without us. We'd meet at the designated campground in Lago Legarda (Lake Legardo) in Italy. We turned back to Garmish, where a mechanic was confident he could fix the problem.

After spending the night, we arose in the cool of the morning for our second attempt. At four we started out, and the kids were soon asleep in the back seat. However, we had to stop every five minutes to let the engine cool. Finally, after six hours, we pulled into the camping ground in Italy.

Our friends were patiently waiting for us, cooling some Italian wine. They knew Dave and I would have a great thirst, and we proved it. Have you ever seen the cartoon of the guy with the world's worst hangover? Actually that guy was a gal; I sat for the sketch.

A few days later we reached a campsite known as Union Lido, on the shores of the Adriatic Sea. Years earlier, the press had glorified Union Lido as the largest open-air health resort in Europe. It contained 60,000 square metres of building—the size of a miniature city. The campsite was complete with restaurants, sidewalk cafes, clothing and grocery stores, a daily market, churches, hairdressers, nightclubs, horseback riding facilities, shuffleboard, tennis, golf—you name it, it had it. More than 30,000 trailers camped there.

Security police with guard dogs patrolled the grounds at night. The dogs were the biggest German shepherds I had ever seen, in fact, their nostrils looked like the front end of a double-barrelled shotgun. We were advised to take all valuables from our car and unlock the doors. Who would be foolish enough to even attempt a break-in?

Siesta occurred each day, and the campsite shut down from noon to three with the gates locked to both incoming and outgoing traffic. If you wanted to sightsee, you did it before noon. On our first day we travelled by ferry to Venice and spent most of the day exploring the city. The next day the troupe preferred to laze on the beach, including Dave and my kids. I maintained that they could swim anytime. You couldn't visit Venice anytime. Obviously, my theory didn't hold water.

We camped at Union Lido for three weeks, and every day I made the daily trek to Venice alone. I'd lumber back around suppertime, exhausted. I toured museums and walked the lanes and streets seeking treasures. I sat in St. Mark's Square and lunched at one of the many sidewalk cafes. I sampled so many different pastas, cheeses, and wines that I practically became a connoisseur of Italian cuisine.

I became extremely adept at sidestepping. During the 1970s, the human population of Venice was about 350,000, but the pigeon population was about 400,000. Take a tip from a Cape Bretoner! When you visit Venice, wear sunglasses, be it day or night, and please try to restrict your urge to view the ornamental architecture on the tops of buildings.

I marvelled at this ancient city with no cars and watched with astonishment as the gondolas transported goods and supplies. Everything the city requires is assembled and shipped by barge. I watched children play by themselves on the canal banks and quivered at the risk. But a drowning is no more frequent here than anywhere else. Everyone is raised to respect the water. Most of the young men in Venice learn early in life how to row or pole a gondola, and when they become teenagers, many take up the trade of gondolier.

It's a wonderful treat to ride the canals with a tall, dark, and handsome gondolier, dressed in a striped shirt. The oars move to the rhythm of his singing, and I am certain that in order to become a gondolier, you must have a beautiful voice. They all sounded like Mario Lanza to me.

Long ago the Bridge of Sighs carried prisoners to the gallows, and the people of Venice say that if you listen attentively in the still of the night, you can hear their sighs of despair.

After the third week of camping at Union Lido, the troupe decided that it was time to move on to Pisa, Rome, and Monte Carlo. Everyone hitched up and off went the Canadian contingent once again. But this time, we went separate ways. The four families had perhaps seen enough of one another. To tell you the truth it was a relief. If you book a tour, the itinerary is planned. But in our case, everyone wanted to do something different. We all had different tastes. So, it was a friendly decision to divide and go separate ways.

Dave and I coupled up with Bill and Betty Spicer and their three children. The Spicers and we always had such fun together in Brunssum. We felt that this vacation together would not be an exception.

We followed one another on towards Pisa, and looming in the distance, we saw the world-famous leaning tower. We eventually parked our vehicles and walked through the crowded square towards the tower. But how many were Canadian families?

The freestanding bell tower of the cathedral of Pisa was begun in 1173. Construction took 200 years, partly because of delays caused by the tower's persistent structural problems. By the time the first three stories were completed, one side of the tower had already begun to sink into the soft soil. Construction was halted for 100 years before it was finally finished in 1350.

The climb to the top was, at best, 294 lung-burning steps up a spiral staircase. I rested on every landing, but that still did not prevent me from feeling sick. It felt as if the tower moved and swayed. It probably did. Eventually we reached the top, but when I looked down, everything appeared crooked and tilted, including the cathedral. Although the tower's ancient bells remain in place, they are no longer rung. Thank God for that. All I needed at that point was to be deafened.

Galileo conducted his famous experiments with gravity and the relative speed of falling objects from the tower's top storey. Although it used to tilt a bit each year, the tower will never tumble as Italian architects and engineers have recently arrested its off-centre movement. And no one else will experience that horrible woozy feeling; the tower has been closed to the public since 1990 due to safety and conservation concerns.

Seventy-five miles outside of Rome, we set up camp at "Camping Hawaii." We were astounded at the numerous pine trees there. They stood so tall they almost obliterated the sun, and they produced the biggest pine cones I've ever seen.

We headed for the beach with its wonderful white sand that stretched as far as the eye could see. There, we passed a small sign written in Italian tacked to a tree. I hoped I'd remember to ask the campsite owner about this upon our return.

The bright turquoise water sparkled crystal clear. We had this part of the Mediterranean all to ourselves as there was not another soul on the beach. Maybe this was unusual, but then again we were in another part of Italy. It was 4 p.m., and siesta times could be different. The sun shone on our private beach, and we felt that heaven couldn't be much better than this.

We spread out blankets, smothered our bodies with sun tan lotion, and sipped on cold lemonade. We frolicked in the surf, snorkelled in the clear water, and floated aimlessly. We paddled our rubber boat to an area where huge waves rose and fell and got caught in the thrill of it rushing us towards shore. In and out of the water we threw the frisbee. When the sun went down, it was back to the campsite.

That evening after a feed of pizza in the pizzeria, I asked the owner why there hadn't been anyone on the beach. I had forgotten to ask him about the sign.

"You were on the beach? Did you not read the sign that says 'Swim at your own risk'? You were very lucky people. The entire beach is a haven and breeding ground for the great white shark."

Everyone knew this but us. In and out of that water—I still quiver at the thought. We had yet to see the movie *Jaws*.

The following day we parked our cars at the train station in Orthebello and took the train into Rome. European trains are unique. Every car has separate compartments with sliding doors and seats for about ten people. There are three classifications: third class with wooden benches, second class with leather seats, and first class with plush velour seats. We were split up and took whatever seat was available. The Italians travel with snacks—sausage, cheese, bread, and wine are staples—and everyone appeared to carry a wicker basket. The aroma emitted when the baskets opened was phenomenal.

Thank God we left our cars behind. Roman drivers are crazy. And did all Italians drive a Fiat? It seemed so. By comparison, a Volkswagen looked the size of a Cadillac. I couldn't imagine a family fitting into one. But as dwarfish as these cars looked, they zipped through the streets of Rome like a rocket. The Italian race-car drivers must be trained on the streets of Rome. Pedestrians ought to say a prayer when they cross a street.

The first thing we did was find a sidewalk café. No Italian on the train offered us even a morsel of food, and we were ravenous. Our meal cost about eighty cents—cokes, $2.50. But we were seasoned travelers and did as the Romans.

To be frugal, we drank the wine—the adults, that is. A strolling mandolier stopped at each table, strumming the strings of his instrument. His tenor voice made you feel you were drinking wine in an opera house. We didn't know the lyrics, but the more wine we poured, the more we harmonized with him.

Our first taste of Rome as a family and we loved it.

Our tour of the city had been arranged through the American USO, and the air-conditioned bus was a delight in the heat of the day. It must have been 110 degrees.

We marvelled at the sites of this ancient city. I had been there before, so I knew what to expect, but Glenn and Alan were transfixed walking through the living history book. What a marvelous opportunity for them to be standing on these historic sites! We visited Capitoline Hill, the Roman Forum, and the Coliseum. It is mystifying to comprehend why people had been thrown to the lions in this arena, simply because they were Christians. We know arenas are for sports—a playground—but in this playground, bets were made about who would survive the attack—the Christian or the hungry lion?

I had last thrown coins into the Trevi Fountain twelve years before. One of those coins obviously granted me my wish—to live my life with Dave—so I believed in the power of this fountain. However, this time, as I turned around and tossed a coin over my shoulder, I could see from the corner of my eye a group of Italian boys jump into the fountain and retrieve my "wish."

"Get out of there!" I hollered. "Leave my coin alone. I want my wish to come true, again."

This time my wish was self-indulgent. I wanted to become a millionaire. We'll see. The boys scattered with my coin held firmly in a grubby little hand.

Every Wednesday the Pope held a general audience at the Vatican. By general, I mean that 80,000 people gathered in the square to receive his blessing. He then appeared on his balcony, raised his arms heavenward giving his blessing, made the sign of the cross, and then waved goodbye to the people. It took about fifteen minutes. Some people travelled all night from various points in Italy and other countries to be present at this event. We opted to watch the ceremony later on television. We figured we were sinners anyway and his blessing wouldn't do us much good.

Instead we decided to visit St. Peter's Cathedral. When I approached the main entrance, a guard stopped me and told me I was inappropriately dressed to enter. I was wearing a sleeveless sundress. This was not respectful enough; therefore, he handed me a plastic wrap with sleeves and a sash that tied in the middle to hide my immodesty. Reluctantly, I put the quasi-garbage bag over my dress. I had no choice: don't do, don't see.

I'm sure I could have assisted Pope Paul without him ever realizing I wasn't a nun.

Once again I was in awe, and upon entering the Church of St. Peter, I felt the ever-present sense of tranquillity, splendour, and serenity. But being of the Protestant faith, I also felt like an intruder and outsider, so that day I feigned being Catholic. Unfortunately, our day in Rome drew to a close much too quickly. We hobbled to the train station for the trip back to Orthebello. We all were exhausted. It felt so good to remove shoes from aching feet.

The train again was packed, and we had to split up into different compartments. Betty and I managed to find two seats together next to a handsome Italian gentleman.

There are a few rules you must know when travelling by train in Europe. First and foremost: you must remain alert for your stop. The train stops for approximately three minutes, allowing you one minute to get up from your seat, another to gather up your luggage, and a third to get yourself off the train.

Our conductor spoke a little English and told Dave there were two more stops before we reached Orthebello—another couple of hours. Meanwhile, Betty and I were having a great time with the handsome Italian. He spoke excellent English and gave us a dramatic tour of the scenic countryside. He said he'd let us know in plenty of time when to get off. I hadn't had the chance to tell this to Dave, and I didn't know that Dave had spoken to the conductor either.

After the train made the first stop, Dave appeared at our door and told us to get ready. We only had one more stop. Betty and I looked at our friend and he shook his head.

"No, no, you're not near Orthebello at all."

Dave paid no attention. Only because I trust my husband, I paid no heed to what our newly acquired friend tried to tell us.

Dave had the five kids, three adults, and himself congregated near the exit waiting for the train to stop at Orthebello. The train slowed, but didn't stop. The doors didn't open.

Remember the three minute warning? If we didn't get off, God only knows where the next stop would be. Naples, perhaps!

We were all in a panic. Unfortunately, in momentous situations, I tend to find predicaments such as this hilarious. I can't stop laughing. My hilarity became uncontrollable and, obviously, very contagious. Everyone laughed now, that is everyone except Dave. He was not amused.

He found the emergency exit, then he pulled the brake cord. The brakes locked, and the train's wheels screeched and squealed on the tracks. The train gyrated and shuddered. Then it came to a blissful stop. Dave pushed and pulled on the steel bar of the emergency door until it opened. Then, he disappeared. There were no steps.

We looked out the open door and found him screaming for us to get off the train. But we wouldn't budge. Poor Dave! He looked up at us from a distance of about twenty feet. The tracks stood on an embankment, and it's a miracle he didn't fall over. His eyes held sheer panic. He pleaded for us to jump.

We all looked out the door and up the track. We didn't see any lights. We couldn't see a station or even any people. No way we were getting off that train. Passengers left their compartments to see what the disturbance was all about.

Betty and I spied our Italian friend and he shook his head unbelievingly. The conductor sprinted up the corridor. I'm sure he frothed at the mouth as he shouted at the top of his lungs.

"Not Orthebello, not Orthebello, next stop, Orthebello." He was furious.

In the meantime, Dave yelled at us from the track.

"Hurry, we don't have much time. Jump!" He was at his wits' end.

He almost jumped—out of his skin that is—when the whistle blew and the train began to move. He figured he'd better hop aboard pretty quick. We reached down, pulled and tugged, and with help from the conductor, hauled him back in. It's a wonder we had any strength left, we were still laughing so hard.

The comment by the conductor said it all.

"Stupido Canadese."

We travelled one more hour before we reached Orthebello. As I said earlier in this book, there are times when I follow Dave's advice and there are times when I do not. God only knows what could have happened. *Arrivederci*!

Bright and early the next morning we packed for the Italian Riviera and Monaco. There were many places we still wanted to visit, but time was of the essence. We had been holidaying for almost four weeks, but we could not end this trip without a visit to Monte Carlo. We drove through dozens of tunnels, up and down winding narrow hills that seemed endless. Finally, as we came over the crest of what would be our final hill, we saw Monaco. It bordered the clear turquoise waters of the Mediterranean Sea.

Monaco is known as the pink city-state and is defined by harbours and high-rises that cling to the rocky Mediterranean coast of the French Riviera. It has no poverty, pollution, unemployment, or income tax; is half the size of New York City's Central Park; and, with a population of about 31,000, has a fraction of the congestion.

Every building, street, and sidewalk is tinted pink. The look is affluent, clean, healthy, and crisp. When we jokingly asked our waiter at the sidewalk café whether food colouring was mixed into the concrete, he chuckled. He advised us that the coral in the waters of the Mediterranean near Monaco is pink and because of that, it's incorporated with the landfill.

After lunch, our walking tour of the seaside resort revealed a never-ending array of pictures of the royal family. It was obvious that the residents of Monaco revered their principality and adored their prince; therefore, no excursion would have been complete without a tour of the Royal Palace.

Again, another winding narrow road lay ahead. The raised imperial flag signified the royal family was in residence. We hoped to catch a glimpse of the children or maybe Grace Kelly herself. But our guide indicated that they resided in a special wing of the palace, not accessible by the public.

I remember when my mother and I toured the palace during the sixties. Both of us were positive that our tour guide had been Grace Kelly. I even commented to her that she was the spitting image of the princess. She replied, but in a very stiff British accent, "Thank you for the compliment. I've been told this many times before. I'm very flattered."

When we finished our tour, our guide tapped me on the shoulder, and with a twinkle in her eye said, "Sometimes the princess has been known to appear in public incognito and have some fun."

Once she said that, I knew my mystery guide had to have been her.

The next landmark would be Monte Carlo, the town in Monaco famous for its casino. We walked up many steps to the front entrance. Our kids were turned back, as the age for admittance was twenty-one. They glumly sat on the bottom step waiting while we contributed to the economy of Monaco.

The stay on the steps was not too dismal for them. They had their attention diverted by the many dozens of Mercedes, Porsches, and Rolls-Royces parked nearby. Even today, neat-looking vehicles mesmerize kids, especially little boys. It may be a Mack truck, a BMW, or perhaps even a 1991 Camaro with a T-top that can catch their attention.

I know I'm getting ahead of myself, but I must tell you a little story before I forget.

Can you guess? We have a 1991 Camero T-top that Dave and I drive during the summer. We take off the top and buzz around town. The other day, I stopped for a red light. On the side of the road waiting to cross was a young boy about my granddaughter's age, maybe around six.

"Nanny, look at that neat car."

"Where, son, I don't see it."

"Over there, Nanny. See . . . an old lady is driving it."

I pretended not to hear. Nanny and I looked at one another and smiled.

The kids watched as chauffeurs dressed in full regalia stood next to the cars. Every so often a runner ran down the steps and handed a chauffeur a zippered bag. He would unlock the vehicle, place the bag inside, and re-lock the doors. The sentry protected the vehicle and no one dared to ramble within close range.

No one ran for us, and we were determined to return one day to visit our money.

The following day we headed homeward. Our next stop would be Switzerland and the famous Bernard Tunnel. The official name for the tunnel, the Great St. Bernard Road Tunnel, was the first transalpine tunnel in Europe.

Reports from fellow Canadians who climbed the mountain with trailers in tow had not been encouraging. We were scared to death and weren't looking forward to the journey. The tunnel is three miles long and goes straight over the mountains. On each side of the road are covered galleries that protect the road in all seasons. It also prevents falling rocks. The road was so narrow that our trailers bumped against the side of the cliff in order to stay away from the sheer drop on the other side. It was a scary ride all right. The only mountain I had ever crossed before had been Kelly's Mountain on the Cabot Trail in Cape Breton. Its elevation of 1,740 feet was high enough for me.

The Alps must be treated with respect. Never once did any one of us look down. It was a harrowing journey.

The grand finale to this holiday was Glenn and Alan spending time in the hospital at the Canadian base at Baden. We had no idea that the quarry at the campsite had tested high for bacteria. We didn't understand the signs there, either, that said in German, "Swim at your own risk."

At the end of twelve continuous hours of vomiting and diarrhea, Glenn and Alan emerged not quite their usual frisky selves, but glad they were alive.

Why do I continue to pay no heed to road signs? I read English rather well, but how is it possible to have accumulated so many demerit points?

CHAPTER TWELVE

Have you ever made contact with a thirty-pound sewer rat? Did you know they travel in packs? Could they be compared to their Canadian cousins? Dave shivered and shook the day this wet furry animal scurried up the handle of the shovel.

Time and time again our neighbours heard the shovel hit the earth. Dave was furiously digging at a mound on the ground. Suddenly he noticed a motion in the murky water and bubbles rose to the surface—big round dirty bubbles. He thought he could see two eyes, but passed it off for a second, that is until he saw what he thought was a furry body swimming.

In the spring of 1975 we decided to move to a larger home, preferably one that stood further back from the sidewalk. We found a house we liked in Vaesrade, a community of about 500 families. The town had all the main Dutch essentials—church, frit shop, and bar. Our brick house was semi-detached, but, once again, sat almost directly on the sidewalk.

Sidewalk at the front door or not, what a house! There were three floors and the inside had been completely modernized and lavishly furnished. The first floor contained a large ceramic-tiled foyer, a two-piece bath, roomy living and dining areas, and an American-style kitchen. According to Dutch standards, the kitchen was to die for. There was every convenience imaginable, including a dishwasher, an electric stove, and a refrigerator with side-by-side doors. The island—a bar-type table surrounded by six tall oak stools—was unique and served as our kitchen table. Five small crystal chandeliers hung from the ceiling above the island, and sliding glass doors opened onto a patio. An awning covered the outside courtyard.

The remainder of the downstairs was furnished in oak. Our dining-room table, hutches, and chairs were oak and upholstered in burgundy velvet. The couch, armchairs, and draperies were also of burgundy velvet. The tie-backs for the drapes were showy gold tassels.

An open-concept staircase led to the second floor where we had an area set aside for another couch and chairs that overlooked the courtyard. Two bedrooms and a so-called modern bathroom and laundry room completed this level. The bathroom had a gas-fired boiler over the tub for our hot water. The tank for the commode was suspended above your head, and "personal droppings" did not fall into water but onto a flat porcelain surface in the toilet bowl. After evacuation, you pulled the chain. We later learned that this old style of toilet had primarily been used to collect manure for farmers' crops. Much to our delight, this practice had been outlawed for years.

Another open-concept staircase led to the third floor and a loft, which Glenn claimed for his bedroom. Perhaps because he was the older brother, he assumed he had the choice. Alan never put up much of a fight when his brother dictated, although I'm sure he wanted to.

Glenn's bed had been constructed below floor level for some reason, but thank goodness skylights brightened the room during the day. Every time I made Glenn's bed, it gave me such an eerie feeling, as if I was peering into a huge coffin. It frightened me.

I thought something was odd the night we met our landlady. She opened the front door wearing sunglasses, and the lights in the front room were dimmed. I wondered how she could see anything.

She told us her job required much of her time, and because she had recently divorced, this home was now much too large for her needs. She owned a hotel in another town and told us she'd be moving there.

We spent the better part of the evening with her, and it wasn't until we got up to leave that she removed her glasses. She sported the biggest shiner I had ever seen. The entire side of her face resembled a raccoon. It was obvious she hadn't missed the door she bumped into. She offered no explanation, but, oh! how I was dying to ask what had happened.

A hotel? Well, yes, it was a hotel for sure and the largest one in Amstenrade. It was named La Cartouche, and it was a brothel. Our landlady was a madam, and she employed young Dutch and German girls. As the hotel windows were also covered with burgundy velvet drapes tied with gold tassels, I couldn't help but think that perhaps our house was used as back-up when La Cartouche was full. I told Dave that we must change the locks.

The oldest profession in the world is legal in Holland, and it had been a well-known fact in the small community of Vaesrade that our landlady's courtesans were young, healthy, and clean.

When Dave went to the hotel to pay the rent, young women immediately surrounded him. Our landlady told her girls that this particular gentleman was out of bounds. He was not a paying customer. Dave told me that he would quickly run in, quickly pay the rent, and quickly exit. I chose to believe him, but it was an endless source of teasing.

Word spread throughout the military community that the Russells' landlord was a "landmadame." Suddenly Dave had more male friends than ever. All wanted to accompany him on rent day.

Aside from a few problems, we enjoyed living in the farming community of Vaesrade. One of those problems was that we were convinced that the farm behind us raised only roosters. Then, next to this farm, the church bells chimed every morning at six o'clock. Our next-door neighbours raced pigeons, and the farmer beside us had some kind of obsession with his "honey wagon." He ran it all the time. So, combined with roosters, chiming bells, cooing pigeons, and that fresh, minty smell of pig manure, we never got to sleep in past six in the morning. But, what the heck, we had lots to do, and who wants to sleep their life away? How many people get to live in Holland for three years? We cherished every moment.

Being so busy working and travelling, Dave and I never got to know our neighbours very well. When we did have spare time, it usually was spent at the ball field, hockey rink, or tennis courts. Glenn and Alan made friends with the kids on the street, and they played street hockey, baseball, and basketball.

We were quite the novelty amongst the kids in this small town. None of the Dutch children had ever eaten a Canadian-style hamburger or hot dog, and those foods became a staple at our house on weekends. Before long, Glenn and Alan spoke some Dutch and their friends, pigeon Canadianese.

We found that a Dutchman's joy not only comprised his love for flowers, but also his home. The Dutch are extremely proud of their front rooms. Drapes are never closed on these exquisitely furnished rooms. On daily walks, people take a discreet peek through shining windows as they stroll by.

Many of these strollers also walk their dogs, but had never heard of pooper-scoopers. Therefore, you trod carefully on your own lawn. I always felt pity for the Dutchman who never owned a dog.

At the top of our street was a beautiful park where Dave often jogged in the mornings. One day, he noticed a dignified older Dutch gentleman walking a huge Newfoundland dog.

"Good morning. Nice dog you have there," Dave remarked.

The Dutchman beamed with pride, "*Morgen*! *Ja*! Newfoundland dog."

Dave went over and petted the familiar breed. "Yes, I know, I'm from Newfoundland. I grew up with these dogs." He pointed to himself.

The Dutchman had a puzzled look on his face and shook his head. "Nay, nay, Newfoundland dog—you a man, this a dog."

Dave tried to explain, but he couldn't get him to understand. He believed that this man and his dog wanted to get the hell out of that park. Both were jittery. They walked away quickly. The Newfoundland dog practically dragged his master, and over the dog's shoulders, Dave saw the Dutchman glance back at him. This man kept shaking his head in disbelief.

I believe Dave should have barked and wagged his tail.

Compared to most Dutch homes, ours was quite modern, with an American-style kitchen and bathrooms. However, we seldom used the bathroom off the foyer, because we had a problem with the toilet. It kept backing up. So, every now and again, Dave would go to the front of the house and lift up a cement block that covered the collection tank. I had never heard of a collection tank before and shuddered at the thought of its contents. But, why had it been placed on the front lawn? What was wrong with the backyard? Usually a few swipes with a pick would unclog the blockage and everything would flow freely for another week or so.

One afternoon, after a procedure of lift and poke, Dave was determined to dig to its depth and solve this problem once and for all. He took a large shovel from our shed and stamped to the front of the house. He lifted the cement block and as he began probing in the murky water, an animal emerged. A sewer rat that weighed at least thirty pounds thrashed, spurted, and scurried up the shovel blade and onto the handle that Dave held.

Dave's hands and eyes were glued to the shovel. For an instant he froze. He couldn't believe what he saw. He nearly had a heart attack right then and there. As did the rat.

Dave and the rat screeched in fright. Dave threw the shovel half way across the lawn, and the huge Dutch sewer rat bounced off and scurried towards the ditch on the other side of the street.

"What's wrong? What's the matter?" Our neighbours came running over.

When Dave caught his breath and was able to speak, he told them what had happened. He wasn't happy with their response.

"Meneer! Where there is one sewer rat, there's bound to be another close by."

I promptly forbade anyone from using that chamber pot until we found this monster. I piled the heaviest things I could find in the house on top of the toilet seat—encyclopaedias, from A to Z.

We phoned the town council of Vaesrade, but our news didn't alarm them. They confirmed our fear—where there's one rat, there's sure to be a relative close by. They told us to keep a close eye out for both and promised to be at our house first thing in the morning to take care of the problem.

I remember saying to Dave, "What do they mean, first thing in the morning? The council must realize that you've destroyed their home? What happens if these creatures decide to invade our house? Besides, did I hear right about them travelling in packs?"

Morning was too far away. We decided to catch the rat ourselves. At the hardware store, we purchased the biggest mousetrap I've ever seen. The mousetrap was so large that a pound of cheese would be required to tempt him or her. However, with this baby in stock, we figured this wasn't an isolated problem. Why were these huge wire traps even manufactured? And why did the store have so many of them?

We assumed the Dutch rodent was similar to its Canadian cousin, but obviously not in size. The small field mice I saw in Canada were cute. We'd take a broom and shuffle them out the door. I wondered whether sewer rats were the same size worldwide, or was the Dutch mammal larger because of the continuous rainfall.

Neither Dave nor I wished to kill this animal. We only wanted it to find a new home. We placed the trap in the opening over the septic tank, activated it, but left nothing inside to tempt the rat. Perhaps he'd back in and we'd catch the end of its long scaly tail. Maybe we would find it a new home.

But as we waited for our visitor to appear, we pondered whether an unsuspecting animal could be lured to the ambush. We would never forgive ourselves if our snare caught a poodle that had just finished pooping on our lawn, or maybe the Newfoundland dog Dave petted that day. The laundry basket placed over the trap for the protection of others was dismantled.

"Let's leave the rat business to the professionals," Dave said.

Later that evening as Dave parked the car, I noticed a couple of shadows near the front of the house. The moon was bright that night revealing animal silhouettes on the ground. I didn't want to open the car door.

Dave tried to reassure me. "Jeanette, don't be silly. The rat has no home now. Trust me, he's long gone."

I opened the door and stepped out. I heard a strange noise. It sounded like a high-pitched squeal. I felt something brush against the bottom of my coat. I almost jumped out of my skin. I looked down and saw two cats chase one another across our lawn.

Cats? They weren't cats, they were rats!

"Lord in heaven, they're back," I cried.

I sprinted indoors and raced to our bathroom. Thank God, the encyclopaedias had not shifted.

The next day the rat destroyers from the town council arrived. We were informed that the problem had been solved.

From that day forward, whenever I entered the downstairs bathroom, I became extremely vigilant before I sat down.

The summer of 1976 was a roaster. Record-high temperatures raged throughout Europe; a heat wave like that had not happened in more than a century. And as many buildings and houses had no air conditioning, stores selling fans enjoyed record sales. Within a week, no cooling apparatus could be purchased. We had to rely on homemade fans.

My mother came to visit that summer. She was a seventy-one-year-old modest widow, but she wandered throughout the house in her bra and panties when she got the chance to be alone.

My mother was quite the talker, extremely vivacious, and remarkably witty. She couldn't believe I had lived in Vaesrade for over a year and hardly knew my neighbours. One afternoon I came home from work to find her sitting on my next-door neighbour's verandah.

"Jeanette, I'm over here. Come and meet your neighbours."

Oh, my! Mother, what have you done? The Rietras lived next door and other than "*Goede dag,*" that was the extent of our conversation. How did it feel to have my mother, all the way from Canada, introduce me to my neighbours in Holland? Foolish, that's how it felt.

The Rietra family didn't understand English, but knew some French. My mother was bilingual, but her Quebec French had a dialect different from the language spoken in Europe. They barely understood each other.

I sat in my neighbour's parlour. I drank tea and nodded my head until it creaked. I only grasped the conversation when my mother translated, but even her decoding didn't make much sense.

My neighbours had a toy poodle called Wolf that weighed maybe four pounds. He looked harmless. He was harmless. But, regardless of a dog's size, he will protect his home.

My mother was fond of dogs, especially small ones. So, when we were about to leave, she put her hand out to pet Wolf. He lunged and drew blood. Mrs. Rietra ran to get a bandage. My mother couldn't understand exactly what Mrs. Rietra tried to tell us, but we assumed by her hand motions that Wolf had been inoculated. We were not to worry.

Back home, Dave insisted we phone the doctor. He certainly didn't want his mother-in-law taking a fit of barking and frothing at the mouth in the middle of the night. Against her wishes, we went to the British Medical Centre.

The doctor examined the wound, which was deep enough to require a couple of stitches, and urged us to obtain proof from the owner that the dog had been vaccinated for rabies. We were to phone him immediately when we found out. He suggested to my mother that she receive a tetanus shot. She insisted she felt fine. We had been invited out for the evening, and my mother wanted nothing to interfere with a night of partying. She allowed the tetanus shot only after the doctor said she could have a glass or two of wine.

When we arrived home, the Rietras were at our front door with papers in their hands. And, yes, Wolf did have his rabies shots.

"I didn't mind getting stitched up, but that needle hurt," my mother chuckled.

We convinced her that in the event another toy poodle was lurking around a corner somewhere, she wouldn't have to go through the same procedure again.

We went to our dinner party, and my mother was in great form. Combined with the mixture of tetanus toxin and rum, she had a ball. The next morning she asked us how the party went and if she had enjoyed herself. She danced all night, we told her, and sang her favourite song, "After the Ball Was Over."

> *After the ball was over, Mary takes out her glass eye,*
> *Puts her false teeth in a tumbler, next to a bottle of rye.*
> *She kicks her cork leg in the corner, hangs up her hair on the wall,*
> *And that's what was left of poor Mary, AFTER THE BALL.*

There's a restaurant in Maastricht called Knijpke's, famous for French onion soup, escargot and cheese boards. That's all they serve, and what a gourmet delight it is. It wasn't unusual to get a craving for this trio at ten in the evening. Although we had to drive nearly thirty miles, Dave and I made the trip about three or four times a month.

Maastricht, capital of Limburg province, is situated near the Belgian border and beside the Maas River. The townspeople are proud of their city, which was founded in the days of the Roman Empire. Maastricht, the oldest fortified town in Holland, is renowned for its many medieval ramparts, gates, and French bastions. You can explore a six-mile labyrinth of chalk tunnels on the city's western outskirts.

Knijpka's is located in one of these tunnels.

Once inside, it is practically impossible to see through the smoke. You know people are there because you actually smell them. No perfume, in my estimation, can mask the scent of tobacco. Dave was amused that I couldn't differentiate between the smell of marijuana and cigarette smoke.

The restaurant is located below ground and never had an immediate vacancy. A waiter wrote your name on a chalkboard, and when a table became available, he'd lead you down a narrow winding set of stone steps. Cobwebs grazed your face and parts of your body while you trod carefully in the dark. I was glad for the candles that furnished even a dim light. A spider's web I could handle—the eight-legged insect that spun the web might be a different story.

Combined with the smoke from the kitchen and the marijuana and hashish in the dining area, it was nearly impossible to see.

Fortunately, the cooking area comprised stainless steel stoves and dishwashers. Had this area not been visible when I first stepped into this dungeon, I would have been long gone. At least the dishes would be sterilized and the food well cooked. I took it for granted that food poisoning would be non-existent.

We never got tired of eating the same thing, over and over. How could you when the French onion soup came loaded with onions and was encrusted with double, sometimes triple, layers of mozzarella cheese? Escargots were topped with mounds of succulent garlic butter. Freshly baked French baguettes were hot and crusty. And the ultimate—a cheese board piled high with every cheese imaginable: Roquefort, brie, havarti, Camembert, Gouda, and feta. But my all-time favourite—the house cheese—filled with garlic and herbs, practically melted on your tongue.

Pitchers of red and white wine emptied quickly.

Knijpka's was our number one priority when company arrived. Friends from Moosonee days, Jean and Terry Warner, came for frequent visits. Terry, an exchange duty communications officer at a British military establishment in the Malvern Hills area of England, had been transferred from Moosonee the same time as we had. They had no children and were able to vacation any time of the year.

Terry and Jean were well known for their dinner parties in Moosonee—different dinner parties. We always approached their dinner table with apprehension. Meat-and-potato parties, they were not. They always cooked up some exotic dish—ostrich, pheasant, and sometimes octopus. Even today when I see a bag of ordinary cheesies on the grocery shelf, I quiver. Terry loved to hide chocolate-covered ants in them.

We chose to have dinner with Terry and Jean that night in Maastricht, and Dave and I decided to tell a little white lie. We told my mother and our guests that a dress code was usually in effect for Knijpka's, but because the summer had been so warm, it had been lifted. Casual attire would be sufficient. They were hungry and excited.

We arrived in Maastricht, parked our car, and trotted down the cobblestone streets, rounding the corner to the alley. About to enter Knijpka's, I glanced at my mother and our friends. Their eyes were huge as saucers. It appeared they were very wary of what was behind that door. In we went, sat at the bar, and ordered a drink. My mother ordered double rum that night, likely as an antiseptic. A short time later, the waiter announced that our table was ready. As we descended the staircase, I was glad that the spiders were slothful that night, at least in this area. I overheard Mom whisper to Terry and Jean, "Lord in heaven! I can't believe my eyes? They actually come to places like this? Do you know what I would call this so-called restaurant? A dive, that's what. God help us all!" She had the Warners in stitches.

Before we sat down, we had to wipe the crumbs from the table—just a swipe and swish and they were gone, onto the floor. Candles smoldered in the stone walls, the resident spiders scurried up and down the waterspout, and the smoke and smell of marijuana was thick enough to cut into chunks.

Despite earlier skepticism, our friends were ecstatic when the waiter served the bubbling, cheese-encrusted soup. They couldn't wait to try it.

However, my mother wasn't so enthusiastic. She lingered and wouldn't put the utensils anywhere near her mouth. We had to reassure her that the dishes and utensils had been sterilized in a dishwasher.

"Look, Mary!" Dave said. "See all the steam coming from that dishwasher over there. Everything sparkles. No need to worry."

She toyed with her soup and finally tasted it. She was not impressed. She preferred homemade chicken soup, she said. Then, over her unwillingness, we ordered escargots. When they arrived, she took one look at the dark little devils and nearly passed out. Her eyes glazed over as she stared at the ceiling. She shivered and shook and pushed her plate in front of Dave.

"Mary, just try them. Try one . . . just one. Believe me, you'll love them. Now, Mary, open up! Come on now!"

Surprisingly, she obeyed, and Dave popped a snail into her mouth.

Her expression was priceless. She chewed with her mouth still open. A horrified look came across her face. Her eyes bulged.

"Serviette, serviette," she cried in a muffled voice.

"Mary, just eat it. You'll see how delicious escargots really are."

I knew my mother would never eat that slug. But how would she solve her problem and discard what she had in her mouth in a ladylike fashion? She didn't think too long. She turned her back and spit into her hand. She didn't need a napkin at all. She tossed that slug into the ashtray. It was impossible to contain our laughter.

Years later when we asked if she wanted a feed of escargots, she'd glare at us.

"Are you crazy. I can't imagine anyone wanting to put those mollusks with the wormy body into their mouth—garlic butter or no garlic butter."

When Dave and I revisited Holland twenty-five years later, we made the trek to Maastricht. At the end of the lengthy cobblestone street, there it was. Knijpka's in all its glory. It remains the best escargot café in the heart of the well-preserved town centre. The familiar and delicious taste brought back fond memories.

The pilots of the Hercules aircraft based at Lahr were assigned designated ports of call on a regular basis. They flew mail, supplies, and personnel for the Canadian Forces. Their route took them to Brussels, Beek, and Gatwick, and military personnel in any city could take advantage of space available and board free of charge.

How lucky we were to be part and parcel of the Canadian Forces. On this occasion, there were four seats available, and we decided to visit Terry and Jean in England.

The flight was uneventful until I looked out the window. That's when I saw another plane—directly below our plane. We were practically piggyback. My blood pressure had to have hit the roof. I know my ears rang as if I heard a set of bells strike a hammer. I panicked. I looked to Dave for reassurance. He mouthed something, but I couldn't hear. I know he saw the other plane, too. He simply nodded and smiled. But why did he point his two thumbs downwards?

Those who have flown in a Hercules aircraft know that the noise is so loud that earplugs become a necessity. Because I couldn't hear what Dave had to say, he gestured. Thanks for the comfort, Dave!

My God, were we going to crash into one another? When I looked around, no one appeared to be aware of any danger. They obviously weren't looking out the window. Passengers munched on the box lunches provided for our flight. People read. Others slept.

Was I the only one with mental anguish? Did they have blinders on? I silently prayed we would land safe and sound.

When the plane finally touched down, I couldn't help but notice the sweat from Dave's brow dripping on to his big nose. Tough guy, eh, Dave?

We boarded the train at Victoria Station. The English countryside is spectacular. Tourists who visit London and fail to include a side trip to the countryside miss the best part of England. You can have your Buckingham Palace, Westminster Abbey, Tower of London, or even Hyde Park—just give me the hills, valleys, and dales.

Malvern Hills is widely known for its exclusive private schools. Sometimes I wondered whether it was education or the prestige that encouraged most of the British military to send their children to private schools. Actually, no tuition could be a determining factor.

Children are enrolled in these special schools at the tender age of only seven or eight. They are virtually raised by the school system. Headmasters become the parents, and the children go home only for the holidays.

These youngsters must be so melancholy when they get lonely or sick. How they must wish their mother and father were there to comfort them. But I suppose like all things, you learn to adjust. Stiff upper lip! That's the British way.

We were wined and dined by Terry and Jean, and if the quaint inns and restaurants we visited had spiders, they were no doubt camouflaged.

Glenn and Alan were introduced to air shows while still in the cradle. It always astounded me that at two or three years of age, they could look into the sky and accurately identify any plane. Their knowledge of aircraft far surpassed their father's. To this day, Dave has never won "the challenge." So, the side trip to the Farnborough Air Show was perfect. Had our two boys not inherited myopia they might have become members of Canada's aerial acrobatic team, the Snowbirds.

We topped off our weekend by attending a play. Thank heavens we didn't take the kids along. Although it had played in London for over twenty years, we knew that *Oh, Calcutta!* had been banned in Canada and the U.S.

The cast was nude. Did I make comparisons? You bet!

Sadly, a few years ago, our friend Jean passed away.

CHAPTER THIRTEEN

Vasectomy became a household word in the seventies and for Dave not so much of a Dutch treat. He lay naked on the stretcher, breathless, in line, waiting his turn. Would he survive unscathed?

Glenn seemed jinxed on school trips—X-rays, broken bones—but it was nothing to what Dave had to go through. Poor Glenn! Poor Dave! I don't know for whom I felt sorrier.

The consensus of the international staff of AFCENT School was that school trips be made a couple of times per year. It presented an opportunity for all nationalities to know one another outside of the school setting. Glenn and Alan took advantage of the school trips, but also participated in excursions planned by the International Boy Scouts.

During school break in February, the Scouts sharpened their skiing skills on the slopes of the Zugspitze, the highest mountain in Germany, with an elevation of 9,718 feet. As the mountain borders Austria, the Scouts stayed at a chalet in the Austrian town of Biberwier, a famous ski town that attracts people from around the world.

This was the first time since Glenn and Alan were born that Dave and I were home alone. We decided to go on a second honeymoon. With no plans or direction, we simply toured the countryside, in and out of little towns, eating at out-of-the-way restaurants and stopping when there was something unusual to see. We spent a glorious week, just being alone.

We arrived home to hear the phone ringing. It was the Boy Scout leader calling from Austria. Glenn had fallen on the slopes the first day and broken his ankle. The doctor from the town had encased his leg in a plaster cast from knee to toes.

The Boy Scout oath, "pledging to keep myself physically strong, mentally awake and morally straight," was practised by all of the Scouts that week as they cared for Glenn. He travelled by sled all week, and they never excluded him from any activity. He hobbled off the bus sore, but glad he had gone.

Another year went by and come February the Boy Scouts went back to Biberwier. Glenn didn't want to go this time, but we convinced him that he'd be fine. The possibility of another broken ankle was remote. He believed us.

We received a phone call. He'd done it again. On the last day of the trip, Glenn had fallen and broken his leg. The same doctor set the fracture (he remembered Glenn from the previous year) and gave Glenn two X-rays.

"A souvenir from Austria," he said as he hugged his favourite patient.

Glenn came home encased in plaster of Paris once again—from hip to toes this time.

The day we received the phone call from Austria, Dave had a vasectomy after being on a waiting list at the hospital in Heerlen for more than two months. So many vasectomies had been executed at this hospital, Dave felt as if he were on Death Row. Finally he was notified that the knife was sharpened and that the hospital looked forward to proceeding with the "ceremonial cutting."

Dave drove to the hospital, parked, and walked to the emergency entrance. A nurse guided a jittery and embarrassed military man to a room, handed him a robe, and told him to undress. As Dave tiptoed from the room, clutching the thin material provided for cover, the nurse pointed to a stretcher in the corridor and motioned for him to hop aboard. Dave was twentieth in line.

Men of all shapes, forms, and nationalities sprawled out on stretchers lined up back to back. There was no privacy. Doctors, nurses, priests, nuns, and visitors scurried past, seemingly oblivious to the stretcher brigade. Dave wondered whether anyone knew what they were lined up for.

At regular intervals, a nurse appeared to wheel yet another nervous, jittery, and fidgety male into the operating room.

Finally, it was Dave's turn. As the nurse wheeled him in, he said a prayer that the doctor would still be alert after seeing so many scrotums and that his hands were steady and the equipment sharp. But when Dave saw the six-inch blade shining under the lights, he passed out.

The doctor slapped him awake and assured him he wouldn't feel a thing. The doctor then bent over and, zap! Dave didn't feel a thing. Just like the doctors said. Zap! It was over! Nothing to it!

After a brief rest in the corridor, he sat up on the gurney, wished his compatriots good luck, found his clothes, carefully walked out and sat in his car, and drove home.

"Piece of cake," he chirped as he bounced in the front door.

My first question wasn't about how he felt, but did he have a cover-up while he waited?

Can you imagine if one wasn't provided? The cavalcade of limp penises awaiting their fate would certainly have made for some interesting chitchat.

The doctor informed Dave to take things easy and relax for a few days. And by no means was he to do any heavy lifting.

Meanwhile, the cast on Glenn's leg weighed almost as much as he did. (The Austrian doctor must have depleted his plaster of Paris supply.) Glenn had to learn to balance himself on the crutches, for if he didn't, he'd topple over. So, despite the doctor's orders, Dave became his prime source of support when he needed to move.

Glenn's bedroom sat at the top of a long steep row of stairs, and because of the cumbersome cast, he could hardly drag himself up the steps. So Dave carried Glenn piggyback-style up and down those stairs for over a week. Finally, Glenn mastered his crutches.

Dave woke up one morning feeling mighty uncomfortable. He lifted the blankets and ogled and winced at what appeared to be two small basketballs wedged between his legs. He quickly determined the balls were attached to his body.

Poor Dave. What a time! He spent the next month on antibiotics and sitting on the softest of cushions that were added to every chair in the house. Needless to say, Glenn's skiing career was put on hold.

CHAPTER FOURTEEN

To tour Paris with friends could be dangerous. The French bouncers appeared to be seven feet tall. They were not happy with us. We had no choice . . . we had to pay.

Easter weekend in April 1976, we travelled to *Gay Paree* with our compatriots, Ron and Eileen Halfpenny. We had met Ron and Eileen the first week we arrived in Brunssum. They also had two boys, Patrick and Brian. Ron was Army and the administrative clerk for the Canadian contingent at AFCENT. Before his posting to Brunssum, he had been with the Airborne Regiment. Eileen's pretty face, blond hair, and huge blue eyes turned heads

Escapades with the Halfpennys, Paris, France, 1975

whenever she walked by. Her dad had been a Jesuit brother for more than twenty years before he married, so I assumed that when the Lord was giving out good looks, Eileen was definitely on the top of his list.

We left on holidays knowing our boys were safe in the hands of a capable live-in babysitter. Our Chrysler and caravan were weighted down with a heavy cargo (we carried a mini grocery and wine store in the event we didn't like French cooking and wine). We always travelled prepared.

Just outside of Paris we found a great campsite with city transportation at our doorstep. We couldn't fathom taking the car into Paris and returning alive. French cab drivers have a nasty reputation for a heavy foot on the accelerator. Brakes last the life of the car with little or no wear and tear.

We planned a barbecue that night and attached the dining tent to the caravan. Dave lit the hibachi, while Eileen and I made a salad, cut up cheese, sliced French bread, and opened wine. Four enormous porterhouse steaks dangled and smoldered over the sides of the small hibachi. The aroma travelled throughout the campsite.

A couple of British joggers slowed up as they ran past. "My, God, man, where's the army? Who's eating that meat? Or should we say that small cow?" They both licked the drool from their lips.

"Are you blokes feeding the whole campsite? Should we gather up our families and have a communal buffet?" They shook their heads in disbelief.

"We've never seen steaks so large in our entire lives. In the name of God, mates, who is going to eat them?"

Dave pointed at Ron and said, "That guy over there, and me."

The British joggers laughed, "That heifer you have there would feed the wives and kidlings for a week. Anyhow, mates, enjoy. Sorry we can't join you. We have to go home and take out the liverwurst and chips."

Throughout the evening eyes gazed at us from behind windows and doors, while curtains fluttered in the breeze from almost every caravan in the campsite. We felt guilty at our extravagance. Perhaps we should have shared?

The following day, we rose early, showered, checked our wallets for sufficient funds, hopped a bus with the local populace, and sped off to Paris. The bus driver scared the hell out of us, and we wondered if the local psychiatric hospital had issued an early release. Our bus driver definitely assumed the appearance of someone unhinged.

No one followed a traffic pattern. Cars weaved in and out. Tempers flared. Car horns blared. Hands and arms made obscene gestures. Everyone screamed and shouted. It was crazy. On almost every street corner, someone sat waiting for the police. Fender benders and cars wrapped around poles were a common sight. The city smelled as if it had been doused in brake fluid.

After surviving this hair-raising trip, we took a guided tour of the city and this time had a chauffeur who followed a reasonable speed limit. We visited most of the historic sites in Paris, walked the Champs Elysees, and sat on the banks of the Seine. We ate lunch at a sidewalk café at the base of Notre Dame, the church where Napoleon Bonaparte and the Empress Josephine were crowned in 1804.

Of all the historic sites we visited, the Palace of Versailles was by far my favourite. History tells us that it was originally a hunting lodge, but in 1661, Louis XIV commissioned Louis Le Vau to renovate and extend it. It eventually became the permanent abode of Louis XVI, the great-great grandson of Louis XIV and husband of Marie Antoinette.

The exterior lands are spectacular with thousands of flowerbeds, acres of lawns, an army of statues, and oceans of water displays. Magnificent gardens surround the palace. The inside of the palace is adorned with paintings and sculptures created by the greatest artists of the seventeenth and eighteenth centuries. They achieved a standard of greatness that is found nowhere else, for to receive a commission from the king was an honour that impelled them to reach a level of craftsmanship that exceeded all else.

Rituals were prominent in those days. Ceremonies were performed when the king and queen retired for the evening. They had no privacy. Even the birth of the royal children took place in public. Do you suppose the public viewed the conception as well? I wonder!

The French Revolution ended the reign of Louis XVI in 1792, and the furnishings of Versailles were sold and the palace was turned into a museum. Because Marie Antoinette and her husband, the king, sided with the those who opposed the revolutionaries, they were subsequently executed. He was beheaded in 1792 and she, the following year.

Come dusk, we decided to take our own walking tour of Paris by night. We dined at a sidewalk café where I tasted my first and last frog's leg. We strolled to the famous Pigalle section of Paris. We had tickets for the Moulin Rouge to see the famous cancan dancers. The cancan became popular in the music halls of Paris about 1840, but was considered vulgar. The name of the dance is derived from the French word for scandal. Regardless, the music had everyone moving to its beat. It sure put us in a festive mood. We'd remember this night for a long time to come.

Across from the Moulin Rouge were bars, lined up side by side. It has been said that one never leaves Paris without going to a bar. It appeared to us that they all had similar entertainment—exotic dancers and French singers. We looked at several marquees and chose the one we thought would be the most entertaining. We climbed a long flight of stairs and entered a small, dark, and smoky room.

The stage was at the far end of the room, with tables and chairs topped with buckets of champagne surrounding it. Because we had been pre-warned by friends to avoid sitting close to the entertainment, we opted for a secluded corner near the bar at the back of the nightclub. We later learned that millionaires sit up front, the working class at the back.

We sat down at a table for four. The waiter took our order—four beers—which arrived warm and in small Coca-Cola glasses. We were not impressed but didn't complain. Our saving grace was the cask of beer waiting for us at the campsite.

The entertainment started. A spotlight shone on three scantily clad women on the stage, and musical instruments began to play. It sounded like a comic opera. The women, however, did not sing. Instead they peeled, in unison, and gyrated around the stage.

Drums rolled, and when we looked up, three nets came tumbling down from the ceiling with a thud. The strippers climbed into the hammocks, and men from the audience joined them. The hammocks began to swing and sway.

We were certainly red-faced as the act became raunchier and raunchier. Body fluids sprayed everywhere.

"Hey, that's enough for us, let's go." We beckoned to our waiter to bring the bill. He handed it to Ron.

Ron's face turned white. He mumbled.

"Dave, look at this." He handed him the slip of paper.

"Are my eyes deceiving me? How many zeros do you count?"

"Waiter!" Dave exclaimed. "Excuse me, but I do believe you have too many zeros on our check. You obviously miscalculated and made a mistake."

Dave took out the calculator that he always carried and determined that each beer cost $60 in American funds, for a total of $240.

The waiter looked at us with a frown on his face. *"Que, Monsieur! Il n'ya pas trop de zeros."*

Dave and Ron stood up. "We're sorry, but we will not pay this amount. You have made a big mistake. No one charges sixty American dollars for a small glass of beer."

"S'il vous plait! Fermez votre bouche, fermez votre bouche!" We turned around and noticed that the bare-naked women had left their nets and now lay across tables. The attending patrons still had the strength to tell us to shut up.

The waiter clicked and snapped his fingers. Immediately, four burly bouncers surrounded us. They looked to be over seven feet tall.

"Monsieur, Madame, avez-vous une probleme?"

"A small problem perhaps, Gentlemen," Dave said softly. He didn't want to antagonize the giants. "I believe we have been overcharged for our beer. We only had four of them. We will only pay what we feel is fair. The total on our check is outrageous. I'm sure you wouldn't even pay this amount. Do you understand what I'm saying?"

They stood there with arms folded. Oh, yes, they understood what Dave was saying. They slowly shook their head. Pay up or else was the look.

Ron leaned over to Dave and whispered, "You take those two over there, and I'll take the other two."

Right, Ron, fine for an old paratrooper to say. You were Airborne Regiment and tough. You jumped from planes while I sat at a desk to keep them in the air. Big difference here, my man!

By this time Ron resembled a raging bulldog. His eyes were glassy. Bubbles foamed at the corner of his mouth. His chest rose and fell. You could nearly hear his heart pound. The veins in his neck protruded. Eileen thought he might have a heart attack right on the spot. We decided we had better have a fast consultation while we still breathed.

It didn't take long to conclude that we'd better pay the absurd bill and get the hell out of there. We pooled our 960 francs together, crumpled the bills into tiny wads, and defiantly threw them on top of the table. We accidentally spilled our unfinished warm beers over the francs and the tablecloth. Unfortunately the Coca-Cola glasses fell to the cement floor and shattered.

As we made our way to the door, Ron turned halfway and flicked his cigarette, hitting one of the four bouncers with it. They chased us down the stairs.

"*Vous, les americains, sacrez vous-en de Paris et revenez pas.*"

Once outside, Ron stood boldly by the open door and wouldn't budge. While the doorman tried to drum up business by calling out to the tourists, "Fuckie, fuckie," Ron in turn bellowed at the top of his lungs.

"The show is a rip-off. Save your money and go next door."

It took three of us to drag him away from that door. He continued frothing and drooling for the better part of an hour.

With only mothballs left in our wallets, all we could afford for our romantic "Paris by Night" escapade was a stroll through Pigalle and window shopping. We window shopped all right. We ended up walking through the heart of the red-light district!

Hookers paraded their wares on street corners. Other women of the night sat in store windows. In various stages of undress they provocatively enticed anyone who walked by. There were signs that read, "Susie speaks English," "Susie provides clean sheets," "Susie is very experienced," and "Susie will give you a good time." These women looked to be from thirteen to seventy years old. Surprisingly enough, most of them were absolutely gorgeous.

Dave and Ron walked ahead of us and were accosted time and time again by the French women of the night. It looked like our protectors enjoyed every minute of this attention. We wondered what would happen if we took on the role of the women around us. We figured that if our husbands could act foolish, then so could we!

We waited for Dave and Ron to cross the street. They looked back, and we gestured that we'd be there in a few minutes.

Eileen, fluently bilingual, would do the talking. All I had to do was to stand next to her and smile. The hilarious thing is that it worked. Men stopped and asked Eileen what we charged. I assumed she asked a fortune for our make-believe services, for the men looked astounded as they quickly scurried away. Then two Arab gentlemen in full regalia stopped and wanted to know our rate.

"Six-cents dollars pour nous deux. Nous avons des draps qui sont dernierment laver." (Six hundred dollars for the two of us. We have clean sheets.)

The astonished look on their faces gave us quite a chuckle, as they backed away muttering in Arabic. There was no way these millionaires would pay that amount of money for fifteen minutes of fun and games.

An unexpected tap on the shoulder caused us to look around into the faces of two furious Paris hookers. *"Vous deux, partez! Vous êtes dans notre territoire. Nous avons payer pour ceci alors perdez-vous."* (You two vamoose. You are in our territory. We paid for this spot, so get lost!)

Eileen and I concluded that our minutes of hooking should come to an abrupt end before we got ourselves into more trouble. We ran to catch up with our cavaliers! I don't think they had even noticed our small escapade.

This truly had become a night none of us would ever forget. But before a French paddy wagon came round the corner, we thought it best to leave Paris *toute suite*!

We found the bus to take us to back to safety and our trailer park. Ron's adrenaline was still pumping hot through his veins, and there were a few times we had to restrain him from jumping off the bus and running at full speed back to the nightclub. He insisted we all had unfinished business with the seven-foot bouncers.

Apparently, behind most bars in the Pigalle district are wide-open fields. We don't know whether or not to believe our friends, but we were told that confrontations with Pigalle bouncers are kept very private!

The Russells and Halfpennys have an increasingly long history of misfortunes and calamities when they're together.

Mallorca, Spain. It's May 1977, and Dave and I again paired up with our cohorts in calamity, Eileen and Ron, for one more trip. We were a touch apprehensive about our journey and pondered just what would happen this time around. The four of us together seemed to be subject to such adversity that we figured for sure that some catastrophe awaited us there.

We'd been transferred back to Canada, and this would be our last chance to travel together in Europe. A Dutch travel agency offered a great trip to Spain, which included airfare from Holland plus all-inclusive accommodation at a four-star hotel in Santa Ponsa.

We arrived at Beek Airport in plenty of time to board Spandair Airlines. However, the DC9 was delayed because of weather—for over four hours! To pass the time, we raised many glasses in the airport bar. Finally, after asking for the umpteenth time, "Where in hell is the plane?" we heard the roar of engines. We hustled, somewhat water-logged and a bit tipsy, to the counter. There was no such thing as a seat assignment for the flight.

"First come, first served," informed a bored clerk.

For those who have travelled with Dutch or German tourists, you know you have to be quick. They were born scrambling. When they're on holidays, look out! Timid is not the trait to display.

Before we knew it, we had landed at the back of the pack, and had to enter the plane amidst much pushing, shoving, elbowing, and mad clamouring. I dropped into a front row seat, Dave ended up at the back, and Ron and Eileen found themselves somewhere in the middle. Packed together like a can of sardines, we couldn't move.

During the flight, we'd find one another in the crush, make eye contact, and wave. The DC9 shook and rumbled. There were times I wondered if I'd ever see the light of day again. I tried to think of a reasonable prayer so that when we landed, I wouldn't be obliged to live down the indebtedness.

I remember that the three stewardesses kept disappearing and reappearing, each time in a different uniform. Three times they did this. I couldn't figure it out. Did they feel the change of uniform somehow altered their appearance? Why they wanted to confuse the passengers still boggles my mind. From the meal we received, I knew it would have been impossible for them to soil any clothing. Our gourmet delight consisted of day-old sandwiches wrapped in cellophane. Some of us caught them in mid-air.

The heavily accented captain was just as weird. "Good evening ladies and gentlemen. Welcome aboard Flight 347. We are expected to arrive in Palma at two a.m. The temperature inside the plane is seventy-five degrees Fahrenheit. Outside the plane, it's thirty-five degrees below zero. Enjoy your flight, and we'll see you when we land."

After this broadcast, I immediately crawled from my seat to find Dave. Why should we be concerned about the temperature outside the plane when we were 30,000 feet in the air? Dave had to explain this to me. But I couldn't reach him.

Man, this plane is eerie. The people aboard are spooky. Stewardesses keep changing their clothes. A pilot who can hardly speak English is concerned about the temperature outside the plane. Our meal is tossed at us from the aisle. Oh, God, I pray we land safe and sound. Dave, can you hear me? I love you. I love you, kids!

Finally we landed at Palma. The time was two a.m. The door opened and a mad scramble of perplexed passengers made their way to the exit. Poor Dave was sandwiched in between a couple of people. When he stood up, he almost collapsed. He's six-foot-three, and when he rose, he felt five-foot-four. He felt as if his elbows and knees were glued together. We gathered our luggage and scuffled aboard a bus that would take us to our hotel in Santa Ponza, another two-hour ride.

The Playa de Mallorca had been listed in our guidebook as a four-star hotel, with all rooms facing the Mediterranean. But no matter how hard we looked, we could not locate two of the stars. And only a daredevil with a set of binoculars would lean over the balcony to view the ocean. Oh, well, the hotel wasn't fancy, but it was clean.

Santa Ponza is a small seacoast town on the southwest coast of Mallorca that had not yet been discovered by most tourists. It's about two hours outside of Palma, the capital of Mallorca. The town had a natural charm, with sandy beaches, fishing boats in the harbour, sheep and hogs roaming the fields, and palm and olive trees swaying in the gentle breeze. We were content.

Had it not rained for seven days and six nights, we probably would have frittered away our days on the beach. Instead, we planned excursions each day, and with umbrellas in hand, we walked the city, visited churches, and haunted the shops and boutiques. Combined with paella and sangria, each meal became a paradise. We didn't care if raindrops splashed all around us. My God, we were in Mallorca! Once again had it not been for Dave's and Ron's jobs, we would never have been able to afford this luxury.

Every morning we sat by the pool and sipped our juice. Lamamba was the specialty of the house. The cognac-laced chocolate milk started our day with purpose. While it might seem that all we did was consume alcoholic beverages, this occurred largely during vacation. After all, Dave and I are from the East Coast where a change from our national drink, Orange Pekoe Tea, is always welcomed.

One evening, we joined a group of tourists from the hotel and attended a medieval barbecue at an ancient *casa* once owned by a famous count. I've since forgotten his name, but the Count of Monte Cristo wouldn't have been out of place. The hacienda was typical of Spanish times when the main action took place within the walls. A huge windmill was centred in the large hallway, and visible through the open doors to the ballroom were long tables heaped high with chicken, pork, potatoes, soups, salads, bread, wines, and liqueurs. Try as we might, we were not able to stop salivating.

Minstrels strummed "Viva Espagne" as we were seated at the long narrow tables, and an orchestra provided backup music for the Spanish dancers and their castanets. The master of ceremonies introduced a dancer who would perform the flamenco and recounted the history of the national dance.

The flamenco is a genuine Spanish art and at one time was performed only by gypsies. The flamenco has always been an intimate performance where there is nothing but the voice, the guitar, and the body of a dancer moving in the moonlight. It combines acoustic guitar, singing, chanting, dancing, and staccato hand-clapping and is performed with passion, fervour, and tortured expressions.

The lights dimmed. We hoped the presentation wouldn't be too painful. It wasn't. However, following the performance, the showdown began. Everything happened so fast.

Waiters sneaked behind us, grabbed our heads, and tilted them back. From the flasks held firmly in their hands, they poured wine directly into our mouths. The liquid ran down our throats, making us gasp for air. You either gulped fast or drowned in the attempt.

Were we having fun yet? Try drinking soup cupped in your hands. Try breaking apart a whole chicken and ripping a leg off a pig. In medieval times, cutlery was unheard of and hands were put to good use. By the time the evening was over, we were exhausted, splattered with grease and food from head to toe, and outrageously drunk.

I don't think I had fun—maybe the others did. I'm from the old school where I was raised to be pampered and taught to appreciate fine things. I like fine dishes, fine wineglasses, fine knives, forks and spoons, and a fine meal looking fine upon my fine plate, and all finally placed on top of a fine tablecloth. I bless the fact I was conceived in the twentieth century were there are so many fine things.

The next day after our morning lamamba, the cobwebs gradually being swept away, I knew I'd make it through the day. Of course it rained. Dave and Ron wanted only to lounge around and try to recover from the previous evening, while Eileen and I itched for another sightseeing expedition. We took the bus into Palma.

Eileen had a girlfriend who lived in Palma. She had married a Spaniard and moved to Spain a few years before. Now divorced, she was settled in Palma, where she worked for the Spanish government. I thought it was neat to be in a foreign country and actually know a Canadian who lived there—someone not connected to the military.

Eileen's friend, Marion, escorted us through her city, showing us places unknown to any tourist. Overlooking the sea where private yachts and ocean liners were moored, we lunched at a café—paella and sangria. What else!

We visited the haunts that Errol Flynn and Ernest Hemingway frequented in the forties and fifties. They were well known for teasing the affections of Spanish women, and each summer they left behind many heavy hearts. We toured castles and explored coves once occupied by Black Beard and other notorious pirates. We wandered through dark and mysterious streets picking up treasures here and there.

Sadly the day came to an end. The sun shone gloriously that day in Palma, but we had to return to our men and the rain. Our Canadian tour guide dropped us off at our bus stop. Another street corner! Paris came to mind. And yes, it happened again!

What was it with our looks? Did we resemble ladies of the evening, harlots, or Spanish courtesans? Why were we getting all those stares and looks from people passing by? Were our features so unusual?

Unexpectedly, two Spanish men approached us. They smiled and started talking to us in perfect English. We tried to ignore them.

"What is your fee?" one of them asked.

"Our what?" I exclaimed. *Oh, no, it's happening again. They think we're hookers.*

Aghast, Eileen and I looked at one another. I could hardly keep from laughing, but I managed for the moment.

"Sorry, Gentlemen, but our talents are not for sale. We're simply two Canadian tourists waiting for a bus. Perhaps a couple of Spanish girls could fill your needs. Get lost!" They shrugged their shoulders and moved on.

We giggled like two schoolgirls and hoped our transportation would hurry. We just wanted to get the hell out of there.

Almost instantly a bald-headed man, well dressed in shirt and tie, headed our way. He had a camera slung over his shoulder, and we assumed he was another tourist. That is until he stopped directly in front of us. He introduced himself and indicated that he was a movie producer from Argentina. He said he had been watching us and was captivated by our clean looks. We were perfect for a part in a movie he was producing. He wanted to take some pictures.

I had visions of a limousine squealing to a halt and the chauffeur throwing us in the back seat. For the second time on this lonely street corner, Eileen and I had been approached by strangers. We became more and more paranoid of Spanish men. Our newfound friend insisted we take advantage of his offer.

"I will make you rich and famous. A few pictures won't take that long. My hotel is just around the corner, Señoritas."

From the corner of my eye I could see our bus approaching. I nudged Eileen. We must have been nothing but a blur to our "friend" as we hopped aboard. You never saw two women mount three tall steps so fast in your life. With the door barely open, we almost broke our necks. We stumbled, but we were off that street. Adios!

Once in the safety of the bus, we rolled down the window.

"Señor, good luck on your star search. We'll be sure to watch for the movie when it comes out. By the way, what's your name again?"

He mumbled something we weren't quite sure of. He stood on the corner looking astonished as the bus sped away. Did he think he could hoodwink two seasoned travellers?

On the ride back to Santa Ponza we convinced each other that we probably were fairly good looking. Horsing around I said to Eileen, "Dave and Ron had better start appreciating us a little more. And, if they don't, then maybe we'd just find a street corner in Holland to frequent; or better still, I may take over my landlady's job and start collecting rent at La Cartouche."

A thousand stars lit up the night—our last evening together in Santa Ponza! After the rain we had endured for the week, it became yet another night to remember. We skipped our scheduled dinner at the hotel in order to devour paella just one last time. At a neat little café in a limestone cavern we ordered two pitchers of sangria and a large dish of paella. We joked most of the evening with the bartender. He gave us his recipe for the sangria, which I make to this day.

Following dinner, we aimlessly strolled for hours through the streets filled with Spanish tradition. We marvelled at the bright, warm night. At four a.m., we decided to call it a night, and the four of us sat on the dock overlooking the sea. We took off our shoes and dipped our toes into the warm waters of the Mediterranean. All of us vowed that someday we would return—maybe with canes and hearing aids—but one day! Eileen bawled her head off. Even my eyes welled up.

When I stood up, I felt something warm on my backside. I reached back. My hand came back covered in a thick, brown slime. No pooper scooper had been used that night on the dock. Although my pure silk pants were taupe in colour, the brown doggie poo clashed considerably. The new silk pants I had saved for our last night would be but a memory.

Funny what you recollect as being important. Over the years when I reminisce about our travels in Spain, it isn't the people, the place, the food, or the drink I recall, but the ruin of a wonderful pair of pure silk pants.

CHAPTER FIFTEEN

The images of Athens I carried on the airplane were of a white rocky hill with a ruined but glorious temple on the top, a Greek soldier in his traditional skirt with pompoms on his shoes, or perhaps a Trojan horse at the entrance to the city. But, my first impression of Athens was nothing like that. Despite the unmistakable signs urging everyone to drink Coca-Cola, I was left with no doubt that we were indeed in a Mediterranean country.

While Alan cruised the Mediterranean, my friend Viviane (Crowell) Lafraniere and I journeyed to Greece. Alan's experience was filled with history and geography, while Viviane's and mine delved into the absurdities of, shall we say, human relations?

My pal Viviane Lafraniere, Athens, Greece, 1975

Viviane and Avery Crowell! Well, where do I begin! They have three great kids— Wanda, Carol, and Jeff. Viviane met Avery during her career as an airwoman in the Royal Canadian Air Force. They were quite a contrast: the East meets the West, a giant from the waters of Nova Scotia and a petite gal from the farmlands of Saskatchewan. Viviane left the Air Force when they married.

We met in Brunssum shortly after our arrival. I don't know what it was about that era, but we became instant friends with many of the Canadians stationed there. This is odd, as I'm not a person who makes friends quickly. There has to be something to like and admire about a person. Dave and I agreed that if you wouldn't befriend an individual with unattractive traits in Canada, then why would you go against the grain in a foreign land? With Viviane and Avery we didn't go against the grain. We became soul mates.

Viviane and I had lots in common, and it was ironic that both of us worked at the AFCENT school, she as secretary for the Canadian Section and me as secretary to the director. Her daughter, Wanda, a high school student, became my "girl Friday" at the office and ran numerous errands for the school.

Our families bonded, and we spent many weekends camping together. Every chance we got we sampled foods foreign to us. It was Viviane and Avery who introduced us to Knipka's. How many times did we receive a phone call in the middle of the night? "How about going to Knipka's for a feed." It's a wonder we didn't become as big as houses.

In February 1977, staff and senior students of AFCENT International School left to take part in a two-week educational cruise on the Mediterranean. Those years of having lunch with the "Brass," combined with a determined mother who was the Brass's secretary, paid off. The school made an exception so that Alan could participate.

It was definitely an experience for Alan to cruise the Mediterranean at twelve years of age. On the first day of February, the students and teachers left the school aboard a bus headed for Zeebrugge where they took the ferry to Dover in England. At Gatwick Airport near London, they boarded a plane for Malta.

Until I read Alan's journal, I didn't know that Malta has no permanent rivers or lakes and only limited precipitation. A supply of potable water is naturally a problem, so the country implemented a program to desalinate seawater. Up to seventy per cent of Malta's water comes from desalination plants.

The students boarded the cruise ship, the SS *Uganda*, which became their home away from home. During the Falklands War a few years later, the Royal Navy used the SS *Uganda* as its hospital ship.

First-class passengers occupied the top two decks, leaving the lower decks for the students who came from across the British Isles. Two Canadians were aboard, Alan and his friend, Mike Patterson.

During the next two weeks, these kids received the educational experience of their young lives. Each student was required to keep a journal of their land excursions and also a logbook to report activities aboard ship. Alan received an A+ for this composition. It was clearly a unique experience for a young man.

Excerpts from Alan's journal:

February 3rd, woke up at 7:25 and got dressed. I had a shower and made my bed. At 8:15 I had missed breakfast but the cooks decided to give the others and me breakfast anyway. I should have missed it. We are still sailing to Santorin today. We will arrive in the morning. We had a lecture on Santorin. It is a volcanic island which sank into a hole 18.2 miles underwater. The force of the explosion was estimated at 5,000 atomic bombs. We are staying at Santorin for one day, then going to Israel. The time is 11:43 and I am changing ten pounds into drachma. I need drachma (Greek money) because that is the currency in Santorin.

February 4th. Got up at 7:25. We were in sight of Santorin. I ate breakfast, then went up on the top deck to watch the crew lower the boats to bring us ashore. We got to Santorin and we could either walk up 600 steps sideways or take a donkey up. I did not take a donkey. I walked. By the time I got up, I was sweating. The temperature was about 75 degrees. When I got to the top I drank a Coke, then went out to do some shopping. The thing to do when you are shopping is to bargain—for instance, I bargained a 500-drachma object down to 200 drachmas.

February 6th. Today I woke up at 7:25 and made my bed, then went to breakfast. We were in Haifa, Israel. We disembarked at 9:30, got on our bus and had a three-hour ride to Jerusalem. When we arrived, we went around and saw some sights. Next we went to buy some souvenirs. After that we went to Bethlehem and saw where Jesus was born. After that we came back into Jerusalem and went to a holy church. There were guards with sub-machine guns. Next we saw where Jesus was killed and where he was born. After that, came back to the *Uganda*.

February 9th. Today I woke up at 7:25 and ate breakfast. By this time, we had arrived in Turkey. We were to go to our classrooms and disembark. When we got ashore we went to our tour buses and toured Ismar, Ephisius, Seljuk and other small towns. At Ephisius I bought a fez. We saw old Roman, Greek and Turkish ruins. After that we went shopping and I bought some souvenirs. We arrived back at the boat at 3:55 p.m. and we were allowed to go shopping by ourselves. We did not find anything to buy so we went back to the ship, and are now sailing to Venice.

February 11th. Woke up at 7:25 and made my bed. I went to eat breakfast at 8:03. The breakfast was rubber eggs, rock bacon and fish sticks. We are still on our way to Venice. At 9:00 we had our first class, which was deck games. We had played ping-pong. Next there was a church service which was cancelled until 11:00 because we were off the coast of Albania. In Albania, it is rare to see inside the country because nobody can go in and nobody can go out. After the morning classes were over I ate lunch. After lunch I went up top and went to my classes. At 5:00 we were free and I ate supper—then went to our dorm and retired.

The excerpts broke me up. Alan walked on an island that history tells us may have been the basis for Plato's writings on the lost continent of Atlantis. He traded coins with Israeli soldiers on the Golan Heights and visited a church protected by armed guards in Jerusalem. He saw the birthplace of Jesus in Bethlehem, a place most people only dream of visiting. These experiences were made possible because his father was a member of the Canadian Armed Forces. How many children outside of the military would have had this experience at twelve years of age?

In the meantime, Viviane and I travelled to Athens.

Originally, we had planned a trip to Moscow, but soon learned that because of our husbands' involvement with NATO, there would be lots of red tape to cut, and did we want to do that? We would have to travel by way of our home base at Lahr, West Germany, for a briefing before entry to Russia and a debriefing upon our return. We would also have to watch our Ps and Qs. The Russians had been known to detain foreigners for reasons only known to them. Maybe we'd never return. We might be kidnapped and held for ransom or worse.

What kind of a holiday is that? God only knows what might have happened if we'd followed through. After all, it was still the Cold War. Our husbands were the enemy. We decided to play it safe and made plans for Greece instead.

We left from Amsterdam's Schiphol Airport and flew directly to Athens. Talk about a bunch of rowdy tourists on board this plane. When the Dutchmen and Germans go on vacation, their strait-laced attitudes go out the window.

We sang when the songs were in English, but otherwise hummed along to that distinctive German oompah sound, a tone we had become so familiar with during Oktoberfest. After the Dutch stewardesses joined the choir, I periodically looked towards the cockpit. I hoped the pilots were British and not bilingual. We certainly didn't want them to take part in the singsong.

We landed safely in Athens all fast friends. If you have lived in Europe you know what it's like to shake hands. We said goodbye for twenty minutes. Our arms were limp. We wondered if we'd have the strength to hold a glass of ouzo.

On our ride from the airport we passed through rundown suburbs of two-storey white houses with flat roofs. We saw women dressed mostly in black surrounded by small children, dogs, and goats.

Once we entered Athens, we encountered a sophisticated city with spacious squares, terrace cafés, and avenues filled with shops. In the centre of Athens is a large open area known as Constitution Square, around which rise tall apartment blocks as luxurious as any others in Europe. The American Embassy and the Hilton Hotel overshadow some of the nineteenth-century embassies. The main shopping quarter extends to both sides of Hermes Street, which is appropriately named after Hermes, the god of trade. If only we could afford a silk Hermes scarf.

Our hotel, the Pythorgorian, was located close to Omonia Square, an area we learned was a regular meeting place for the townspeople. The Pythorgorian had a typical class C rating. It wasn't the Hilton, but it was clean and included a continental breakfast. We were the only Canadians registered. We carried our luggage to the tiny room that would be our home for the next couple of weeks.

It was nine o'clock at night and we were famished. We hadn't eaten since lunch aboard the plane, and that had been pure liquid. We looked through our tourist guidebook and found a restaurant that appeared interesting—a steakhouse owned by a Greek-Canadian. It definitely appealed to us.

We asked the hotel manager to phone for a taxi, but learned that you don't call a cab in Athens. You only have to step into one. Taxis are everywhere. The one stationed in front of our hotel had two passengers, the driver and another male in the front seat. Greek cab drivers prefer to take more than one passenger at a time, so sometimes the ride can be endless. God only knows how long the passenger had been waiting. We pondered whether we should get in the car or not. We didn't like the idea of two men sitting up front. Would we be able to defend ourselves if anything out of the ordinary happened? Our growling stomachs overcame the risk factor, so we hopped in.

The ride was disconcerting. The driver and the man in the front seat were much too friendly for our liking. Back home, you tell the driver your destination, and that's it—no conversation. But this cab driver and his front-seat passenger talked endlessly. Their English was limited, but we understood. Viviane and I whispered to each other that if matters got any more amiable, we might have to make a quick exit at the next light. We breathed more freely when the driver pulled up to a house and his passenger got out.

The next stop was ours. The driver turned down an alley, a dark alley. There were no lights. There were no people. Glued to our seat, Viviane and I didn't want to move. Should we go back to our hotel? We didn't know what to do. The cab driver interrupted our thoughts and told us he had to be on his way. He couldn't make money sitting there. He told us to pay and leave. We paid him and stepped onto the street. It was pitch black. In front of us stood a darkened restaurant. We went up to the door and knocked. We pounded relentlessly. Help! Help! Help!

We didn't notice the slot in the door until it slid open. It reminded us of the Chicago nightclubs and prohibition. An eye appeared, the door opened, and a huge man wearing an apron stepped forward. He said something. We assumed he told us the restaurant was closed. We must have looked like two damsels in distress. We were two damsels in distress.

"Do you speak English?" I asked.

"Yes, I do," he said. "And for some reason, I can depict your accent. Could you be from Canada?"

"Yes, yes! We are. We're from Ontario."

"Canada! You're from Canada? Well, if that's the case, how can I leave two of my favourite people standing there in the dark? Please, please come in."

We were rescued.

We were the only people there. The restaurant had closed about an hour earlier.

"I'll prepare something special for you," the owner offered. True to his word, we dined on T-bone steaks, baked potatoes, and Greek salad—a reminder of our homeland, he told us.

Our host had been born in Toronto to Greek parents, but he had moved to Athens five years previously and opened the first steakhouse in the city. He introduced us to the national drink of Greece. I'm not a liqueur lover, but ouzo's licorice taste definitely has an appeal.

Although we had only been in Athens less than a day, our fellow Canadian made us feel special. He must have had connections for he called a taxi to take us back to our hotel. We didn't pay for our meal or the transportation. First impressions are lasting.

I knew the remainder of our holiday would be as pleasurable, and we couldn't help but promise to return. The taxi arrived with headlights shining. We hopped in and the driver whizzed us back to our hotel with nary a word.

Our hotel manager liked us, too. Viviane and I were certain that he had a cousin living in Toronto. Everyone else we spoke to thus far had a relative there, including some of the people on our flight. Sponsorship was a word they were all familiar with.

Our good-looking manager served us at breakfast, assuming the role of waiter, porter, and door attendant. He was here, there, and everywhere; he was almost unavoidable.

We finally accepted an invitation for dinner and a tour of his city. We looked forward to a traditional Greek dinner at one of Athens' most famous restaurants.

From every window in our hotel the lights of the Parthenon cast a glow across the sky from its home high atop the Acropolis. I loved the myths and legends associated with the country and felt fortunate to have this great opportunity to discover it first hand. Our good fortune, once again, compliments of the Canadian military. Had Dave not been transferred to Europe, this lifetime dream for me would never have happened.

The Parthenon was created in the fifth century B.C. and was dedicated to the Greek goddess Athena, for whom Athens is named. Did you know that Athena created the first olive tree? To this day, every time I have a martini, I raise my glass in a toast to Athena.

At the base of the Acropolis is the Plaka. During World War II, the Germans promised city officials that the Acropolis would remain untouched by military intervention. They wanted to preserve the historic treasure. Not all of them were crazy like their leader Adolf Hitler. During the war, thousands of Athenians built small one-room houses in the Plaka knowing they would be safe there. These houses were later converted to small tavernas and nightclubs and eventually became the main night-spot area of Athens. Viviane and I spent many evenings in the Plaka.

At midnight when coaches turn into pumpkins, Athenians turn into swingers. Until midnight all the bands sound like Guy Lombardo and the singers like Tom Jones. Come midnight, the whole atmosphere changes. The local night owls start arriving, the bouzoukis are plugged in, and the air fills with bittersweet Greek melodies. They all keep blasting away until three or four in the morning or until the last plate has been thrown.

We bounced from taverna to taverna. As more men than women frequented the clubs, Viviane and I became somewhat of a novelty. Throughout our travels in Greece, we rarely saw women, especially after dark. Equal rights had not yet surfaced in Athens.

The Greek equivalent to our familiar proverb, "Let's go and paint the town red," is "Let's go and break a few plates together." It's an old Greek custom that when you enjoy the theatre, a play or a nightclub act, you show your appreciation by throwing plates upon the stage.

We watched the Greek folk dancers swirl to the music of the bouzouki, whipping the crowd into a frenzy. The audience was most definitely alive and rowdy. Gyrating belly dancers and delirious sounds of the bouzouki had people cheering, bellowing at the top of their lungs, and clapping thunderously. Our waiter explained that there are occasions when the music, the stars on stage, the stars above and even Dionysus, the Greek god of wine, combine to rouse the audience to a smashing pitch. Flowers and baubles simply are not adequate prizes.

Consequently, waiters hand plates to the audience, enticing all to join the insanity and throw them onto the stage.

The plates were paper thin, chip- and shatterproof, or so we were told. Still we hesitated. Should we or should we not? Because history has a tendency to repeat itself, could the waiter be believed? Helen of Troy came to mind. Might she have been in a crowd such as this before the Trojan War? After all, her beauty was the direct cause of the war. We certainly didn't want to be left out. We hesitated some more, but then tossed a few. We also ducked. Imagine having plates whiz by your ear! It sounded like mosquitos nesting.

Plates thrown in olden days were glass and shattered into pieces. Police eventually banned the custom, and the practice was replaced with the throwing of flowers and plastic baubles instead. Can you picture the casualties in the days before the flowers? I maintain that Greek embalmers, if in fact embalming occurred in those days, did not contest the old practice.

What a night!

Each morning we walked to the American Express USO office and booked a tour for the day. One day, we visited Trikala, a village famous for flokati rugs, which the Greeks have made by hand for centuries. Originally the rugs, which are made from a combination of sheep and goat's wool, then softened under a waterfall to make them feel like velvet, provided shepherds with warm clothing and bedding during the long winter months. How could I resist?

My rugs were luxuriously thick and heavy and huge—they measured eight by ten feet. One was a natural colour while the other was patterned in orange, gold, cream, and black and was called the Wedding Gift. That particular pattern covers some beds at the Waldorf Astoria in New York.

The bus driver nearly had a seizure when I stumbled up his steps dragging my new purchases. The only space available on the bus to house my rugs was the centre aisle, and some of the passengers were not happy when they had to step over them to reach the exit.

Someone told me that there are two things you must purchase while in Greece. One is a flokati rug and the other is a mink coat. Dave blessed me that I opted for the rugs.

When we arrived back in Athens later that afternoon, Viviane and I gathered up the rugs and hobbled off the bus. We definitely required a taxi to get my load back to the hotel. But in Athens, unless your destination makes the fare worthwhile, the driver won't allow you to enter his cab. They simply wait for something more lucrative to come along. The Pythorgorian was only a couple of blocks away, therefore, no sale!

"Hey, don't be unreasonable. We'll pay whatever you want. Why not pretend to drive us ten miles. Charge us for that amount. We don't care. We'll pay the fare."

It didn't matter. They couldn't understand English.

"What's wrong with you cab drivers? Are you nuts?"

Viviane and I stood tall and must have resembled two damsels in distress, but the Greek men could care less. If we were in Canada and sat by the side of the road with two huge rugs, someone would surely have come to our rescue.

Disappointed with the entire city at this point, we picked up the rugs by the heavy ropes that tied them together. We pulled and tugged the magic carpets through the streets to our hotel. I hated flokati rugs at that point.

It took nearly two hours to reach our hotel. When we finally staggered through the front entrance our hotel manager set us free. He picked up those two rugs as if he lifted two feathers. What a hero! We called him our Dionysus.

It was also on one of our daily trips that we met Mrs. Sebastian. She was American and lived on the island of St. Thomas in the Caribbean. She and her late husband had been pioneers in the 1930s, developing the Caribbean tourist industry. They opened hotels on St. Thomas and Tortola and entertained heads of state, kings, queens, and movie stars. She now travelled the world with a small black poodle.

Mrs. Sebastian met us every day at the USO tour office, and we became a threesome throughout the week. We tramped through ancient ruins, sat on cliffs overlooking the ocean, munched on pistachios, and quenched our thirst with freshly squeezed orange juice. She mesmerized us with tales of her life experiences. However, there were times when Viviane and I glanced at each other with an eyebrow raised, sometimes skeptical whether or not she was always truthful. Her appearance didn't convey wealth. She had no jewellery, she wore a variety of wrinkled denim dresses, she carried a small camera and a small ordinary purse around her neck. Her wrinkled face had only a smidgen of makeup. Of course, we never asked her age, but guessed it had to be at least seventy.

We later discovered the reason for this pauper look. She travelled extensively and defensively and knew the tricks for staying safe.

With three days remaining before our return to Holland, Mrs. Sebastian invited us to be her guests for lunch at the Athens Hilton. We wondered about accepting her invitation. We still questioned her authenticity.

"Why not? We do like her, don't we? Maybe she is a trillionaire like she says? For sure, we'll never meet another in our lifetime. Let's go for it."

Our cab pulled up in front of a massive hotel surrounded by flowering trees and marble pillars. The hotel doorman ran to open the cab door. What a contrast to the Pythorgorian! We paid the driver and followed the doorman into the hotel, where we were captivated by the interior fountains, waterfalls, aquariums, and period furniture. Quite noticeable were the flokati rugs covering the floors, walls, and ceilings.

Dave is going to be so proud of me for making such a tasty choice.

The doorman escorted us to Mrs. Sebastian's suite, which occupied almost the entire penthouse area. We knocked on the door and were met by a small black poodle. Instead of barking, however, he practically gave us a bath. Mrs. Sebastian introduced us to the doorman.

"Aristotle, I'd like you to meet my newfound friends, Jeanette and Viviane."

Aristotle sat on a small chair in the foyer and told Mrs. Sebastion that he'd be close by if anything was required. He had to be her private concierge, but we didn't ask.

She guided us to the living room where French doors accented with bevelled glass led to an enormous patio that overlooked the Acropolis and almost the entire city. When we saw the magnificent private pool, Viviane and I looked at one another with two eyebrows raised. There was little doubt left in our minds now of her authenticity.

Mrs. Sebastian gave us the grand tour of her suite. Each room had luxurious antique furnishings and silk and velvet draperies. We marvelled at the bathrooms with their marble floors, gold-plated fixtures, and crystal chandeliers. Imagine having a chandelier in your bathroom! We also learned that the Greeks invented the toilet and the tub.

Come to think of it, my horoscope and astrology sign is Aquarius—the water carrier. Suddenly it struck me why I love the water the way I do. Just give me an ocean or a bathtub and I'm content.

Following our eye-popping tour, we returned to the patio to relax by the pool. The doorman appeared with a bottle of Dom Perignon and took our order for lunch. We dined on filet mignon in an olive cognac sauce, nestled on a variety of fruits. How wonderful everything was. The little girl from Saskatchewan and her pal from Cape Breton Island were mesmerized.

For the rest of the day we heard, "Can I get you anything, Mrs. Sebastian? Can I do this for you? Can I light your cigarette. Can I? Can I?"

No sooner had the Dom Perignon emptied than another bottle appeared. The only sober one in the room was the small black poodle, and I sometimes wondered about him, sitting upon her knee. Dogs do hiccup.

Mrs. Sebastian's next excursion was to Africa by tanker. She hated cruise ships. She invited us to accompany her, and it did sound tempting. Had we not been wives and mothers . . .

Why the tanker? It was a mode of transportation she had not yet taken. It intrigued her. There are tankers that take some passengers, usually about ten, depending upon availability. Travelling aboard one is unique. The tankers travel sea lanes and stop in ports different from cruise liners.

Mrs. Sebastian travelled with a trunk, a couple of denim dresses, a small black dog, and a heavy wallet full of traveller's cheques secured around her waist.

What a delightful afternoon! Everyone promised to keep in touch, and for awhile, postcards arrived from various ports of call. But as time passed and circumstances changed, Viviane and I lost touch with Mrs. Sebastian. I often think of our friend and wonder where she is today. Viviane and I were privileged to have known her.

The following day, bright and early, we walked to the USO office and purchased tickets for our last tour—a cruise ship that would take us to the islands of Aegina, Poros, and Hydra. We boarded at the Port of Piraeus, the port made famous by the movie, *Never On Sunday*, starring the Greek actress, Melina Mercouri.

Still feeling the effects of our Dom Perignon, we feared that the swinging and swaying of the boat would cause throbbing heads and nausea. However, a few hours of lying on lounge chairs inhaling the warm Mediterranean air soon cleared our heads.

We felt exceedingly rich. The combination of the sea plus the islands and natural harbours made this cruise unlike anything we had ever experienced. The scenery was breathtaking. It explained why Jacqueline Kennedy had married Aristotle Onassis. She had to have been awestruck by the beauty of Greece, the islands, and the magnificent Aegean and Mediterranean Seas. Unfortunately, privately owned islets, such as Skorpios, were not on our tour.

Of the 1,400 Greek islands, only 166 are inhabited. They have a few things in common. The sun shines about 300 days a year and many of the island waters are warm enough for swimming, even in January. The islands are dotted with whitewashed houses, huddled around narrow alleyways and strung along narrow streets leading to a tiny harbour where cafés and tavernas can be distinguished by their red, blue, and yellow awnings. Remnants of antiquity can also be found, including columns, Byzantine churches, and fortresses. Others have little to see besides secluded coves, beaches, and valleys filled with vineyards and trees, including olive, lemon, and pistachio. Many of the islands have no cars; horse-drawn carriages and donkeys provide transportation.

Our first port of call was the island of Aegina. It's about sixteen miles southwest of Piraeus and has an area of thirty-two square miles. It's a mountainous island with a town perched above the sea. Athens' more prosperous citizens spend their summers there, while the locals earn their living mostly from farming. A tour of a pistachio plantation left our lips stained red for days. The main street comprised a few cafés, a bakery, and strangely enough, a movie theatre.

Our next stop was Poros, where the ship squeezed through a strait so narrow you could almost touch the land on either side. Poros is a conical, volcanic island with a tiny village that's a classic of its kind. It's also famous for lemons. The island owns a huge lemon grove called Lemonodasos, which contains more than 30,000 trees. Whitewashed buildings are piled high above the harbour all seemingly decked out with brightly coloured awnings. The café tables come right to the water's edge, which inspired us to have a glass or two of our favourite aperitif made from grape stems and flavored with anise. You guessed it—ouzo!

Hydra, our third stop, was my personal favourite. Until our boat slipped into the harbour, all you could see was a bleak and rocky island. As we neared the island, it became immediately recognizable from a thousand photographs. The town centre is built like an amphitheatre around the port.

Hydra had its heyday in the time of Napoleon when more than 30,000 people lived there. When we visited, the population was about 2,000, and most residents were artists, writers, and jet-setters. The town is different from the others we visited. Terraces rise up from the harbour and house a type of mansion dating from the eighteenth century, called the Hydriot Palazzo. The harbour is also known to be one of the prettiest of the Saronic Gulf. Dozens of stores selling souvenirs and handcrafted items line the streets. It was here where we met a young woman from Montreal. She had originally come to Hydra for a visit, and like us, fell in love with this island and its people. She stayed and opened a boutique where she sold paintings and crochet work created by the local people. I purchased a watercolour of the island painted by a local artist and a crocheted dress that now, unfortunately, fails to mould to my body.

I can't remember who said that a picture is worth a thousand words. But, that's exactly how I've felt over the years about any painting I've purchased. Whenever I look at that watercolour or any other picture that I've acquired throughout our military career, I repeat the same phrase, "When I'm ninety years old (and oh, yes, I intend to be that age one day), this military wife will look back with joy and say, 'Memories are such fond echoes.'"

All too soon the day ended, and we sailed back to the Port of Piraeus. The sun was low in the sky but glistened on the sea. By the time we reached port, long shadows were giving way to a star-studded night.

Viviane and I found the Greeks to be lively, friendly and fun-loving, although sometimes a little too exuberant. They take great pride in their country, its heritage, and its symbols of ruined glory. Hospitality is an admirable Greek trait, and even the fishing villages open their homes to tourists. The staff at the Pythorgorian were no exception. They treated us with kindness and liberality, especially our hotel manager.

Dimitri looked like a Greek god. He was taller than many of the Greeks we had seen and had amazing light blue eyes and dark curly hair. He might have been in his early thirties and was unmarried, or so he said. I couldn't imagine any male with his looks not being pursued by hundreds of women. He spoke excellent English and appeared fascinated with Canada. He asked us questions about our customs, people, and climate and the job opportunities for Greek immigrants. There was no doubt that he knew the meaning of the word "sponsorship." We flirted with him from time to time, only because we didn't want him to forget the promise he made the night of our arrival. We had been looking forward to having him take us out on the town. Besides, it probably would be more fun to break plates with a true Greek.

Viviane and I made reservations to dine at the Roof Garden of the Astor Hotel, and asked Dimitri to join us for a nightcap when we returned. We wanted to ensure that Dimitri would fulfill his commitment for the following evening.

The Roof Garden, which is known for its fine cuisine, overlooks the Acropolis. We sat at a large round table near the window with a clear view of the Acropolis and the Parthenon. The table was made from cherry wood and topped with a glorious white crocheted tablecloth. I haven't seen too many restaurants that have tables set with fine china and real crystal. We knew the food would match the presentation and be delicious.

We ordered a bottle of Santa Elena, a retsina wine well known in Greece. We scanned the menu, but didn't have a clue what to order. Everything was written in Greek. We had to rely on our waiter's expertise to choose something delectable. He came across first class. First of all we had egg-lemon soup called *avgolimono*, followed by *moussaka*. Then we dined on *gourounaki souvlas* and a Greek salad of tomatoes, onions, and feta cheese. It was unfathomable for us to skip dessert, but Viviane and I felt like a stuffed vine leaf. The *baklava* remained untouched on our dessert plate. Sinful!

The night was bright with hundreds of stars blazing across the sky, and it was warm enough to walk back to our hotel. There were no women on the streets, only men. They congregated on street corners and sat alone in bars and parks. We wanted to sit on the park bench and star gaze, but so many insolent men approached us that we thought it best to make a quick exit. Obviously, their women entertained themselves. I suspect they were not allowed out after dark. However, I was a little miffed that only the elderly gentlemen, who had probably been congregating there since the days of Zeus, were attracted to me, while the young Adonises charmed Viviane. I couldn't figure that one out. Was it because of my red hair? Did the colour give me the mature, maybe non-virgin look that was attractive to the older generation? Who knows?

Around midnight, we reached our hotel. Dimitri had already changed from his uniform into white pants and a white shirt. He looked like a Greek god, and we hoped he would conduct himself in a godly fashion. He picked up a tray that carried a bucket of ice, Coca-Cola, and three glasses as he followed us to our hotel room. We offered Dimitri our only chair. Viviane and I sat on the twin beds.

We opened our bottle of Canadian Club whisky, and the three glasses were filled with the liquor, Coke, and ice cubes. Together we toasted Greek and Canadian culture, once, twice, three times. We were all having a merry time.

Our fascinating Greek deity gave us a free history lesson. Dimitri was extremely knowledgeable about his country's traditions and customs. But perhaps it was nothing more than his natural sense of drama—the opportunity to take the stage with little prompting. To any Greek, the entire world's a stage, just as it always has been.

Greece is the cradle of civilization, the origin of the West, the birthplace of democracy . . . Dimitri got the clichés out of the way. Nevertheless, it's hard to imagine what civilized life would be like today without the influence of Ancient Greece. The Greeks invented drama and the amphitheatres to perform it in. They invented the Olympic Games. Euclid and

Pythagoras formulated the theories geometry students slave over to this day. (Now I remember why the name of our hotel was so familiar. I hated geometry.)

Until Dimitri spoke, we had forgotten that as children we learned about the ant, the grasshopper, and other characters from Aesop's Fables. Greek myths have become so interwoven with our consciousness we sometimes forget just where they came from.

During the evening we had quite the study session. Viviane and I agreed that, indeed, the Greeks greatly influenced Western history. We also acknowledged that there's probably not a computer programmer who hasn't studied the logic of Aristotle and again an athlete who hasn't watched the Olympic Games. In fact, Dimitri convinced us that the Greek influence has been so strong throughout our heritage, so ubiquitous in our every day lives that a visit to Greece is like a prodigal's return. As the Greeks tell their visitors, "Welcome home, you've been away too long."

Dimitri obviously took this sentiment to heart as he then staggered over to our beds and with bleary eyes said, "Welcome home! Which one of you would like to make love first? It's getting late, and I have to work in the morning?"

We were flabbergasted!

"Did he say what I think he said?" I asked Viviane.

"Yep! I think so. Sounds to me like he wants to make love."

"Of course I do!" exclaimed our Greek god. "But I do prefer to make love to both of you at the same time. I shall make it an evening you will never forget."

He stood in front of us with squinty eyes and a greasy furrow on his brow. He started to unbutton his shirt.

That poor fellow never knew what he was in for and never realized a redheaded Irish girl from Cape Breton could have a sinful temper.

"Okay, Mister, out the door you go. Out! Out!" I screamed.

Dimitri appeared puzzled. Then he spoke ever so softly. "What did I do wrong? Did I say something offensive? I won't hurt either of you. You'll enjoy it. I'm certain of that!"

We didn't know what to think at this point. He looked calm and certainly was not outraged. We probably were safe. After all, this was a hotel, a prestigious hotel. Nothing out of the ordinary would happen here. But, how did we know that?

Viviane and I both raised our voices. "Please leave right now. Get the hell out of our room. Our talents are not for sale."

He still sat there by the table with a grin on his face. He didn't move, but he did whisper for us to calm down. He worried that someone would hear the commotion and want to investigate. "Okay, then, I'll leave, but only because I don't want to lose my job. Management is not supposed to fraternize with hotel guests."

I flew into a rage when he said that. "If you're not out that door before I blink again, you'll be sorry. Now, beat it, Mister!"

He jumped like a rabbit from that chair. He grabbed his tray, ice bucket, empty Coca-Cola bottles, and the three empty glasses. Viviane and I hustled our God of Love out that door and into the hallway. We slammed and bolted the door behind him.

Viviane and I couldn't believe what had happened. It was so ludicrous that we couldn't contain our laughter. We tried to muffle the sound, but it didn't work. We fell across our beds in hysterics.

To be honest, we likely gave the impression of being two sex-starved fun seekers. We presumed our Dionysus wanted to make the night so pleasurable and gratifying that more frolicking could occur in Canada when we took him back home with us.

In the morning, there was no one behind the counter in the lobby. We walked into the breakfast room and for the first time had to wait in line for a table. It seemed that the staff avoided eye contact. A waitress finally served us. She told us that it had been a busy morning and that the kitchen had run out of croissants, eggs, ham, and cheese. She knew that's what we ordered each morning. We settled for some fruit loaf and juice. Funny, though, that the hotel patrons around us munched on eggs and ham. Could our manager have had influence in the kitchen? After breakfast we passed through the lobby and there he was, at his post. Two red and bleary eyes dropped quickly to the floor.

Our hopes were still not dimmed that he would take us out on the town that night, but the minutes and hours ticked by. He stood us up. Imagine that! It may have been fun to break plates together with a Greek god. But, on the other hand, maybe not!

We struggled with suitcases and heavy flokati rugs down a seemingly endless flight of stairs. No one was there to open the door or to hail a cab. Our last day in Greece with no service or farewell was bittersweet.

We did not tell our husbands what had happened that night until many months later. They were not impressed. Over twenty years have passed since our memorable trip to Athens, but every time Viviane and I get together or talk on the telephone, the first thing out of our mouths is, "Do you want to make love?"

We arrived at the Athens airport for our return flight to Holland only to discover that everyone was on strike—no ticket agents or pilots. The only people in sight were grumpy passengers and police patrolling with machine guns strapped over their shoulders. Hijackings were fairly common in those days, and almost every European airport had armed guards.

A couple of hours passed before we boarded, but our plane sat on the runway for most of the day while negotiations took place with airport personnel. Once again the plane was filled with German and Dutch tourists, many of whom we recognized from the flight two weeks before. During the delay, we were wined and dined in true Greek fashion and time flew by. When the crew finally boarded, cheerful passengers gave the V for victory sign. An agreement had been reached. We fell asleep with that unmistakable flavour of licorice caressing our tongues.

Dave had been waiting at Schiphol airport for hours. He could only drink so much Heineken and smoke so many cigars. Patience wasn't one of his virtues.

Our plane landed safely in Amsterdam, ten hours late. Viviane and I were shuttled into the customs area where we waited for our luggage. Upstairs, behind glass windows, people waited for the late arrivals. My heart jumped when I saw Dave. My hero, patiently waiting for his wife.

I got his attention and pointed to the conveyor belt that held our luggage. From it tumbled a huge bundle of brown paper tied with rope onto the floor. The package contained one of my eight-by-ten flokati rugs, rugs that Viviane and I carried across Athens. I looked up at Dave, nodded my head, and mouthed, "That's mine." It took him minutes to stop shaking his head.

A short time later another huge bundle of brown paper tied with rope tumbled down the conveyor belt. It plopped on the floor beside its mate—the second eight-by-ten flokati rug. I looked back up at Dave. I nodded my head and smiled tightly, "That's mine, too. It's called the Wedding Gift."

"Hey, Viviane," I asked. "Can you make out what Dave is saying?"

"Jeanette, he doesn't look happy. I think he's saying . . . What the hell?"

"Oh, well! He'll get over it."

My guardian angel must have been on duty for the customs officer didn't go through my luggage. But, it was after midnight, and I suppose he just wanted to go home and sleep.

In Greece, I collected seashells and various rocks and stones for Alan's collection. They were in my suitcase. Had the customs officer searched my luggage and found the treasures I had retrieved from some of the ancient sites we visited, I probably would have been tarred and feathered. One never knowingly smuggles antiquities from Greece. Under no circumstances are you to disturb any stone on the Acropolis or elsewhere in the country. Why didn't my Greek god tell me that?

Some day, if you should hear of an archeologist searching for one last piece of a puzzle, forget about what I just said. I mailed all antiquities back to Greece.

Greece, however, was left with my promise to someday return.

Kheh-reh-the Athens!

CHAPTER SIXTEEN

The station clerk looked amused at the look of fear and desperation on my face. "You remind me so much of my wife, and I would hate to see her stranded in a strange country with no money. So, Mrs. Russell, because it is Jubilee Year, I am sure our queen would want you looked after." He handed me my train ticket.

Hammock-type seats spread down each side of the aircraft and no washroom facilities existed. A port-a-potty was concealed by a curtain. No complaints from me! The price was right, and I knew I'd get there safe and sound. My only prayer was that my bladder would not require emptying during my flight aboard the Hercules bound for Gatwick Airport, London.

The Canadian military had a weekly mail run to England, and depending upon space availability, often took passengers. I was one of those passengers in July 1977.

I arrived safe and sound at Gatwick Airport, with my nose print embedded on the small window while I searched the air space for additional planes that might be in close proximity. I took a bus to Victoria Station and then the train to Worcester. Jim and Coleen Gould were waiting for me. Jim was in the British Airforce and he and Dave became acquainted at AFCENT. I was given the grand tour of Worcester, a picturesque city on the Severn River and famous for the production of Worchestershire sauce.

I had budgeted for my trip back to Gatwick, not a penny less or a penny more. However, I could not leave England without purchasing the traditional British classics. A camel-hair suit and a Royal Stewart plaid wool kit were on the top of the list. Only one thing was missing–a cashmere sweater. The red one I chose went perfectly with both. I felt somewhat guilty about the total price, but convinced myself that I'd probably never again have the opportunity to shop at Harrods. Besides, it wasn't like me at all to leave a country without contributing to the economy.

I didn't think I would need extra funds as I would have no expenses. My flight back to Brussels had been taken care of by the Canadian Military. For the first time in my travels, I had a small reserve of money left—at least enough for a souvenir or two. Dave would be proud.

With my luggage and shopping bags in tow, I walked over to the military airline desk to check in. I was flabbergasted when I heard the news. Because of severe weather conditions, the military flight to Brussels had been cancelled.

"Cancelled? Did I hear you right? The plane is not going to Brussels?"

Oh yes, I heard right! No plane! No free ride!

The clerk offered his condolences, but there was nothing he could do. The other passengers had been contacted earlier about the cancellation. He had been waiting for me to arrive. He had tried phoning Dave to give him the news, but Dave and the kids had already left for SHAPE in Brussels to pick me up. Brussels was a three-hour ride from Vaesrade.

Now what am I going to do? I have a few pounds in my purse, but very few. Oh, boy, this is not good. Here I go again! But I suppose there's no point in panicking and elevating my blood pressure any higher than it probably is already. Jeanette, you've sure got yourself in a quandary this time. Think, girl, think!

"Excuse me, Madam!" The clerk's voice interrupted my thoughts. "Have you considered taking the boat train back to Holland? One leaves the dock at ten o'clock this evening."

I thanked him for his advice, but was too embarrassed to tell him that I didn't have enough money to pay the fare. I suppose that could have happened frequently in the days before credit cards. So, surrounded by my luggage and shopping bags, I contemplated what my next course of action would be. Should I phone Coleen and have her come and get me, or should I attempt to obtain a train ticket on compassionate grounds?

I had no choice but to find some way to purchase a ticket for the boat train. Holland seemed a million miles away.

Queen Elizabeth II celebrated her Silver Jubilee in 1977. The country was crowded with well-wishing tourists. Wasn't I a tourist as well? A poor one, mind you, but nevertheless a tourist? I was sure the British people wouldn't let me down once they heard my tale of woe. Ever so anxious, I slowly sauntered to the wicket. Of course I looked dejected, perhaps somewhat shameful, too. As quietly as I could, I explained to the clerk my dilemma.

"Hello! My name is Jeanette Russell, and I'm from Canada. Umm . . . well, I'm from Holland now because my husband and I live there with our family. We are in the Canadian Air Force. Aah! Umm! Well, my husband is in the Canadian Air Force . . . not me." I babbled on.

"Mrs. Russell, that's nice, but what can I do for you?" he asked quickly.

"Well, Sir! I'm on holidays, you see. I visited friends for a week here and unfortunately spent most of my money. I was supposed to be a passenger on a Canadian military flight that was to take me back to Holland, but the plane was cancelled. My husband would have a fit if he knew I had spent my money on clothes and neglected to keep some for an emergency. I have a few pounds left, but not enough for the full fare, I don't think."

He looked amused at my look of fear and desperation. "Mrs. Russell, how much do you have?"

I sheepishly handed him a couple of small pieces of currency. The station clerk cleared his throat. A wide grin etched his face. I hoped that was a smile I saw.

"Mrs. Russell, you remind me so much of my wife, and I would hate to see her stranded in a strange country with no money. So, Mrs. Russell, because it is Jubilee Year, I am sure our queen would want you looked after."

At this point, my heart raced for joy. I had a good feeling about what he was going to say next. "I'll tell you what I'll do . . . I'll buy your ticket."

He handed me two tickets—one for the boat train and the other for the transfer from Amsterdam to Heerlen, a town close to my home. I couldn't believe my good fortune!

"Have a pleasant journey home. And good luck!" His face lit up with the most pleasant of smiles.

I leaned over the counter and put my hands on his cheeks. I gave him the biggest kiss he has ever had I'm sure—in public and from an unknown passenger, anyway.

It was obvious that people behind me were tuned into our conversation. Everyone cheered and clapped. Was I embarrassed when I came to my senses? I was mortified.

I asked the clerk for his name and address. I wanted to send him the money when I got home. But, he told me it was a gift. As I left the wicket, people patted me on the back and wished *bon voyage*.

I couldn't believe it. I had a ticket to go home and, the best part, Dave would never have to know the circumstances. I floated onto the train, bags and baggage, another crisis over. I shall always have a fondness for the British people, especially ticket masters at train stations.

The train arrived at the dock, and I boarded the cross-channel ferry. I shared a cabin with four people, none of whom could speak English. I was famished, but paid no attention to the growlings in my stomach. Oh, for just a crumb, I thought. Convincing myself it was time to shed the pounds I had gained during the week, I climbed into the top bunk.

It looked as if my roommates intended to stay up all night, as none of them undressed for bed. I tucked my passport into my bra and made a makeshift pillow with my booty from Harrods. Having gone through what I did to get there, I was determined no one would rob me. I slept that night dreaming of a luscious banana split topped with two cherries.

We arrived in Amsterdam in the early morning, and I transferred to the train bound for Heerlen. I nearly kissed the ground I walked on. During my trip home, I sat with a young university student from Maastricht who got the greatest charge over my exploits. He must have heard my stomach growl because when he opened his haversack, the next thing I knew we were both eating croissants and cheese. Never had anything tasted so good.

Meanwhile, back at the ranch as they say, Dave had no idea where I was. I wasn't at SHAPE, as he found out after a three-hour ride, and he knew I wasn't in Worcester either. He'd called Coleen and she'd informed him that the last time she saw me, I was sitting on the train headed for London. She had no clue what had happened after that.

Dave didn't panic for the time being. He suspected I was broke and with my track record he figured I'd survive somehow. Once again history repeated itself.

I arrived at the station in Herleen that afternoon. Twenty-four hours had gone by since I had left England. Before I got off the train I imposed once again on my Dutch student friend. I bummed a guilder so I could phone home. Dave answered.

"I'm at the train station in Herleen, please come and get me."

A few minutes later he pulled up with a frown instead of worry on his face. I sat on the curb surrounded by luggage and bags from Harrods. I tried not to look as frazzled as I felt.

There was no kiss of welcome.

"Not one word!" I stated between clenched teeth.

CHAPTER SEVENTEEN

The Dutch police suddenly appeared from out of nowhere. They came screaming from behind shrubs and bushes, around corners and driveways. Their lights were flashing and their sirens could be heard for miles.

Fall was edging closer, and with it, our transfer back to Canada. I hate going-away parties, especially when I'm the one leaving. Our family had met many special people at AFCENT, so not only were we leaving behind Canadian friends, but German, American, British, and Dutch friends as well. Parting this time would certainly be sweet sorrow.

Our going-away party was held at the NCO Club in Brunssum, and everyone was in a festive mood. There were no boring speeches after dinner—only party time. We danced the night away, and I shed the odd tear when dear friends told us how we would be missed. That makes you feel so good. In the military, parting is inevitable, but you learn to live with it, and surprisingly enough, you do adjust. You simply consider it another adventure and something to look forward to. Besides, our postings kept getting better and better.

The evening was winding down and the threat of the "Marechaussee" loomed near. The Dutch police (The Royal Marechaussee) are highly respected in the Netherlands. I would say that only a Formula I racecar could outrun the souped-up Porsches the police drive. Despite this, there is only one traffic rule in Holland that everybody should abide by: don't drink and drive. The police have no tolerance for transgressors.

As our party ended about three in the morning, we had to plan a strategy whereby we would all get home safe, sound, and not arrested. Most of our cars were in the club's parking lot, but there were some parked on the streets surrounding the club.

The Marechaussee knew when parties were being held at the NCO Club, so they lurked in the dark and waited for their prey, with a breathalyzer machine on the front seat of every vehicle. On this particular night, the police had the club surrounded, eagerly anticipating someone weaving out the door. The law in Holland declares that you can be arrested for drunk driving without starting your car. All you have to do is sit in it. Once the door is opened, the intent to drive is made. Some people found sleeping in their back seats have been arrested for drunk driving.

A U.S. soldier from North Carolina, a good friend of Dave's, told him he had an idea about getting everyone home safe and sound. Bob, a born-again Christian, was a tall African-American with a heavy Carolina drawl. He didn't smoke or drink liquor, but he did like to gamble. He was always broke. That night money was more important to Bob than the sin he committed to get in that state. He told Dave that for a small sum he would be willing to help us out. We knew he was the ideal guy to elude and fool the Marechaussee.

All of us gathered in the hallway, close to the club's main entrance. Keys in hand, we stood in wait for the signal to sprint to our vehicles. Bob tugged at the front door, stumbled outside, then turned back and waved. We could hear him whistling and singing at the top of his lungs. He was creating quite the noisy scene. He then staggered throughout the parking lot looking for his car, which he seemed to have great difficulty locating. He'd peer into one car window and shake his head. He'd then stagger on to the next car and so on. It was an Academy Award performance.

About ten minutes later he finally found his car. Then, everything happened faster than lightning. He jumped in, started the car, spun his tires, and ripped out of that parking lot at a speed that would have impressed Mario Andretti. This was our signal.

The Marechaussee suddenly came to life. There must been a half dozen Porsches with motors revved up and tires squealing. However, at the same time, a mad scrambling exodus turned the club parking lot into the Indianapolis Speedway. We bolted to our cars, everyone laughing hysterically.

"Gentlemen, start your engines!" I heard someone yell. We jumped in and sped out of that parking lot, steering our cars into various side streets. When we knew we were in the clear we slowly, but ever so slowly, drove home.

Bob told us he deliberately took a narrow lane, so the cops had no choice but to stay behind him. But before he wrapped himself around a tree, he squealed to a halt, about two miles from the club.

The Marechaussee were not happy. With guns drawn, they instructed him via the loudspeaker to get out of his car and lie flat on the pavement, where they handcuffed him and waited for backup. A van, similar to our paddy wagon, took him to police headquarters.

Headquarters was mystified. They couldn't detect the slightest whiff of alcohol on Bob's breath, nor did they suspect drugs. They realized a breathalyzer or a blood test would have been a total waste of time and money. They were not impressed.

Bob's commanding officer was summoned, and he was not impressed either, especially at four o'clock in the morning. He apologized to the Dutch police and explained that Bob was a fine soldier and a deeply religious man who meant no harm. It was a fact that Bob had been raised in a U.S. state where racing cars was a passionate pastime. He even had aspirations to become a race car driver, but was drafted to Vietnam. The commanding officer knew all this, and even though he was not impressed by Bob's behaviour, he assured the police that this would not happen again. Bob was released, but not before they charged him with reckless driving and had given him a heavy fine.

We often wonder whether the police ever found out they were hoodwinked. If they had gone back to the club, they certainly would have discovered our caper. The club was in darkness and the parking lot empty.

The following day, those people involved in the practical joke met at the club. Bob was declared Speed King of the Road and made hero of the day. The rich hero of the day! Everyone chipped in enough money to pay the fine and make sure our hero lived comfortably for some time to come.

Now it became time for my personal going-away party.

The AFCENT International School faculty and management had a "do" for me at the estate of the director, Herr Rudolf Bewer. It was quite an honour to have so many people attend—principals, headmasters, teachers, cooks, and maintenance staff.

Herr Bewer knew I loved windmills and decided this would be the inspiration for the perfect gift for me. He asked his friend, a Dutch artist, to paint me a windmill. Laeven lived in Heerlen and worked at the Dutch State Mines (DSM) in the printing and graphics department. A large number of his paintings are found in plants around the world owned by DSM. Although he never visited any of these plants or factories, a photographer would be sent out to capture a look that Laeven eventually painted. These paintings, in turn, have been published in DSM calendars, which are collector's items.

Laeven has been compared to Rembrandt or Van Gogh, in terms of skill. All of his paintings are indexed with names and addresses, and his fingerprints, preserved in the oils he used, are found on the back of my painting. Perhaps I have in my care a future masterpiece.

When asked by Herr Bewer if he would paint a windmill, Laeven was reluctant. He had never been satisfied with any windmills he had painted in the past, but because Rudolf Bewer was a dear friend, he told him he would try again.

For me, Laeven painted the mill at Groot Genhout, a village near Beek. However, he was so pleased with the results, he told Herr Bewer, that he wanted to keep the painting for himself. He determined the reason for his success this time was that he had painted "my" windmill on a grey and dismal day. Before, he had always painted on a sunny day.

"No, Sir!" Herr Bewer exclaimed. "The painting must go to Jeanette."

The masterpiece hangs on the wall above my sofa and presents itself exactly how the artist described it—dark and dismal. Periodically I stare at it, and the more I do, the better I like it. I think.

When we got back to Canada, I took the painting to a local art gallery to have it framed. The owner was an art collector, and he fell in love with the painting and offered to buy it. He told me that it exhibited a procedure so unusual that it's almost unheard of in the art world today. Every brush stroke the artist used seemed to be a compass measurement.

When an expert showed that much interest, I thought that perhaps I'd better take a closer look at my painting and learn to appreciate fine art. When I got home, I took out a ruler and actually measured the spaces between each stroke. Surprisingly enough, they were all the same distance. I really do love my windmill more and more each day. It brings back wonderful echoes of the past.

We were wined and dined by friends and colleagues at other parties, and for the time being, I had mixed feelings about returning home. Once again we were leaving close friends, I had to resign from a job I loved, and Glenn and Alan would say goodbye to their friends and school. That lonely feeling resurfaced. We would miss Holland, but life does go on in the military.

CHAPTER EIGHTEEN

Back to where it all began and to a somewhat quieter life. But before long, we had all settled into our routines—kids in school, Dave back to work at CFB North Bay, and me in a new job with the police department. Sometimes I wished I worked somewhere less realistic. My job was not glamorous.

With the help of friends, we unpacked tons of furniture—well, it certainly seemed like tons. Furniture that had been in storage for five years, furniture from Europe, and furniture recently purchased for the first home we had ever owned. What a fun time we had when we discovered the crate packed solid with liqueurs! That evening we managed to find a place for everything, even through our haze.

Life was humdrum in the beginning, but I soon adjusted to a new routine. It may not have been that easy for Glenn and Alan. Since kindergarten they had attended school on a military base, where everyone knew that within a couple of years, their friends would part and reside in a different part of the world. But this year they were enrolled in a public school—Glenn at West Ferris Secondary for Grade 10 and Alan at Silver Birches for Grade 8. The school year started the day after Labour Day, but Glenn and Alan's first day was not until October 22. Would they be shut out from friendships that had already been formed? Would they have difficulties catching up with their classmates? There were so many questions I wanted to ask, but didn't. I knew it would be an adjustment. But we also recognized the fact that most military children adjust well to challenges. We never heard a complaint from either of them.

Although Glenn entered the second year of high school at West Ferris Secondary, the Grade 9 curriculum at AFCENT had been American-based and subordinate to the Ontario standard for that grade. But with little effort Glenn was soon back on track.

Do civilian parents have much influence over their children's profession? Do we, as military, want more for our kids? Do we feel guilty because we moved from place to place? Maybe, but I truly feel that military kids admire their parents tremendously. It's not easy for a military child to adjust to different cultures, religions, and customs. They must learn tolerance, and they look to their parents for that guidance and strength.

On the other hand, civilian kids who have been raised in the same town, and go to school with the same kids their entire academic career, lead a different style of life. They receive lots of guidance from people they've known their entire lives—their parents, grandparents, friends, doctors, ministers, and teachers. Military children miss out on that closeness with others. They rely on their immediate family for solace. However, ask any "military brat" if he enjoyed his growing up years, and I bet he'll say, "Is there any other life?"

My next-door neighbour knew I had been job hunting. Mel Janveau, a constable with the North Bay Police Force, informed me that a secretarial position had become available at his office. I filled out the application form and was called for an interview.

I waltzed into the interview wearing the new camel-hair suit I had purchased at Harrods in London—the suit I protected with my life during my perils in England. It must have had some magic to it, for I was hired on the spot. I always told Dave that one day that suit would sell itself. I worked there for seven years.

However, sometimes I wished I worked somewhere less realistic, such as when I read first-hand details about a dear friend's suicide, rape victims, assaults on children.

Working for the chief of police had its advantages, however. When Dave was posted to northern Canada for six months, the chief had a cruiser stop by my house in the wee hours of the morning to make sure no one of dubious character lingered in the neighbourhood.

On one occasion, our next-door neighbour woke up around three o'clock in the morning. She heard a noise that appeared to be coming from her backyard. When she looked out her window, she noticed two policemen wandering around, their flashlights beaming.

"Is anything wrong, Officers?" she asked when she opened her back door.

"Sorry we disturbed you, Madam," they said. "No, there's nothing wrong. We're just checking on Jeanette."

Police Chief William Wotherspoon died on July 9, 1996. I will miss him!

CHAPTER NINETEEN

CFS Alert wanted Dave. We weren't sure we wanted CFS Alert. Dave's problem was living six months in isolation in the Northwest Territories. My problem was coping alone with two teenagers, a dog, two hamsters, a job, and no husband. Our problem was communicating—via ham radio.

In January 1979, Dave received the surprise of his life with the notice of a single transfer. Alert demanded Dave's expertise. Having no choice, Dave left us in March and returned in September. Dave's sole consolation was that it would be daylight in the Arctic for most of his tour. There is no night, as we know it, in Canada's northern regions. Six months of the year is light, six months is dark.

Located off the northwestern coast of Greenland, Ellesmere Island, where CFS Alert is located, forms part of the Arctic Archipelago. The island is 460 miles long and 300 miles wide, and much of its surface lies under a glacial ice cap. Herds of caribou and muskox roam some of the ice-free regions on the island. Human habitation is very sparse with only a few scattered communities. One of these communities is CFS Alert, a radio and weather station. It is the northernmost settlement in the world.

I had no idea what Dave's new job entailed, but suspected that the Russians were involved somehow.

Eva Janveau, my next-door neighbour, jokingly told us that she might have been able to avert this posting. Three plainclothes military police had approached her, as well as just about everyone else in the neighbourhood, asking questions about the Russells. Their last stop was Eva's. "Do you know your neighbours well? Do they have a good family unit? Have their kids ever been in any kind of trouble? Do they have many parties? Does WO Russell ever talk about his job?"

She could picture the surprised look on the investigators' faces had she told a few fibs: "Well, if I were the government, I'd look elsewhere because I feel Dave Russell will probably go nuts in isolation. He definitely will party, and without strict guidance from their father, those boys will go wild. Besides, I've always had a suspicion that he's a spy."

Eva's conscience, however, wouldn't let her lie.

When I found out about the interviews with my neighbours, I was furious with the military. How dare they go behind our backs and ask for details about our family life from virtual strangers? Dave understood their motive, but didn't let on to me. Later I learned that confidential interviews are a necessary military procedure when a security clearance is required. Alert was classified as top secret on the operations side—on the domestic side, the clearance was secret. However, that didn't make me feel any better when I saw neighbours I barely knew looking suspiciously at us.

I had no problems becoming a single parent for six months, but I wore many hats. Glenn and Alan were good students with good friends, and I was thankful for that. Good friends are essential for a child's future. If more parents would weed out the friends with trashy attitudes and remain on top of things, they wouldn't raise a "follower." For all the weeks alone with my boys, my patience sometimes wore thin, but I never had a day of mental anguish. During those six months a special bonding took place among us that will remain forever. Surprisingly, time passed quickly.

Dave phoned once a week using a ham radio operator in North Bay to connect us. In between static and speaking delay, our conversations were often hilarious. I kept forgetting to say, "Over," after each sentence, so half the time, Dave never got to hear what I had to say. The delay, meanwhile, nearly drove me nuts. He also reminded me time and time again not to discuss financial, domestic, or personal problems over the air, as the whole world could be listening to the frequency we were on. For me not to talk about important issues was difficult to do. Finally, we got the bright idea to record tapes, which we exchanged regularly.

One famous tape was recorded when our friends, Ron and Eileen, came to visit. They were stationed in Sault Ste. Marie. Craving company and a party, I invited two more couples, and at the end of the evening, we began to record messages for Dave. We all took a turn and visited with Dave over the microphone. When he received the tape with accompanying pictures, he listened to it for a couple of minutes, then put it back in its case and into a drawer for safekeeping. When Dave returned from the Arctic Circle, he wanted the authors to attend a hearing. We were all to listen to the tape—cold sober! I have it around somewhere. I must dig it up. We'll keep the memory alive.

Also around this time, Walter and Bert died. They were hamsters that had been named after Walter Peyton and Bert Jones, two favourite football heroes. I was suspicious of their untimely deaths. They had separate cages, and both died on the same day. An autopsy would have shown that they died from pneumonia and not from natural causes. Alan confessed he had given them a bath with Windex window spray. Alan felt terrible.

I was at work the day I learned of their demise, and I had just got off the phone from talking to Alan when it rang again. It was long distance. Dave was playing in a volleyball tournament at the U.S. air base in Thule, Greenland, and had access to a real telephone. I was so excited to hear his voice and that I didn't have to say, "Over," that I hardly gave him a chance to say a word. The main topic of conversation was Walter and Bert. I kept rambling until I heard the click that Dave's time was up! As I sat and listened to a dial tone from Greenland, I realized that I hadn't asked my husband how he was doing and what was happening in his life. I never lived that one down.

Shortly after the rodents' untimely end, Sammy, our Maltese dog, began to bark near the dining room table. She would sprint from the kitchen into the dining room and start to yelp. I looked carefully, but couldn't see anything out of the ordinary. If it continued I would plan a session with a doggie psychiatrist. I assumed it must have been her shadow she barked at. But, oh no, it wasn't her shadow!

With warm weather on the horizon, I began summer rituals. I planted flowers, repainted the deck, and swept away cobwebs from outdoor furniture. The lawn chair cushions needed some reviving, so I brought them into the house and laid them on the dining room table. They had spent the winter with the rest of the furniture in our shed.

The explanation for my dog's insanity lay under my dining room table. A huge red squirrel. It must have been two feet long from his head to his bushy red tail. I was frozen with fear. Visions of the rat-infested bathroom in Holland flashed through my mind.

My next-door neighbour, one of North Bay's finest and my saviour for the past six months, would know what to do. I knew no red squirrel could outsmart Constable Janveau.

He came to the rescue wearing a long-sleeved shirt and heavy jeans and carrying a baseball mitt. A scuffle between man and beast occurred. It reminded me of the Disney characters, Tom and Jerry. Mel the cop and Jerry the squirrel raced through the house, up and down stairs, up and down curtains, in and out of rooms. What a racket! I screamed, Mel huffed and puffed, the squirrel scolded and chirped, and Sammy never stopped barking. Ultimately, the baseball mitt was too much for our furry friend, and she was apprehended. Mel hustled her out the patio door.

A minute or so later we looked at the door and there she was, peering defiantly through the glass. Perhaps she had rabies and was back for the kill?

When we thought the coast was clear, Sammy started to bark again, and this time, at the cushions on the dining room table. We could see some movement from one cushion and could hear small peeps coming from it. Then we spotted six little heads with sleepy-looking eyes. Mother Squirrel had nested in the cushion that sat in the shed. From the patio door, she was telling us that she wanted her kids back.

With the baseball mitt still on his hand, Mel picked up the cushion and carried it to the woods behind our house, followed closely by Mother. The cushion was left under a pine tree and became the family's permanent home.

A family of red squirrels that might be the offspring of the babies we rescued spends the winter in our shed and taunts our little dog Puffin during the summer in the backyard.

Because the kids and I were never sure what Dave did during his service in the Air Force, we named him 0010 (Dave Bond). He insisted he monitored the weather in Alert. The turbulence between Russia and the Free World could create an atmospheric condition, I dare say. However, while I'll never know what his roles have been during his military career, one thing remains certain: Dave will never be court-martialed for revealing military secrets.

September drew closer, meaning Dave would soon be home. To say we were excited, as a family, would be an understatement. Even Sammy sensed her master would soon pick up the leash and squire her back to her favourite stomping ground at the beach.

One day I received a phone call from the base padre. He told me to expect a letter in the mail and asked that I study it carefully.

"If you are at all concerned about the content of the letter and you have any questions, please get back to me." *Hello! Am I concerned? I think so!* The padre then assured me that everything would soon be back to normal.

"What the heck are you talking about . . . back to normal. Who's this letter from? Is my husband okay?" I was quite annoyed actually. Was this padre in a habit of phoning military wives and scaring the pants off them?

Finally he talked some sense. He must have known from the tone of my voice that he'd better explain a bit more than he had. The five-page letter would be mailed from National Defence Headquarters in Ottawa and was sent to all wives and families informing them of what to expect upon a member's return from an isolation posting—what to expect in terms of personality changes and readjustment to the populated world.

Had this husband of mine been brainwashed? Would he have some type of post-traumatic syndrome? I was certainly anxious to receive this letter.

The letter stated that isolation and separation affects some people adversely. I could understand that to be the case for some, but not for my husband. Dave was and remains mentally well adjusted and can deal with whatever situation arises. He was neither depressed nor unhappy to take this posting. He was a military man and would go wherever needed, no questions asked. I put the letter back into the envelope and hoped that I'd remember to show it to Dave when he got home.

Dave flew from the Arctic Circle to CFB Trenton aboard a Hercules aircraft on September 8, 1979. I wanted to make sure that our first meeting in more than six months would be a night to remember. After all, a healthy Newfoundlander is known for his virility and cannot remain a celibate for even one day past a six-month period.

Before I made the trek to Toronto, where we had agreed to meet, I had the four essential components necessary for the return: I indulged in a new hairdo, a facial, a manicure, and a pedicure. Everything had to be perfect, from head to toe. New lingerie, perfume, and bath salts completed the picture.

Wouldn't it be nice if I could get the bridal suite at the Chelsea Inn? But, just how could I wangle that? Then I thought back to the clerk at Gatwick who purchased my train ticket. *Perhaps I could persuade the hotel manager to feel the same way and be sympathetic.* Anyway, it was worth a try. I seem to have a way with managers.

When I walked into the Chelsea Inn, I asked for the manager. I mentioned the homecoming and the fact that Dave had been in the Arctic Circle for six months with the Canadian Air Force.

"Sir, this homecoming is important to me as maybe it should be for all of us. My husband has lived in isolation for over six months. His role is to defend our country and keep it safe for our children and grandchildren.

"I want everything to be perfect upon his return. Many of our soldiers find it difficult to be away from their families for such a long period of time. I know that if the shoe were on the other foot, so to speak, I'd be depressed as well. I simply want to make the journey's end something for my husband to remember."

Before I could even pose the question—Is the bridal suite available?—my room was upgraded. I noticed a tear cloud the manager's eye. Suddenly a porter appeared and put my luggage on a cart. He told me to follow him.

I walked into this magnificent room. The first thing I noticed was a heart-shaped bed topped with dozens of red cushions—very unusual. The bathroom contained a large Jacuzzi, marble floors, and brass faucets, and large fluffy white terry robes were neatly folded in the closet. There was even a telephone in there. (I couldn't imagine what you'd need a telephone in the bathroom for.) The only bathroom that could compare to it would be the one in Mrs. Sebastian's suite in Greece.

As I unpacked, the doorbell rang. A waiter brought in a large bowl of fresh fruit and placed it on the table. Next came an ice bucket containing a bottle of champagne!

"Compliments of the management," he smiled as he closed the door.

Can't get much better than this.

I unfolded the black silk baby dolls I had recently purchased and ran the water for the Jacuzzi. I laced it with my favourite lavender bath salts. I felt sensuous even before I hopped in. I soaked for over an hour, and only when my body started to resemble a prune did I decide to make my exit.

I ordered hors d'oeuvres from room service and placed them next to the chilled bottle of champagne on the dresser. I settled back to wait for my man to return. He was due to arrive about 7 p.m., and I wanted everything to be perfect. I planned to hand my husband a glass of champagne as soon as I opened the door. So, around 6:30, I popped open the bubbly. Everything was set.

At 6:45 the phone rang. A telephone operator from CFB Trenton informed me that Dave's flight had been delayed due to inclement weather. He was now expected to arrive at 11 p.m.

Oh no! What can I do with this open bottle of champagne? There won't be any fizzle left by eleven o'clock. I guess I have no choice . . .

Dave's flight finally arrived at Trenton. Everyone, including the flight crew, stepped from the Hercules attired in parkas and boots. They looked quite the sight as they made their way across the runway. Of course, they fooled around. The temperature in Trenton was ninety degrees Fahrenheit.

Dave stopped at customs. When asked if he had anything to declare, he stated, "Yes . . . ME! And I'm back to stay! Thank God."

It was after midnight, and I had been in bed since nine with a belly full of hors d'oeuvres and a bottle of champagne. A faint knock sounded at the door. I thought I was dreaming at first, but then I heard it again. My head felt like it had separated from my body, but I managed to rise from the bed and slowly make my way towards the door. I opened it and there he was—My Hero!

"Oh! My head!" I could hardly see. Never had I been plagued with such a tremendous hangover. I mumbled, "Welcome home, Sweetheart. I'll see you in the morning. We'll talk then." I don't remember anything else.

Life became normal once again, and I resumed the role of pledging allegiance to my husband. No post-traumatic syndrome, Dave was fine. Just fine! But he did make the comment from time to time that the only way he'd return to the far north was if the Forces promoted him to a four-star general and provided him with a flight crew and a Lear jet.

Two years later, in 1981, Dave was transferred to Ottawa. For the first time in our career, this posting created a problem. Glenn was in Grade 13 and Alan in Grade 11. Although we both knew that the posting would be advantageous for Dave's career, we could not interrupt our children's education at this point. It simply wasn't fair.

The Canadian Forces agreed that the family could stay in North Bay, and Dave would go alone for one year to the capital. At least we had a year to figure things out.

However, this wasn't an isolation posting, so circumstances would be much different. There would be no need for ham radios and tapes, and the military provided Dave with comfortable accommodations—a one-bedroom apartment, maid service included. Who could be so lucky to have a house in the country and an apartment in the city? The weekends that Dave didn't come home, I went to Ottawa.

Ottawa was a desirable posting for most military personnel, and many of our friends were stationed there. You could remain in Ottawa for years, transferring from job to job, and not uproot your family. We had a marvellous time becoming reacquainted with our friends from Moosonee and Holland.

Dave's bachelor year in Ottawa ended. And for once, the gods were on our side. Dave was transferred back to North Bay. Glenn graduated from Grade 13 and would attend Nipissing University. Where had time gone?

Is there a distinction between a wandering newspaper life and a wandering military life? You adjust—like my mother adjusted in 1983.

My mother had devoted her life to my father's career, which was similar to a military career in terms of promotion, relocation, and readjustment. You simply moved on with your life. When a place began to feel like home for my mother, my father took another job, in another province. Like the dutiful wife she was, she followed her husband, but still muttering to herself about the newspaper business being a man's world. When my father received word that his next job would be Sydney my mother cried, "Oh, no! Now I have to move to Australia."

When she discovered that this Sydney was on Cape Breton Island, she did follow her husband without a word of discouragement and said a small prayer that Nova Scotia would be her last move.

She stayed there for forty-two years, until 1983, at the age of seventy-eight and now a widow, she packed up once again. Her destination: North Bay, a choice that gave her renewed vigour.

Even though I had my mother back in my life, she didn't take the place of my children who had left to further their education. I still felt a little lost with the empty nest syndrome.

In September 1983, Alan left North Bay to attend Memorial University in Newfoundland. Alan had wanted to join his friends at an Ontario university, but as parents, we determined that if Alan wished to pursue a career in medicine, Memorial University had to be his choice. Alan left North Bay with a heavy heart.

Ken Kellough, Alan's seventh grade science teacher at AFCENT School, had been adamant that Alan's academic future would be assured in science, especially in biology. He laughed and said that Alan could dissect a frog better than he could, and never got squeamish.

From very early, Dave and I recognized Alan's academic talents, and we encouraged him to excel in whatever field of study he enjoyed. It's the parents' obligation to recognize a gift or aptitude in their child—whether it be academic, musical, or artistic. We acknowledged Alan's talent in science, but unfortunately not Glenn's in art. Why had there been a difference? Professions, obviously! A doctor has a secure future treating people's health problems, and people will always have health problems. People buy art because they like it, not because they need it. Money changes hands differently.

Dave and I didn't have the luxury of a high salary during our military career. We had to seriously consider the cost of a university education that would allow both our sons a better life with no financial struggle. A doctor certainly would have that—an artist, perhaps not.

The medical school at Memorial University has a high rating in Canada, but getting accepted into medicine at any university has some degree of politics attached. We figured it wouldn't hurt for Alan to attend Memorial, where the Russell name was well known. Many of Dave's relatives had attended the university in the past, plus, his brother Wilson and his wife had taught there for a few years previous to Alan's arrival. And let's not forget that Alan was the son of a Newfoundlander.

Memorial University accepted a small number of students from other provinces each year. This initially posed a problem for entrance. Ontario's spots were taken. However, once the university registrar learned that Dave was a member of the Canadian Forces and was born in Newfoundland, the admission rules were changed. Because Dave had the privilege to vote in a federal election in his home province, Alan was deemed to be a Newfoundlander.

We attempted to boost Alan's spirits by trying to convince him that St. John's, a modern city with a huge university, was a far cry from the small fishing village he imagined it to be. He only remembered visits to his grandfather's home in the small community of Bay Roberts. He assumed the rest of the province was the same.

Come to think of it, how many people actually know anything about Newfoundland? They associate the island with crazy jokes and a funny accent. Unless you have visited it, you cannot appreciate its beauty or dynamic capital. Alan was one of those people.

Dave's brother, Bob, took us on a tour of St. John's. He met us at the airport and showed us everything. The university complex at Memorial was enormous, with underground tunnels going from building to building. The newly constructed Health Sciences Centre housed an elite staff of medical doctors.

Bob ended the tour by raising Alan's spirits even more, telling him that the best-looking women in Canada came from Newfoundland.

I obviously had no choice but to object.

We hated to leave Alan; he would be so far away. Alan had never been away from home for any length of time and we wouldn't see him again until Christmas. I had to remind myself time and time again that this separation was a good thing. Not only was Alan attending a reputable university, his stay in Newfoundland would steer him closer to his paternal ancestry. His grandfather, aunts, uncles, and cousins would care for and nurture him.

A mother knows the day will come when her kids leave home, one by one. The times I roamed my house feeling lonely were endless. I sat on the boys' beds and cried. I missed them so much. Life from now on would change for Dave and me.

CHAPTER TWENTY

On my way to visit Dave in Rome, I lay on the top bunk as the train whistled through the Alps. Ice crystals came through the cracks in the window casings. *What if this train slides off the tracks and tumbles down the mountainside? No one would ever find me. I must pray:*

> *Now I lay me down to sleep,*
> *I pray the Lord my soul to keep.*
> *If I should die before I wake,*
> *I pray the Lord my soul to take.*
> *But dear Lord, please don't take my soul tonight*
> *Part the snow and make the night bright.*

Glenn would soon graduate from university and start looking for a job. Unfortunately, North Bay was not on his list. Alan had no qualms about remaining at Memorial, but my mother had never become accustomed to North Bay and was game to relocate. But, I had a great job. Did I want to leave it? Should we or should we not go?

It was 1985 and a transfer had become available for Norfolk, Virginia. In the past, we had always made the right choice, even when that choice was made for us. But this time would be different. We could accept and go to Virginia, or stay put in North Bay. A quandary arose in terms of what would be best for everyone.

The more we thought about living in yet another country, the more we became convinced that this posting would be the opportunity of a lifetime. We'd be foolish to pass it up for a couple of reasons. Dave was in his final years of service and what a grand finale this transfer would be for his career. We jokingly referred to the move as his punishment posting. We also considered another reason for accepting this posting.

My mother and I knew Norfolk and Virginia Beach. My brother Pat lived in Virginia Beach, and over the years we had spent many vacations there. Pat and I were excited by the opportunity for our families to be close again after thirty years. And besides, that old familiar smell of the ocean beckoned to me like a brilliant light shining down from a lighthouse. Salty sea air gets in your bones and the sound of pounding surf never leaves your mind. The ocean called to me.

People not raised on any of Canada's coasts have little idea of the intensity the sea holds for those who have. There is such a mystery to the ocean. Nothing is more invigorating than to be at the edge of the sea and looking straight ahead at the ever-tumbling water. It is mystifying. I shall never forget my love for the smell, sights, and sounds of an ocean.

In preparation for his Virginia posting, Dave spent six months at the Italian air force base in Latina, Italy, where he would study satellite communications at the NATO Communications School. Latina is located thirty miles south of Rome.

For the third time in our career, Dave left the roost. But this time it was so different. I was home alone with only the dog.

Three lonely months went by, when Dave and I decided it was time for a visit. I assured him I'd behave this time. I would not spend a penny until we met in Italy.

I left Ottawa aboard a Canadian Forces Boeing 707 military aircraft and arrived in Lahr, West Germany, about six hours later. The overseas trip cost $11 and included three gourmet box lunches. What a difference from the Hercules aircraft I had flown on for years—a real bathroom this time, no receptacle covered by a curtain.

I booked into the Europahoff, the hotel reserved for Canadian military personnel at Lahr. The following day, I took a cab to the train station, where I purchased a ticket to Rome.

The train reminded me of the Orient Express—old, narrow, and fast. I found my compartment and my three seatmates who didn't speak a word of English. But then again, why was I surprised? After all, wasn't I the foreigner? Why should they speak my language? But thank heavens we were all women. I could have shared this room with men! We had cramped quarters and a microscopic bathroom, but we managed to stay out of one another's way.

The train was scheduled to arrive in Rome the next afternoon at 3 p.m. Concealed under my clothing and tied securely around my waist was my money belt, containing my passport and traveller's cheques. I felt safe in the event my roommates walked in their sleep as I had jet lag and could hardly keep my eyes open.

At bedtime, our seats were converted into four bunks. After taking turns in the bathroom, I hopped up onto the top bunk where I hoped to be lulled to sleep by the motion of the train. This particular locomotive didn't fulfill my hopes for slumber, despite my exhaustion. The motion was neither soothing nor reassuring. It flew over the tracks, shaking from side to side, banging our suitcases against the walls. Anything that wasn't nailed down, fell down. The wind whistled a frightening, eerie sound. It sounded as if someone in the pitch black were shrieking. This night was turning out to be a nightmare. Even my roommates were jittery.

When I squinted out the window from the top bunk, it looked like we were going through a tremendous blizzard. Some of it even managed to come in through the cracks in the window casings.

My God, what if the train slides off the tracks and tumbles down the mountain? No one would ever find me. What in the name of God am I doing here in the middle of the snowy Alps anyway?

It's a well-known fact that Switzerland does not have balmy weather in April. The Alps, not just small molehills like the mountains I'm used to travelling over in Cape Breton, are real live mountains commanding the utmost respect.

I tried to remain calm and convince myself that it was only blowing snow created by the speed of the train and that no blizzard or dangerous conditions existed. Everything was under control. I hoped and prayed that the engineers who drove this monster knew what the hell they were doing.

Finally, morning came. The sun gleamed bright and clear through the windows with not a trace of frost or snow to be seen anywhere. What a relief! Breakfast was served as we rambled through the Italian countryside, with the train stopping along the way to pick up passengers. I marvelled at the beauty of the hills, vineyards, churches, and small villages. Clusters of small homes perched on mountainsides. It looked as if people even lived in caves.

The train pulled into the Roma Termine at three o'clock that afternoon. I don't know how many trains used this station, but as far as my eye could see, there were rows and rows of tracks. The shrill sounds of whistles pierced my eardrums. The odour of fuel and steam assaulted my nose. Hundreds of people milled about, jumping from track to track trying to locate their train. Handsome young men scrambled to help anyone with a suitcase. No questions were asked. My luggage was grabbed from my hands, but the good-looking Italian porter made a quick exit when he saw my guardian angel draw near.

When I pack a suitcase there's not much that remains in my closet. I make sure I have an outfit for any occasion. Dave became my forklift as he led the way to another track I swear was at the other end of the building. I had so much baggage that we had to stand in the aisle of the train we boarded (my baggage got the seats). We had a bumpy journey.

Finally we arrived in Latina and checked into the Europa Hotel that would be our home for the next month. Dave was ordinarily housed in the air force barracks at the Italian base, but for the month I visited, he had been given permission to live at the hotel.

The NATO base was a secure base guarded twenty-four hours a day by armed military personnel with machine guns and guard dogs. The students at this school had a nightly curfew and had to follow a set route to get from building to building. It could be a matter of life or death if the students did not follow the designated path. Intruders would not know of the assigned routes, and sometimes late at night, gunfire could be heard. Maybe the guards firing at rabbits? But on the other hand, maybe not. These sounds sent a chilling message to the foreigners residing on this base.

"Conduct yourself accordingly."

Many of Dave's classmates were military personnel from NATO countries. His roommate, Kidar, was a Muslim soldier from Turkey who prayed many times a day. Dave respected his culture and religion and spent many hours in the common room at the barracks while Kidar worshiped Allah. He and Kidar became soul mates during the six months they lived together. To this day they have a mutual respect for one another and have remained in touch.

Latina's population is around 50,000, and I was surprised to learn that my favourite wine is manufactured there. Castelli Romani sold for $1 a bottle. Latina's town square is surrounded by a beautiful park, is cooled with fountains, flowers, and trees, and is home to clothing stores, small boutiques, supermarkets, restaurants, and cafes.

Our fifth-floor room at the Europa hotel wasn't fancy, but it was clean. We wouldn't spend a lot of time there anyway. The hotel manager spoke excellent English and appeared to be at our beck and call. Whatever we needed or asked for was never a problem. However, his gaze made me feel uncomfortable.

Classes were conducted in two shifts: "mornings" were from seven to three, "evenings" from noon to eight. When Dave had the late shift, he'd leave around eleven in the morning. That's when I began my day. On my way out the door, the manager always bade me farewell, "Enjoy the day."

After a long cold winter in North Bay, the warm Italian sunshine was such a pleasant surprise. I spent many mornings strolling leisurely throughout the town. I'd nod to people as I passed by and wish them a good morning. I suppose I looked foreign to them with my red hair and fair complexion, but that never presented an issue. The townspeople were very friendly.

I came across a sidewalk café that made the best *panino imbottino* I would ever taste in Italy. Every time I was in the café a song was playing. Stevie Wonder had a new release that year, "I Just Called to Say I Love You." Customers sneaked a peek at me while they sang the lyrics in English. It was so funny. I'd join in and sing, too. I had such a great time in that café.

Siesta occurred every day from one to four in the afternoon. Everything shut down, and the town was completely empty for this three-hour period. Iron bars encased shop windows and shutters closed on houses. Families took naps.

I'd usually head for the park, maybe to read or simply to relax and enjoy the sunshine. The only people I'd ever meet would be men, usually old men, either reading or napping on the park benches. I never saw many women or children. One day I noticed a young man watching me from behind a tree. He was so obvious it made me chuckle. We played games. I'd move from one bench to another. He'd move from one tree to another. I knew I was in unfamiliar territory, but after all, it wasn't midnight. The sun was shining. What could happen? But from the sounds of the snores I heard coming from the old men napping on the benches, would a cry for help wake them?

My stalker became more aggressive. He sat beside me on the bench and in almost perfect English asked that I go for a drive with him. He wanted to show me the sights of Latina.

I tried to remain calm, but my heart started to race. I had trouble swallowing. Suddenly I was terrified. What if he gagged me and then hauled me to his car? No one would see it and obviously I wouldn't be able to scream and wake anyone. I simply didn't know what to do. Without a word of encouragement, I got up from the bench and started walking. Worried that he might follow me back to my hotel, I walked to places I knew his car couldn't take him—through the park, up and down one-way streets, and in and out of laneways. It worked—or so I thought!

I couldn't see his car at first, but then I spotted him again. He parked the car and now followed me on foot. I remembered a police station I passed on my way to the park so headed there. I went inside, but no one spoke English. Thank God for my charade parties. One of the policemen understood my dilemma, I think. He came outside with me, but my stranger had vanished. I knew there was nothing more he could do. He shrugged his shoulders and went back inside.

I knew my stranger was lurking somewhere. I could feel his presence, but I had to get back to my hotel without him following me. By this time, siesta was over and the stores were beginning to open. Maybe I could lose him. My plan was to run in and out of stores quickly. If he followed, I'd simply outwit him. I did this for a couple of hours with him hot on my trail.

A small *lavanderia* sat across the street from our hotel. The day before I had taken some of Dave's uniform shirts there to be cleaned. The owners spoke some English and had chatted up a storm with me that day. I entered and noticed my stranger walk by the door, but he didn't look in. When I was certain the coast was clear, I ran across the street and into my hotel. I raced to my room, locked the door, and slowly made my way towards the window where I peered out from behind the blinds. Sure enough, there he was—across the street on the corner and looking my way. I shivered.

Dave wouldn't be home for hours, and I had no way of contacting him. So, I decided to go down to the lobby to tell the manager. He was furious at his countryman. He raced from the hotel and practically flew across the street. I could hear him shout at the stranger. His hands were flaying, and his feet stomped the pavement. Whatever the manager said must have worked, because my stalker turned around and ran down the street with not a backward glance.

"Madam, you can be assured that you'll have no more trouble with that lad."

And true to his word, I never did.

The following day, in the event my unwelcome friend wouldn't heed my hotel manager's warning, I decided to stick close to home. The manager told me about a sundeck on the hotel roof, and if I wanted to sunbathe in private, it would be the perfect place. It sounded like a great idea. I put on my bathing suit, grabbed a towel, a book and a Coke, and went to the roof.

It seldom rains in this part of Italy, and provisions are made throughout the region to trap the water when it does fall. Most roofs are flat and have large barrels and containers for this very purpose. The roofs also make an excellent place for a clothesline, and on this occasion, the hotel maids were busy hanging sheets and towels, as were just about everyone else in the neighbourhood. Laundry of all colours and kinds were blowing in the breeze. I was feeling pretty safe.

There was a small corner set up with a table and umbrella and a couple of chaise lounges. I laid back on one of them and was determined not to leave until my skin turned a golden bronze. Such a beautiful morning! The sun shone brightly in the clear blue sky.

However, I nearly jumped out of my skin when I felt a tap on my shoulder. I looked up into the face of the hotel manager, and visions of Greece flashed through my head.

He had taken the afternoon off and wanted to show me the beach at Anzio. "Your husband will never have to know," he smirked. "I will change into my swimsuit and meet you downstairs. We'll do this in secret and be back in plenty of time. I long for your company."

Oh, my God, here we go again! I felt butterflies in my stomach. My heart began to pound. How much stress could it take? I couldn't believe what I just heard.

"No, Signore, I don't think so. Why don't you ask one of your hotel maids to go to your beach? Please, leave me alone." His expression didn't change. He raised his eyebrows and blinked his eyes a couple of times. But he didn't move. He was waiting for approval.

"Why not, what's wrong? It would be an honour for me to show you a small part of my country, and the beach is very romantic. We'll have a great time and there'll be no tourists to bother us. You'll be safe with me. I got rid of that stranger for you, didn't I?"

"Yes, Signore, you did do that, and I'm thankful, but let me remind you of something. I happen to have a hot-blooded robust Newfoundlander who is six feet, three inches tall, and he wouldn't take too kindly to your invitation. So, get lost, my friend—go find yourself a nice Italian girl."

Had I been discourteous? Of course I had, but he didn't understand that.

"Italians are known to be hot blooded and good lovers, too," he replied. "I am able to show you a good time. You will be impressed. Look at Valentino, you Americans loved him. Give me a chance."

I wondered whether all Italian men were this persistent. Finally I jumped up from my chair and stood nose to nose with him.

"NO! Do you understand the word NO! If you don't go right now, I will scream."

Oh, yes! He understood the word NO! His demeanor quickly changed. He stuttered and stammered. "Please do not tell the maids. I may lose my job."

Where did I hear that before?

The hotel manager didn't care whether or not I told Dave. He just didn't want the maids to know. Brave man? I don't think so!

I agreed, and for the remainder of the month, he made himself pretty scarce.

Dave and I got to know Latina and its cuisine pretty well. Most *trattori* were family owned and operated. There was one we favoured in town, and we became friends with the family. The owner greeted us at the door and reserved a table for us by the window for the remainder of the month. Every day he prepared a small menu—nothing elaborate, but everything delicious. The *cuoco* made us special pasta dishes and referred to them as his *Canadese* specials. His pizzas were our favourite. We followed him to his kitchen and chose the ingredients we preferred.

One evening, I marvelled at the flavour of the Cornish hens. I practically licked my plate clean. However, what I ate that night wasn't chicken or a Cornish hen. It was a rabbit. Dave knew all along what he was eating, but didn't let on to me. He had eaten rabbit many times before.

I once had a pet rabbit and felt guilty that I actually consumed one and enjoyed it. However, I doubt that I shall ever taste another—that is, if I'm not fooled again.

A couple of times a week we joined Dave's classmates at various functions. Many of the wives were visiting that month as well, with German, British, Turkish, Dutch, American, and Canadian making up the nationalities. Dave must have looked more Italian than the other people did for every time we entered a restaurant, he was always given the royal treatment. Later on we learned that the owners were not quite sure whether he was connected with the Mafia or not. I suppose they weren't taking any chances. But I believe that ever-familiar stogie perched in his mouth definitely accounted for him being misidentified as a member of that secret Sicilian order.

Of course, Italians smoke cigars, but then again, Dave has many similar traits with the Italian race; his good looks, dark complexion, Roman nose, and white teeth resemble the handsome Italians I encountered that month.

A couple of times a week we rode the train to Rome. We marvelled over the good looks of the Italian people. In my estimation, the Italian race has to be the most handsome of all. And my hotel manager, despite his odious behaviour, was certainly not excluded. Everyone looked like movie stars, especially the young men and women. We never saw a homely person on that train. Another noticeable detail was that few people wore eyeglasses. Was it because they couldn't afford to buy them or was it because they didn't need them at all. It's my guess that the vitamin C derived from all those grapes might account for excellent eyesight.

We were given good advice on safety from an older gentleman who sat with us on the train. He spoke excellent English, and suggested we remove our jewellery and watches and put them in a safe place. Dave gave me his rings and watch, and I went to the lavatory on the train and put them together with my things in the money belt I wore around my waist under my clothing. The only visible thing left was the camera slung over my shoulder. I kept my calculator out as well and put it in my pocket. I would be lost without that.

Rome, like other large cities around the world, has its share of thieves. Many are homeless or gypsy children, who live on the streets and steal to survive. Gangs of kids are known to drive mopeds up and down streets in search of unsuspecting tourists decked out in jewellery and carrying purses. When they see a "hit," they drive up onto the sidewalk and snatch. The wife of a British classmate had a tragic experience with such a thief on a moped. She was walking on the sidewalk with some friends when a scruffy-looking kid drove up beside her and grabbed her necklace. The necklace didn't break, but the thief didn't let go either and dragged her behind his moped. A hundred yards up the road, he finally let go of the necklace. Her neck was seriously gashed and bruised, her arms and legs fractured. A senseless tragedy with no gain—the necklace remained on her neck. She was airlifted back to England where she underwent extensive surgery.

A clever ruse of gypsy children was to roam the streets with newspapers rolled up under their arms. These forlorn-looking kids with angelic faces are actually the slickest of all. They travel in packs and swarm you like a colony of bees. While one kid begs in front of you, another hits you from behind with the newspaper, hoping to divert your attention. When you swing around to see what in the hell this kid is doing behind you, the one in front grabs your purse and runs. The street urchins figured out we knew about their game. We met the challenge and ended up victorious! But the day had only begun.

I was fleeced, and not by the mopeders or the gypsy children, but by a handsome young man. We were on a city bus that was packed to capacity—standing room only—and we were being jostled back and forth over the bumpy cobblestone roads. My money belt was fastened securely around my waist, and in my pocket held only the essentials—some tissues, and the neatest little calculator that I cherished. It was only the size of a business card and had become my mathematical companion throughout my travels in Europe.

The young man behind kept bumping into me. I peered at him through my sunglasses perched on the end of my nose and thought, "Why did this happen when the bus was stopped?" Then I remembered my neat little calculator. I reached into my pocket and felt around. My pocket was empty. I turned around and came face to face with the most handsome of all Italians. He smiled and winked. I knew that smile was a taunting one.

"Guess what I've got?"

Rome not only captured our pocketbooks, but also our hearts. We walked the cobblestone streets and shopped in the boutiques along the Via Venito. We lunched at the famous Harry's Bar, and from our table watched Rome's elite stroll by. I marvelled at the flowers. April in Canada had hopefully seen the last snowfall, and perhaps with the exception of tulips, flowers had not yet made an appearance. But here in Rome, they were everywhere. Flowers hung from lampposts and were liberally stuffed into wooden boxes on every street corner. Real flowers formed centrepieces on café tables.

Another of our excursions took us to Naples for a weekend, where we had reserved a hotel room at the international base there. Once again, an Italian gentleman approached and motioned for us to remove our jewellery. I thought I had concealed everything. My gold chain was tucked under my collar and my watch under my sleeve. But obviously he could see them. So back to the lavatory I went. Out came the money belt. Once again it would contain rings, chain, watches, money, and passports.

In terms of kleptomaniacs, Naples runs a close second to Rome.

This train trip, which normally took about three hours, lasted eight. Train workers decided to strike that weekend, but the term used for the disruption of the railway was "slowdowns." We weren't sure what that meant. But we soon found out.

Not even halfway to Naples, the train slowed and then came to a complete stop. We looked out the window and watched as the engineers, conductors, and various train personnel left the train and walked up the track. The passengers were left sitting in the middle of nowhere.

"Hey, come back, where are you going?" All the passengers were hollering from the open windows. Everyone was puzzled. We had obviously been abandoned. No one spoke English so all that was left for Dave and me to do was follow the leader.

We picked up our luggage and started walking up the track with the other passengers. We figured there was no point in sitting on a train going nowhere. Dozens of people walked with us carrying their suitcases, packages, and picnic baskets.

"Was that a whistle we just heard?" Yes, it was, and another train appeared on a different track. It actually stopped before it rammed into us, and we breathed a collective sigh of relief.

We all hopped aboard, and exhausted from the stress of the day, we collapsed in our seats. Unfortunately, we only had time to catch our breath before the train slowed again. It stopped. We looked out the windows. The usual crowd of discontented engineers, conductors, and others filed behind one another as they strode up the track.

"Hey, you incompetent morons, get back here!" Dave bellowed.

Once again the weary passengers stepped from the train to shuffle up the tracks, one behind another. By now the sun was scorching hot, and the steel track burned our feet. There was no grass to walk on, only the rails. I had no clue as to why we couldn't see the engineers ahead of us. They had completely disappeared.

We felt a rumble under our feet, and yes, another whistle. We looked behind and saw another huge locomotive barrelling down on us with brakes squealing. We scrambled aboard. This pattern went on for most of the day. Four times we followed the leader. Dave and I were beginning to feel a kinship with our fellow passengers. We walked for miles on those scorching metal rails. Bottled water saved our lives. I hated trains now, especially Italian ones, but the last one we hopped aboard took us right into Naples.

I learned from history books that Naples is known for some of the most beautiful beaches in the world, so beautiful that once you see them and the city, you would rather die than leave. *"Vedi Napoli a poi muri."* However, as we approached the outskirts of the city, the squalor amazed me. Who wrote the history books?

Stinking garbage was heaped high in front of apartment buildings, stores, and on street corners. From what we could see, it appeared that people simply opened their windows and threw out the trash. It was piled as high as snowbanks with rats scurrying everywhere. We were uncertain whether this was a normal occurrence. Maybe garbage collectors were also on strike? We hoped this to be the case. If the picture we had seen was an everyday occurrence, disease had to be rampant.

Dave and I had been told horrendous stories about the train station in Naples, particularly the tunnel we had to walk through to reach the street. Someone said that we would have to sprint through the tunnel as if our pants were on fire. I had no energy left if this was the case.

When we arrived, there were beggars everywhere, and impoverished families sat in various areas on the cold, damp, and muddy floor. Women held babies, small children played in the dirt, old men and women huddled under blankets. They all had the look of destitution upon their faces. How could you turn and look the other way? It was so sad. I wished I had a million dollars. We emptied our pockets into their dirty, outstretched hands.

Through my tears I spotted the ever-present gypsy children with newspapers rolled under their arms. They lurked behind every pillar and post.

At first I thought it was an optical illusion. Now I knew why we were forewarned. Here we go again—Holland and rats, rats, rats! Lord, when will it cease?

Rats, the size of cats, dashed everywhere—dozens and dozens of them. They scurried on top of heaps of garbage. The sounds they made scared the hell out of me; I nearly fainted. I held on to Dave's arm with a grip like a pair of pliers, and we raced through that tunnel as fast as our feet could take us.

I checked all luggage compartments for a slender head, large ears, and long scaly tail. I still shiver at the thought. Bert and Walter were ants in comparison.

We took a cab to AFSOUTH (Allied Forces Southern Europe). This international base controlled all allied military forces in the Mediterranean area. We booked into our hotel, and hardly able to keep our eyes open after dinner, we went to bed, exhausted. I hoped that my dreams wouldn't include railroad tracks or furry critters.

We toured Naples the following day and discovered the beauty of it, which didn't include garbage and rats. Naples is built on the slopes of a range of hills bordering the Bay of Naples, an inlet of the Tyrrhenian Sea. The many harbours are filled with passenger and merchant vessels, fishing and pleasure craft. Cruise ships at anchor in the middle of the bay were too numerous even to count. Never have I seen so many ships.

Visible from the city is the volcano, Mount Vesuvius.

Of special interest was the Cathedral of San Gennaro, which is where St. Januarius, patron saint of the city, is entombed. Crowds fill this cathedral in May and September to witness what is believed to be the miraculous liquefaction of his blood.

Naples is known for its colourful street life, its food (spaghetti and pizza were developed here), and its songs, notably the romantic ones sung by Enrico Caruso. He is hailed as the unequalled opera singer of the twentieth century.

It would have been disrespectful not to have pizza for lunch, and compared to the green peas on our German pizza we had during the seventies, this pizza won top billing. We concluded that the German chefs should preserve their culinary expertise for Wiener schnitzel.

The tour of Pompeii intrigued me most of all. As we walked through the ruins, it was hard to fathom that we were strolling along streets of a city that had been prosperous during the first century. The richest of all Romans had lived there in luxury. Their villas were painted with frescoes by the most famous of Italian artists. But now they were covered and buried in the ash and molten lava that had erupted from Mount Vesuvius many centuries before.

For more than fifteen hundred years, Pompeii had lain undisturbed beneath a blanket of ashes and cinders. Excavation was begun in the eighteenth century, but new discoveries continued to be made throughout the nineteenth and twentieth centuries. Among the most significant aspects is the remarkable degree of preservation of the ancient objects, such as public structures, temples, theatres, baths, shops, and private dwellings. In addition, the remains of some of the 2,000 victims found included several enslaved gladiators who had been placed in chains to prevent them from escaping or committing suicide.

Ashes, mixed with rain, had settled around the bodies in moulds that remained after the bodies themselves had turned to dust. Excavators poured liquid plaster into some of these moulds and the forms of the bodies have been preserved. The forms of two people entwined in one another's arms inspired Elizabeth Taylor to say, "How nice it was for two lovers to have died together." Her remark ended up in the world's newspapers. Must have been a slow news day.

Later that evening on the trek back to our hotel, we noticed a fire burning in the middle of the road. The stench was overpowering. We thought that perhaps the people of Naples were fed up with the litter and decided to burn the garbage themselves. But that wasn't the case. The fire was the result of old tires set ablaze by the "women of the night."

Prostitutes huddled near the fire to keep warm. From what we could see through the window of our taxi, these women came in all shapes and sizes and were aged from ten to sixty. Cars lined up on both sides of the road, and men climbed in and out of back seats. Unlike Paris, these hookers didn't have much of an overhead. Sheets, clean or otherwise, were not required. Our cab driver managed to pilot the taxi around the chaos.

Unfortunately, it came time for me to return to Canada. I didn't want to leave, but I had little choice in the matter. Another adventure in the U.S. awaited the Russells.

Dave took me to the train station in Rome for the non-stop trip back to Lahr, West Germany.

My roommate this time was a gigantic German lady who reminded me of the notorious World War II murderer, Gerta of the Gestapo. I tried to recall whether or not Gerta had been captured.

I kissed Dave goodbye and whispered in his ear, "If my throat is slit in the middle of the night, let's hope the blade is sharp."

The whistle blew, and Dave had to leave. Bells and whistles penetrated my eardrums once again. Loudspeakers announced arrival and departure times in every language imaginable. Vendors hollered their wares as they ran up and down platforms holding aloft bottles of water and bundles of flowers—an endless prattle of people. People dangled from train windows holding hands, kissing, and crying at the same time as they passed food and wine through. The steam and smoke were so thick from the diesel engines, I could hardly see Dave.

As the train started to move, I, too, leaned out the window and kissed him goodbye one more time. At least I thought it was Dave.

"See you in Istanbul!" I bellowed.

I wondered whether he heard me above all the noise. As the train pulled out of the station, I could still see him, and he had a very perplexed look on his face that might have said, "I hope she's only kidding. God knows where she'll end up this time. Let's hope the train has no slowdowns."

Once again over those darn Alps, but the train speeding through the snowdrifts lulled me to sleep. I had more confidence in the engineer this time around. The next thing I heard was, "Lahr, next stop." I hurriedly scrambled from my bunk, got dressed, and said goodbye to Gerta. She gave me a crooked smile with lips that actually resembled the swastika.

I grabbed my luggage and squeezed through the door. I didn't have to ask whether or not the three-minute warning still stood. I was ready. The porter escorted me from the train, and when I looked around, I found myself alone in a huge underground station. I looked at my watch. It was only five-thirty in the morning.

There had to be 600 steps to climb to reach the street. Undaunted, I began the journey. It took me a couple of hours to get my three suitcases to the top. I dragged and pulled one suitcase at a time up those steps, with many stops on the way. By the time my luggage was assembled at the top, I was ready for an oxygen tent.

The station was about ten miles from Lahr. The area was desolate so early in the morning, but a cab driver sat waiting for a fare. I asked him how much it would cost to take me into Lahr. Unfortunately, I didn't have enough money. I couldn't believe it. I had lots of lire and U.S. dollars, but not enough deutschmarks. Why didn't Dave remind me to keep enough marks for the taxi back to the base? It was his fault this time!

Caught again with no money, but, thank God, the driver spoke some English.

"Madam, how much do you have?"

I told him, and he simply shook his head. Somehow I had to make him understand and trust me.

"Sir, I'm from Canada, and I have a plane to catch at Lahr in two hours. I'll tell you what I'll do. If you can take me there, I'll pay double the fare. All you have to do is stop at the gate and wait. I'll get the money and pay you. You can keep my luggage in your cab for collateral." I hoped that the MP on duty would lend me the fare.

"Canada? You're from Canada?" His eyes lit up. "I have a brother in Toronto. Come on, get in. I'll take you home."

He talked non-stop for ten miles about his brother and Canada. He had visited many times. For once someone actually was truthful about having a brother in Toronto.

The MP didn't let me down. I traded U.S. dollars for German marks and paid the driver, who then drove me directly to the airport where I hopped aboard my military flight heading for good old Canada.

Dave phoned the Europahoff, where the desk clerk informed him that I was on the plane headed for home. He breathed one huge sigh of relief.

CHAPTER TWENTY-ONE

Norfolk, Virginia! Salt sea air gets in your bones and the sound of pounding surf never leaves your mind. The ocean was calling me home to where Dave and I were to spend the next five years serving as military ambassadors for our country. We enjoyed every minute of every day of our stay there.

Dave finished his course in Latina and briefly returned home to North Bay before the two of us flew to Virginia Beach in search of a home. The Canadian Forces treated us royally on these house-hunting trips. We stayed at the best hotels, had the luxury of a rented car, and enjoyed delicious meals. I revelled at the thought of living near the sea again. The move to Virginia truly excited me.

The big attraction in Virginia costs nothing, and that's the sea. Virginia Beach has twenty-eight miles of fine blond sandy beaches and fronts on two bodies of salt water—Chesapeake Bay and the Atlantic Ocean. Chesapeake Bay is an important source of oysters, crabs, and other seafood. Then there's the Chesapeake Bay Bridge Tunnel, a seventeen-mile bridge and tunnel link between Virginia Beach and the Eastern Shore. Basically, it's a view, an adventure, and a sea voyage all rolled into one.

On August 6, 1985, North American Van Lines, Glenn, Alan, my mother, our treasured Maltese, Samantha, Dave, and I headed south.

"Yankees. Look out! We're on our way."

We arrived August 9 and took up residence in the Barclay Towers on Atlantic Avenue for thirty days, compliments of the Canadian Armed Forces. The home we had rented wouldn't be available for a month.

Only a witch could brew our shenanigans in Virginia Beach. What could I expect, since Dave and I moved into the subdivision called Salem Woods?

The homes in our subdivision were spectacular, and the community had much to offer in terms of recreation—swimming pools, tennis courts, bowling greens, and shuffleboard. There was even a weekly newsletter that kept residents abreast of all happenings that occurred in the neighbourhood. The streets were lined with trees called crepe myrtles, trees I never heard of before. They bloom for months on end. Azalea bushes blossomed on every manicured lawn. Our house was typically Virginian—southern colonial in design—and never had I seen so many rooms, closets, or bathrooms in one home.

At our end of the cul de sac, we were flanked on both sides by the U.S. military. Our neighbors were a U.S. marine colonel and a U.S. navy commander. Neither family had ever travelled to Canada.

The historical comparison between our two countries amazes me. I'm astounded that many well-educated Americans have little or no desire to visit our country, but yet travel the world. Consequently, many Americans have little knowledge about our country; yet Canadians, on the other hand, learn about the United States in school. Dave is practically an expert on the Civil War, which he started studying while in school in Newfoundland. Americans on the other hand rarely learn Canadian history in school; in fact, much of their studies focus on their own state. Many Americans do not know the name of our prime minister, yet we are neighbours.

Glenn had just graduated from Laurentian University and Alan was on summer holidays from Memorial. Because of a reciprocal agreement between the two countries, dependants of Canadian military personnel stationed in the U.S. were eligible to take up employment there. We registered for a social security card, and they worked in Virginia Beach for the remainder of the summer.

Once again my mother, now eighty years old, would have to adapt to yet another change. This time she would live with us; however, she remained in our home only a few months. My mother had been independent for so many years it was difficult for her to share a space, so my brother and I bought a condo and she moved in as our tenant.

Hurricane season fell upon us in October. While Virginia Beach had not suffered from a bad hurricane since 1956, the memory of that one lingered and the locals maintained a healthy respect for storm warnings, especially since the population of Virginia Beach had more than tripled in the past thirty years. In 1985, Hurricane Gloria headed straight for Virginia Beach, and the city prepared for the storm. All along Atlantic Avenue, shop owners boarded up windows, hotels evacuated patrons, and residents of Virginia Beach and Norfolk were urged to leave the city and head north. Our next-door neighbours drove to Richmond, but not the Russells. We decided to weather the storm and stay at home.

The shelves in large supermarkets and small corner stores were literally empty. People purchased things they needed to survive the storm—canned food, water, bread, ice, mops, batteries, and flashlights. Never in our lives had we been exposed to a weather system of this magnitude, and we did not appreciate the danger. We found the panic somewhat amusing, especially the empty stores.

Although we didn't stand in line at the supermarket, we did pay heed to the warnings and instructions broadcast on the radio and television. We taped windows in the recommended crisscross manner, took in our outdoor furniture, trash cans, and anything else that could move, bolted our doors, and waited. The eye of the storm was headed straight for Virginia Beach.

Meanwhile, evangelist Pat Robertson, founder and owner of the Christian Broadcasting Network, prayed with his congregation. He prayed to the Lord to spare his town from harm. Amazingly, the storm did just that! The eye of the storm veered away from Virginia Beach—to Rhode Island and areas surrounding New York, unfortunately. Although the winds diminished considerably in their drive north, they still caused extensive damage.

Robertson's flock hailed him as a prophet and believed that because of his strong belief in the Lord Almighty, the storm was diverted elsewhere. Maybe he was responsible for the change of direction. When the hurricane reached Virginia Beach, the winds were downgraded to a mere eighty-five miles an hour.

The noise was horrendous and the night, pitch black. Around three in the morning, we heard a loud cracking sound, so I ran to the window where I couldn't see anything but sand and debris flying around. I went back to bed and slept through the rest of the storm.

Morning came to reveal a glorious day. The sky was blue and no clouds floated. The temperature was ninety-five degrees and muggy. From my bedroom window I saw dozens of people milling about on the cul de sac from their cars parked in our driveway and along the street. We went outside and discovered that our neighbour's house had been split in two. A huge one-hundred-year-old oak tree, uprooted by the storm, had crashed through their roof.

The tree had been halfway between their yard and ours. It could have fallen either way. The only damage Virginia Beach sustained to any great extent was this house.

Fortunately our neighbours, a family of four, were safe. The mother (who was seven months pregnant), father, and their two small girls had gathered in the family room behind an upended sofa and slept on the floor in sleeping bags. Thank heavens for the sofa. When the tree cracked in two, it crashed through the children's bedroom, located directly above the family room. Part of the ceiling came down and buried them under the debris. When the parents finally dug themselves and the children out, they found the girls fast asleep.

The story made headline news in many Virginian papers, and it clearly proved to me that when your time on this Earth is up, you'll have no say in the matter. But rather than tempt fate, whenever I hear a warning that a storm of this magnitude is approaching, you won't see me for dust.

Although I had no intentions of working any time soon, I got a job as a replacement secretary for a large company owned by a multi-millionaire and native of Virginia Beach. I had agreed to do this as a favour to my brother, who had a large contract with this company. Besides, it would only be until the regular secretary returned from maternity leave.

The founder and owner of the company was renowned throughout the state of Virginia. Semi-retired and in his late seventies, he had handed the reins over to his son. Married four times, rumour was that he also had many mistresses.

It not only appeared to me, but to others in the office as well, that this older gentleman was smitten—with me! Instead of coming to work once or twice a month like he had in the past, he started coming in every day. In Greece, older men were attracted to me and now it appeared to be happening in Virginia Beach. Why was that?

He reminded me of Rhett Butler in *Gone With the Wind*—extremely handsome and flawlessly dressed. He reminisced over the good old days when he had been a swinger and playboy, running with Big Band musicians. He knew them all, from Doris Day to Frank Sinatra. I got paid for listening.

Every day he paid me a compliment. He loved the way I dressed, my cute accent, and my wiggle when I walked—a wiggle I never knew I had. His attention became more and more of an embarrassment, so much so I hated going to work. However, I humoured the old fuddy-duddy only because I knew the job was a temporary one and the contract my brother held with this company was huge. I'd soon be out of there.

Lunch hour became a problem. I didn't mind going out for lunch once in awhile with him, but soon his friends joined in—his wealthy friends. We always went to restaurants where he was well known. People stared. He'd stop at various tables and introduce me as his secretary from Canada. Lord, how embarrassing was that?

Sometimes I was the only female seated among five or six men. Inevitably, conversations at the lunch table ended up with jokes being told. They were usually murky and sordid. Whether they were jokes based on personal experiences, I was never quite sure, but the old men got a huge chuckle over them as they giggled and roared with laughter. I smiled to be polite, but had the truth been known, I never got the punch line.

I hate long, drawn-out, and complicated jokes. I simply can't be bothered to concentrate. Dave always has to take me aside and explain them. Sure, I get it, but most times I don't think they're funny. Does this mean I have no sense of humour?

My senior citizen drove a custom-made Cadillac with his initials engraved on the dash. Probably in his heyday he had the charm of a gracious southern gentleman, but in his advancing years, he certainly lacked conduct and deportment. I hated getting into his car. He'd take any opportunity to brush against me or touch me in some way. He'd stop abruptly and put out his hand to make sure I wouldn't be thrust forward. I'd quiver when he did that. I felt like whipping around and whacking him one. I hated those rides. There were times I visualized him racing up some deserted mountain road and attacking me. But the truth was that the mildest form of exertion would be in my favour.

Before we went back to the office after lunch, my unwanted admirer always made a special stop. He insisted I accept the presents he bought for me—Godiva chocolates, perfume, or wine. What was next on his list—a diamond bracelet perhaps? Would I still resist?

My phone rang one evening and guess who called? His wife was away at a spa in Texas, and he was home alone. He pleaded with me to visit him that night, have some dinner, and share a bottle of wine. Dave and I were flabbergasted at his audacity. I wanted to say, "Listen here, you old fool!" but I bit my tongue.

"Sir, perhaps you are unaware that my marriage is as solid as a rock. The condition of yours, however, appears to be the shaky one. I'm totally content with my military man. My husband can provide me with whatever needs I may have. So, Sir, I do believe you're fluffing your feathers at the wrong songbird—those days for you are over. If you're lonely, then perhaps you should join your friends at the yacht club for a game of checkers."

Enough was enough, so the following day, I quit. The easiest way for me to get out of this situation and not hurt anyone's feelings was to tender my resignation to the son. Not a trace of disappointment or remorse showed on his face. He was elated. No new stepmother for him. This time, that is!

A couple of weeks later I received a phone call. I couldn't believe it. The position I vacated was still available and did I wish to return to work?

Well, I suppose I missed an opportunity to become a millionairess. But, one never knows. I continue to buy lottery tickets.

Dave's job took him to Europe twice a month for a week or two. But sometimes he flew to Europe for a weekend meeting. My red Hyundai drove to the airport so many times over the next few years that once I left the driveway I set the controls for automatic pilot. Godiva chocolates (this time they were welcomed) filled my cupboards upon his return.

In the summer of 1986, Alan was accepted into medical school at Memorial University in St. John's. He had been staying with us and working at the Barclay Towers as a lifeguard when I phoned him with the news flash. I'll never forget the excitement in his voice. He screeched so loud that he scared the daylights out of the kids at the pool. Everyone was elated, but no one more so than my mother. He had been groomed for this profession.

"Imagine! My grandson is going to be a doctor," she exclaimed. My mother told everyone she knew and even some people she didn't. She thought that now she would live to be a hundred.

Unfortunately in August of that year my beloved mother passed away after a short illness. All of her complaints about the U.S. now seemed so trivial.

Dave and I were in Ottawa after returning from a vacation in Newfoundland when we received word that she had died. We couldn't believe it. Mary couldn't die; she was Dave's drinking partner. Dave had so much fun with Mary that her friends were weary of hearing her say how lucky she was to have him as her son-in-law. She loved my military man.

A memorial service was held for my mother in Virginia Beach and then arrangements were made to have her remains flown to Sydney. Of course her wishes were well known. She was to be buried next to my father.

When Dave and I arrived in Sydney we went directly to the funeral home, only to find out that my mother wasn't there. She and her coffin were still on the tarmac at Sydney Airport. The proper paperwork had not been completed in the U.S., and before her body could be released to Canadian officials, a customs officer had to be called. Would he attempt to ask her what she had to declare? Give me a break! After numerous phone calls back and forth between Canadian and U.S. officials, her body was finally released to us. We received a bill in the mail a short time later for those telephone calls.

The international process of death rights, body disposal, or whatever you call it in a foreign land proved to be a real eye-opener to us. I wonder how many tourists travelling in other lands have not made it back home in death. We knew that my mother must have been cussing from heaven.

"Those damn Yankees! Can't they do anything right? You can bet that I'm never ever going back there—not even for a visit."

When we buried Mary next to my father at the Hardwood Hill Cemetery, an era had passed for me. I'm certain I heard my mother whisper, "Well, Harry, you've been resting long enough now. Move over and make room for me. Do I have lots to tell you."

I often wonder if my mother would have lived longer and been healthier in spirit and mind had we given her the choice to relocate. Hindsight is always twenty-twenty. Who knows? I refuse to dwell on it.

I suspect one of the strongest emotions when dealing with the loss of a loved one is guilt—guilt for not having done more, for not having expressed more, for ever having been irritable, petty, or neglectful. Guilt over the mind-boggling knowledge that time has run out and there is no opportunity to do or undo things. It is so horrifying that it overshadows all the good memories of happy times.

The pendulum always swings, doesn't it? Parents are our caregivers when we are young, but then the role reverses and we become theirs when they get old. It is up to us to make decisions for their well-being and happiness. At the time you wonder whether your decisions are the right ones. When they work out, fine, but when they don't, you sit back and reflect, what more should I have done?

For the most part, I believe our decision to take Mom with us to Virginia Beach was the right one. We became a close-knit family again for that short period, and I know she certainly relished the attention. But, without her saying anything, we knew it was difficult for her to readjust.

My mother tried and with more than a little success to live a life of usefulness. During her eighty-one years on this Earth, she eased many burdens, provided sympathy when others were in sorrow, and lightened paths that were troubled or strewn with obstacles. Neither Harold Adam Shetler nor Mary Veronica Hoobin will ever be forgotten by those who loved them.

CHAPTER TWENTY-TWO

Dave's NATO job introduced us to many new friends of varying nationalities—the more to stir up the pot of fun. How is it that we managed to make friends with people as foolish as us? Do you inherit special military genes?

The Canadian Forces were envied by other nations on a foreign posting. The camaraderie among our three services was unparalleled. We were all Canadians in a foreign land and respected each other at work and at play. Our government paid the troops well, and for a foreign posting, an additional foreign service allowance was tacked onto our salary, which allowed us to live comfortably. So, when these postings became available, no one ever turned them down. However, once again I felt privileged to represent my homeland in another country.

We enjoyed sharing our home on the holidays, especially Canada Day, Thanksgiving, and Christmas. When we had a party, a great deal of thought went into the guest list. We tried hard to not offend anyone, so the list was truly an international one.

Potluck parties were the most fun. You could almost figure out who would bring what; each couple would bring a dish consistent to their nationality. For Germany, it would be schnitzels and sauerbraten; Italy, some form of pasta; Philippines, lumpia; Britain, roast beef or maybe fish and chips. But it was always a toss-up between Canada and the U.S. The Yanks claimed every dish originated in their country, including pizza, apple pie, lobster, ribs, baked beans—even tourtière.

It had been my understanding that Newfoundlanders invented corn beef and cabbage. We were wrong—New Englanders did. So, I had no choice. I would bake a chocolate cake and pop a Canadian flag on the top. However, next to the cake stood a bottle of Newfie screech. No country could lay claim to that one.

For the five years we lived in Virginia Beach, our Christmas party was a tradition. I'd prepare for weeks and rummage through dozens of cookbooks trying to find something unusual to make. It wasn't easy to arrange a menu with taste and gusto that would please international palates. Remember the parties Mary Tyler Moore used to give? No one ever wanted to go. Her bored colleagues always made up an excuse to leave early. Well that was television. This was for real. Before my guests arrived, I crossed fingers and toes that my party would be a hit. They usually were.

Rosemarie and George Roe are one of the most interesting and original couples that Dave and I have ever met. Rosemarie was born and raised in Brooklyn. Her parents had immigrated from Italy years before. George was of German heritage, born and raised in the Bronx, and served as a master chief in the U.S. Navy. Their New York accents were typical of their home neighbourhoods.

George should have had two professions. He is the funniest person we've ever met, and his comedic talents remind us of Robin Williams. He loves to take on accents and has a great ear for them. His Chinese, British, and Russian accents are excellent, but his German accent is true to form. We became very familiar with these accents, as the four of us travelled a great deal, spending weekends visiting various towns and cities in Virginia and North Carolina.

Pals Rosemarie and George Roe, Virginia Beach, Virginia

Dave loves Civil War history and here we were living smack in the middle of it. One weekend we went to Richmond, Virginia, where General Robert E. Lee was headquartered during the war. Richmond was the capital of the Confederate States of America and, as such, was a major objective of Union forces during the Civil War. On April 3, 1865, after many attempts, Union troops led by General Ulysses S. Grant succeeded in occupying Richmond, but only after it had been evacuated and principal sections of the city had been burned by its own residents.

We toured the Museum of the Confederacy. The uniforms displayed were pitiful-looking. Not only were most of them ripped to shreds, dirty, and bloody, but—and this amazed me the most—they were so small. Either the men back in 1861 were small in stature, or the uniforms were taken from children. The museum was heart-rending.

We had booked into a hotel, and after a long, hot day of sightseeing, we went back for appetizers before dinner. We usually set up one of the rooms as the TGIF suite, complete with wine and hors d'oeuvres.

Richmond is a major tobacco market but the Old Tobacco Factory where we had reservations was now a famous restaurant renowned for its Virginian cuisine. It was located near Shockoe Slip, one of four renovated historical areas in the city.

That evening, George was in great form even before we left our room, so I knew we were in for a night to remember. As we left the hotel, George became Heinz from Stuttgart. He put a monocle in his eye, and with his stiff leg (an old football injury), he resembled a young war veteran with the haughty arrogance of a Nazi collaborator. "Heinz" led the way through the restaurant lobby and into the elevator that would take us to the rooftop dining area.

With a throaty German accent he roared to the other people in the elevator, "Hallo! *Guten abend!*" The sound of his heels clicking echoed. "Vere is ze operator? Vere is ze *fräulein*? Vy isn't dere an operator to assist us? Vy do we haas to push ze buttons ourselves? *Nein! Nein! Ja! Ja! Kommt sie hier bitte.*"

He turned to Rose and demanded, "Helga, tell ze people that in Munich and Stuttgart, service is not just a vord but an action. In America, von must do everything themselves. Vere is the servility? Is there no caste? *Schade! Schade! Sprecken, Helga, sprecken.*"

I glanced around at the other passengers. They were unimpressed by this boisterous, overbearing, and arrogant German. I overhead one guy whisper to his friend, "If I don't get off this elevator soon, there's gonna be a dead German at the next stop."

That was all Heinz needed to hear. Now, nothing would stop him. He got louder and louder. We tried not to give him away, but every once in a while, we had to double over with laughter.

Once we entered the dining room, Heinz took over. He wouldn't wait to be seated and marched right past the other patrons in line.

"*Kommt sie hier bitte*—follow me! Ve vill find our reserved table. If other people must stand in line like a bunch of sheep, then that's their problem. *Kommt sie!*"

Although embarrassed over this rude behaviour, we followed behind as if we were robots. I looked over my shoulder and shrugged to the people still in line. I wanted to say, "Hey, he's only play acting. He's rehearsing for a movie. He's really one of us." I might have said something had I not been laughing so hard.

Ignoring the pleas of the hostess, Heinz motioned us to a table near a window. There was a sign on it that said "Reserved." We sat down anyway. It surprised me that nothing was said about the sign. It might have been our table after all. A waiter appeared and Heinz immediately ordered four bottles of their finest German wine.

"But, Sir, you mean four glasses of wine, don't you?"

"*Nein, Nein! Ich habe* four bottles of vino. Ve are vely thirsty, so could you please hurry. *Schnell! Schnell!* Please have each one in an ice bucket."

Four bottles of wine arrived and all in separate containers. In fact, the staff rolled over another table to accommodate them. I knew this was going to be a long evening.

Heinz continued to babble, half in English, half in his pidgin German. He told us some jokes, many of which we had heard before. The more wine George drank, the funnier he became. We wondered when he was going to repent and confess, but he had no intentions. He was on a roll. We noticed that the staff kept looking our way. Some even laughed at his jokes, or at least pretended to enjoy them. The rest of the restaurant patrons stared and shook their heads in disbelief.

"Didn't Nuremberg eliminate all those people?"

After reading the menu, Heinz beckoned to the waiter. "I vant schnitzel. There is no schnitzel on this chart."

The chef came running over when he heard the commotion and tried to convince Heinz to try the house specialty—slow cooked and tasty Virginian pork ribs. "Ribs, ribs, whose ribs? In Stuttgart ze swine is not raised as a food animal, but as a member of the family. He vants to play and have fun in the mud. Obviously your swines don't get that chance to have some fun. How shameful it is to tear the ribs from their filthy little bodies! *Ich* simply don't know vat to think. How do ze *schmecken*?"

"Schmecken?" the chef asked with an anxious look on his face.

"How do ze say . . . taste? That's what I mean in your language."

"Sir, our ribs taste delicious. You will not be disappointed."

It took a few minutes, but the chef convinced Heinz that the ribs would be as delicious as any schnitzel.

"Okay, maybe I will, but I vant you to make sure that all the 'sheit' will be thoroughly rinsed off the swine. I don't want to see any speckles whatsoever, you hear!"

At this point Dave, Rose, and I avoided any eye contact with the rest of the people in the room. I'd bet that if Heinz had choked on his ribs not one person in the restaurant would remember the Heimlich manoeuvre.

Our young waiter, however, liked Heinz. He kept smiling, anyway. He told Heinz that his grandmother was also from Stuttgart and gave him her address. Heinz agreed to look her up when he returned home.

Heinz finally settled down when our meal came. We were exhausted from trying to hold back our laughter. Thank God he was hungry. He dug in. We all dug in. It was delicious. When we left, Heinz stopped by the hostess desk and apologized to her for any disruption he may have caused. She was slightly taken back by this gesture. Hopefully she saw the German people in a much different light.

"Enjoy the rest of your stay in America," she said.

Heinz turned to the people in the restaurant, raised his hand and bellowed, "*Danke schoen! Wir sind zum frühstück* (We'll be back for breakfast)." They glared.

Another night to remember was in the parking lot of Chi Chi's Restaurant in Virginia Beach. We had just finished another hysterical dinner. This time George had taken on the role of a Chinese man. He even looked the part. He has a way of making facial contortions to resemble almost anyone. That night he had taken his own chopsticks and had the restaurant patrons convulsing with laughter. He was fine with the Mexican rice, but then the waiter served him a double-stuffed burrito. Before the waiter had even left our table, George had him doubled up with laughter. Pieces of the burrito were flicked everywhere in and outside of our booth. All we heard was, "Aah so, aah so!" as he tried to saw at his burrito with the chopstick.

After we drank the century plant of Mexico dry—tequila in other words—we called it an evening. We rambled out to the parking lot where George wanted to show us the new Oldsmobile he had purchased that day. He was especially amazed at the size of the trunk. He opened it and said to his wife, "Rose get in and spread out. I want to show Dave how much room we have in this trunk."

Rose hesitated at first. She knew her husband could be up to something, but the effects of the tequila were overpowering her. She stepped up into the trunk, then as quick as lightning, her ever-loving husband slammed down the lid of the trunk, ran to the driver's side, got in, started the engine, and squealed out of the parking lot at the speed of a guided missile. Rose was still in the trunk.

I thought there was no more laughter left in me.

This all had happened so fast that Dave and I looked at one another in amazement. We couldn't believe what we had seen. I was still in hysterics as we pulled into our driveway, and I couldn't wait to get into the house and phone Rose. We hoped that George hadn't had that one tequila too many and forgot that Rose was in the trunk.

Thank God, it was Rose who answered. She said she had a great old snooze before George pulled over at the next stop sign and sprung her loose.

We wondered what might have happened if a cop had appeared on the scene when George opened the trunk. He'd sure have some explaining to do. And, you could bet it wouldn't be with an accent.

We still laugh over that night. Rosemarie and George remain in Virginia Beach and dote on their grandchildren.

We remained astounded over Virginia's historical riches, from Colonial Williamsburg and the Civil War battle sites, to the massive naval and air stations at Norfolk, Little Creek, and Oceana. The naval yards are the largest complexes of navy machinery, ships, and personnel in the world, and from time to time, we'd attempt to navigate our twenty-five-foot boat in the harbour where the aircraft carriers and ships were moored. The huge structures loomed over us. It was breathtaking. The aircraft carriers were the size of two football fields, ten storeys high.

I'll always remember June 23, 1986. We had the pleasure of being invited aboard the aircraft carrier, USS *Nimitz*, as guests of Master Chief Billy Barefoot. Crew members were permitted to bring family and friends aboard to tour the ship and observe operations at sea, including flight operations. Billy was the highest-ranking non-commissioned officer aboard.

Glenn had to work, something he regrets to this day. However, this had to be the thrill of a lifetime for Dave and Alan. You read about the *Nimitz* and its role in peace, you see pictures of it, but never in your wildest dreams do you think you'd ever be sailing in her. We put to sea and travelled 100 miles to the coast of North Carolina.

The commanding officer, Captain E. D. Conner, U.S. Navy, welcomed us aboard. "The *Nimitz* is one of the largest warships in the world and one of the great ships of our navy. We are very proud of our ship, her impressive capabilities, and her important mission. We welcome this opportunity to show you the ship and the skill, dedication, and team spirit of our crew."

The ship reminded me of a miniature city. The total crew assigned to the *Nimitz* when aircraft and aircrew are on board is approximately 5,000 people.

Dave aboard UUS *Nimitz*, June 23, 1986

A tour of the ship showed us firsthand how these men lived for six or more months at a time. From what we observed, the crew endured few hardships while aboard, other than perhaps a feeling of isolation. There was a fully equipped hospital, chapel, dining rooms, lounges, theatre, golf course, and sleeping areas—everything except a bar. That's right, no booze is allowed on any U.S. Navy or Marine ship. On shore leave there must be many a cut-up by crewmembers.

I couldn't feel any motion and had it not been for the sounds of the plane engines, I might have thought I was standing on a city street. Dave and Alan were taken to an area known as

Vulture's Row, the best seat in the house to watch the operational display of takeoffs and landings. Not once in more than six hours did they leave their nest—no food, no drink, no potty.

One of our friends, a former navy pilot, was once stationed aboard such a carrier. He often related to us the harrowing experiences he encountered while trying to land his aircraft on a rolling deck. Sometimes, the seas were so high that the back of the ship was swerving through a figure eight, fishtailing around. If the pilot wasn't lined up properly, he often got a desperate wave-off from the landing director and had to try again. Nerves of steel are a prerequisite for surviving as a pilot.

That goes for both the pilot and the young sailors responsible for launching and recovering aircraft. During launching, the aircraft taxis to the catapult. The launch bar, attached to the nose gear, is positioned in the shuttle on the catapult track. The pilot makes his final checks, and with engines screaming, he waves to the catapult officer that he is ready. The plane is then launched off the carrier deck.

When landing aboard the carrier, a tail hook on the aircraft is lowered, and it in turn must engage one of the steel cables that are strung across the deck. At touchdown, the throttles are advanced to full power, and if the hook misses the cables, the plane must fly past the carrier and try again. For the sailors on deck, you are either quick or you are dead. Sometimes they have only forty-five seconds to handle one plane landing and another taking off. Many times a young sailor has been blown off the deck from the jet exhaust. These young people are as important to the safety of the carrier as the pilots are to the landing of their aircraft. Their average age is nineteen years.

On October 25, 1986, we were invited to the christening of the USS *Theodore Roosevelt*. It was a special honour to be a part of this auspicious occasion, and we were presented with the Order of the Commissioning Ceremony.

The Commissioning Ceremony signifies the acceptance for service and the entry of a ship into the active fleet of the United States Navy. At the moment of the breaking of the commissioning pennant, the USS *Theodore Roosevelt* (CVN-71) became a proud ship of the line. The commanding officer, together with the ship's officers and crew, then accepted the duties and responsibilities of making and keeping her ready for any service required by the nation, whether at peace or at war.

The Commissioning Ceremony has been a tradition of all navies for centuries. It marks the formal entrance of a man-of-war into the naval forces of her nation, and it is the final and perhaps the most significant event of the triad that brings a ship to life: keel laying, launching and christening, and commissioning.

The captain took up the microphone. "From its commissioning day forward, USS *Theodore Roosevelt* will assume a unique personality and become infused with the will, the spirit, and the dedication of those who serve in her. The aircraft carrier also acquires a special international distinction today; wherever she sails, she will project the character and perseverance of her namesake and of the nation.

"We firmly believe that your presence here today will ensure us 'fair winds and a following sea' in all that lies ahead.

"Thank you for coming."

An excerpt of a greeting from President Ronald Reagan stated: "Your aircraft carrier makes an apt memorial to Theodore Roosevelt, who was president when the Wright Brothers first flew and who built our navy into one of the world's finest. I know the sailors and airmen of the USS *Theodore Roosevelt* will carry on T. R.'s legacy of a strong navy, preserving peace and freedom throughout the world.

"God bless you."

Me aboard USS *Theodore Roosevelt*, October 25, 1986

We were escorted to our seats at the Portsmouth Naval Yards. As I looked around, I was reminded of the Ascot Races in England where all women dress in designer fashions, and hats and gloves are a tradition. Military personnel were attired in dress uniforms, guests in black tie. Among the guests that day were John F. Lehman, Jr., Secretary of the Navy, and Casper Weinberger, Secretary of Defense. The oldest child of Teddy Roosevelt, Grace McMillian, christened the ship by swinging the traditional champagne bottle. It broke across the bow.

The captain and commanding officer, Paul W. Parsons, introduced the guests to the audience. After giving us a brief history on the making of this massive structure, which began in October 1980, he said something that I'll always remember:

"God willing, may she never be ordered to launch a strike in anger, but if required, she will be ready."

Then he gave the order, "Gentlemen! Let's bring this ship to life."

Suddenly, out of nowhere, thousands of young sailors in white uniforms appeared from every corner of the shipyard. They ran aboard the ship. They cheered and shouted at the top of their lungs. They took their assigned positions on the various decks and stood at attention. It was a joyful and momentous occasion. At the exact moment when all the men were placed, the Carrier Air Wing, consisting of seventy aircraft, screamed over the top of the ship. What a sight!

Many of these sailors were just out of their teens and probably had dreamed of this moment all of their young lives, but never imagined that they would become a part of naval history. Some wiped tears from eyes shimmering with joy and pride.

Then the bands played the traditional Navy song "Anchors Aweigh." Even I knew the words.

Whistles blew, radars turned, and the whole ship came to life. The range of emotions from the crowd made me proud to witness this unique and historical occasion. There wasn't a dry eye in the house.

CHAPTER TWENTY-THREE

Affectionately known as "The Canuck," I was quite a novelty at first. No employees at R. J. Reynolds Tobacco Company had ever been to Canada, and they had little or no knowledge about my country. The same questions were asked and the same answers were given:

"Yes, we do have four seasons in Canada."

"No, we don't all speak French."

"Yes, we certainly do look like you guys, don't we?"

After my bulldog courage in catering to the millionaire, I had sworn off working in the state of Virginia. But the R. J. Reynolds Tobacco Company made me an offer I couldn't refuse.

How can I describe a non-smoker going to work for the Chain Accounts Manager of a tobacco company? Well, in the beginning, I was the only employee who didn't smoke, but medical reports inundated the media on the dangers of smoking in the late 1980s. It touched home with many of the sales representatives, and, one by one, they threw away their cigarettes. Then it became a difficult task to justify selling their product.

But when you have worked for a company most of your life, what do you do? Throw away benefits or a pension because you have changed your lifestyle? Like it or not, I suppose you carry on the best you can.

With all the controversy about the tobacco industry, I would imagine it's becoming more and more difficult for these companies to defend their carcinogenic products. No matter what restrictions are applied to the sale of tobacco, people have smoked in the past and will continue to smoke in the future. There's some logic to the old saying, "You can lead a horse to water, but you can't make him drink."

And talk about job perks! No one ever wanted to leave the employment of R. J. Reynolds. The tobacco industry was rich. My favourite? Priority seats at the Winston Cup NASCAR races (National Association of Stock Car Auto Racing).

We were a tightly knit group of people who worked and played together. Around every corner lay another adventure for the Reynolds group, whether it was golf tournaments, company picnics, shrimp boils, or birthday parties.

One year, my boss, Bob, planned a surprise party for his wife's fortieth birthday, the best party she had ever had. We all decided to meet at our house and go from there so that we would all arrive at the party together.

Bob and Linda lived nearby. Dave and I often visited them so we knew the route to their house in Salem Woods, a secure neighbourhood with only one entrance and one exit. The homes are huge colonial types and very similar in style. So, if you don't know where you're going, it's quite easy to get lost. Sometimes, the only identifying features were shutters of a different colour, garages on opposite sides, interlocking bricks of various shades, or perhaps a unique rocking chair on the verandah.

The Reynolds group followed Dave and me to the birthday bash, and we parked our cars at the bottom of the street. In the event Linda was around, we didn't want to create any suspicion.

We all walked as quiet as mice up the sidewalk. We had been told not to ring the doorbell, but just to walk in. I led the group, but before I opened the door, I turned around and put my finger to my lips, "Shh! Shh! Not a word."

Once inside there wasn't a sound to be heard. Everything was strangely quiet, eerily quiet. I led the troupe of twenty people down the hall on tiptoes so that we wouldn't make any noise. Over the staggering fragrance of flowers, which obviously came from the bouquets displayed in the foyer, was something that took us a moment to identify. It was incense!

We were not quite sure about two things: why a Filipino gentleman welcomed each of us with a hug, and why the dining room table was laden with food. I had never met this gentleman before and none of the others knew him either. We assumed he was a family friend, but were puzzled as to why he wasn't speaking English. Bob and Linda were both from Alabama, and I knew they didn't speak Filipino. So, just who was this guy?

We approached the family room, where I saw someone on his knees. As we got closer, I noticed there were many people on their knees and humming, it appeared, some kind of tune. We looked at each other in disbelief. I suppose it could have been appropriate if they were thanking the Lord for Linda's birth, but this looked strange.

Then I knew why it looked peculiar. For there in the corner by the window sat a coffin, and in it, an old lady lay. This was not a birthday celebration. This was a Filipino wake. We damn near died as well!

Of course now it was clear why the gentleman hadn't look familiar. We were in the wrong house. The birthday house was right next door.

Well, we tried to explain as best we could, gave our condolences, and left. Can you picture this and hear the laughter that night? One of the guys laughed so hard that he had to borrow a pair of jeans for the rest of the evening. Not only was I the focus for any jokes that evening, but for the rest of my stay at R. J. Reynolds, I was reminded time and time again that only a Canuck could make such an error. Do you suppose my fellow Canadian, Ross Johnston, former CEO of RJR, ever heard this story?

We all concluded that our Reynolds group had to be of good character; after all, we did pay our respects to an old lady we barely knew.

The following night we were all together again, but at our house. I assured the gang there were no vigils I knew of in our neighborhood. But, just in case, I reminded them to look for the Canadian flag flying proudly from our verandah.

That evening we had a great barbecue and even ate outside, which I believe was a first for us. The weather is so humid in the summertime in Virginia Beach that it's almost impossible to breathe without air conditioning. But this was a lovely starlit night, the bugs were at rest, and the moon shone brightly.

Around one o'clock in the morning, we heard someone screaming and pounding at our front door. We all ran to the door and opened it. A young girl stood there shaking like a leaf. Her eyes were crazed, she appeared terrified, and she could hardly speak. Four boys in a white pickup truck had followed her and tried to run her off the road, she said. We couldn't see the truck, but she was so hysterical we had to believe her. She begged us to let her come in so she could phone her father. We thought nothing of it and took her in. After she phoned her father and gave him our address, we called the police.

The girl shook uncontrollably. If she wasn't genuine then she was a damn good actress. We trusted her. I put a sweater over her shoulders and made her a cup of coffee, after which, she calmed down and told us what happened. When she had left her girlfriend's house and stopped at a stop sign, the truck with the four boys in it tried to run her off the road. When she pulled away, they followed directly behind. They shouted and yelled obscenities. She didn't know what to do next until she saw the entrance for Salem Woods. She turned in and frantically looked for a light in a window of any house. Our light was the only one she could see. At one o'clock in the morning, most people are in bed.

Once we had her calmed down and had notified the police, Dave and the others went outside. The white pickup truck cruised slowly back and forth at the top of our street. The driver turned around when he saw the guys. He defiantly squealed his tires and raced into our cul de sac. Four boys screamed and swore at the top of their lungs, as they hung from the windows.

"Faggots, faggots," they yelled.

Dave was pissed off. He ran back into the house and took his Lee Enfield .303 from the closet. Someone had given Dave this gun as a collector's item, and he had hidden it away at the back of a closet. For years I thought it was a BB gun.

He came outside and started waving the rifle at them. "Get the hell out of here, or I'll shoot," he yelled.

Holy Lord! Now it was Dave we had to worry about.

Everyone screamed at this point. Dave bellowed at them, and we shouted at him to get back into the house. Porch lights came on everywhere. Neighbours must have wondered what the hell was going on at the Russells'. The truck continued to circle our street for another few minutes before disappearing.

We finally convinced Dave to come back inside while we waited for the police to arrive. Finally the police cruisers came—three of them. Two cops came to the house and the others were dispatched to cover the entrance and exit to the subdivision.

They were extremely angry with us. "You could have jeopardized your lives had this girl been a plant for criminal intentions. Never open your door to anyone you don't know, especially at this hour in the morning. Go to your phone and call us. Count your blessings that this incident is legitimate."

Thank God, Dave had put his gun back into the closet.

The girl's father arrived and sobbed with relief when he knew his daughter was safe. We didn't recognize his name, but later found out that he held an important position with the State of Virginia. He was grateful we had come to his daughter's rescue. As it turned out, we probably saved this girl's life. Her father phoned us the next morning and told us to read the front page of the newspaper.

There on the front page was the story of a sixteen-year-old girl who had been raped and killed the previous night. Witnesses said the suspects were four young men in a white pickup truck.

The Reynolds group were the heroes of the night.

Someone attempted to break into our house. The doorknobs moved back and forth, and the glass on the double French doors in our family room quivered. Glenn cowered in the corner of the family room watching all of this, afraid to move. I was in bed, unaware of what was happening downstairs.

The night before Mother's Day, 1987, I was home alone. Dave had been in Europe for a week, Glenn was out, and I went to bed around 2 a.m. I hated to be alone in that big house, but I had no other choice. My drapes were always pulled and doors locked. The phone was by my bed and the neighbours lived only a shout away.

Before Glenn pulled into our driveway later that night, he passed a high-speed police chase at the top of our cul de sac. Because they were going past our subdivision, he didn't pay much attention. The cops always seemed to be chasing someone. Sirens were always screaming, day and night.

Around three-thirty in the morning, Glenn was awakened by a noise that came from our backyard. It sounded as if someone had tripped over a trash can. As Glenn crept down the stairs he heard someone rattling the French doors. He could see the doorknobs being turned, but the doors were locked. When I woke up in the morning, he told me what had happened and my heart started to pound. I had slept through it all. Happy Mother's Day!

I asked my six-foot-five protector, "What did you do when you saw the doorknobs moving?"

"See that corner over there?" he replied. "Well, that's where I hid and shook. Don't think I was going to look down two gun barrels."

We assumed it had probably been the person the cops had chased earlier that morning. He must have ditched his car and ran. Thank Heavens he didn't find refuge in our house.

My friends all know I love a party and seldom do I ever refuse an invitation. However, one Christmas Eve, Dave and I were unable to attend one of the international parties.

We'd also been invited for dinner at my brother's home that evening, and because it was Christmas Eve, family was our priority. We were disappointed the two parties were on the same night, as it would have been fun to get together with the international group, especially on Christmas Eve. Everyone could share their different traditions. However, we knew there'd be other parties to attend in the future, and as it turned out, declining this invitation proved a lucky choice.

The party was held at the home of an American soldier in a wonderful safe neighbourhood. About thirty enjoyed a tasty buffet of traditional festive foods and then stood about chatting and visiting. Suddenly the back door burst open and two masked men stood there, threatening the group with pistols.

Because the host hadn't invited any of his neighbours, he figured one of them was playing a prank. "Hey, you guys," he chuckled, "it ain't Halloween. It's Christmas! Playing with your kid's toys? There's lots of food left. Take off your masks and join us."

"This is a stick-up, everyone," one of the masked intruders said. "We want all of you to take off your jewellery and watches and empty your wallets, and we want you to do this now. We don't have much time, so be quick or be dead. Your choice."

"Come on, you guys! Enough is enough. You're scaring me and my friends."

No sooner were the words out of his mouth when one of the intruders pointed his gun and shot the host in the kneecap. Then they both raised their guns and shot a few volleys into the ceiling. At this point a calm came over the room and everyone started moving very quickly. Apparently no one panicked, and although the host was writhing in pain on the floor, he told everyone to do what they said. The guests removed what jewellery and watches they had on and emptied their wallets into the plastic bag one of the robbers held. Within a few minutes, the armed men had left.

Once the coast was clear, one of the guests called 9-1-1, and their host was taken to the hospital by ambulance. After surgery to remove the bullet from his kneecap and a long recuperation period, he was fine.

While this international group will certainly have a special story to tell their families when they return to their homeland, it's one party Dave and I are glad we missed.

When it comes to your safety in Virginia, you learn very quickly to become aware of your surroundings. You never take anything for granted. When you come from a sleepy little place like Cape Breton Island, you trust the people in your town, you trust your neighbours, and you grow up unafraid.

CHAPTER TWENTY-FOUR

My God, this is news no parent ever wants to receive. This is something that's supposed to happen to someone else. But it didn't. It happened to us.

Dave and I were in Ottawa the morning of April 6, 1988. Dave had meetings to attend, and I had gone along for the ride to renew old acquaintances from our Moosonee and Holland days. Around seven that morning, the phone rang in our hotel room. My brother in Virginia Beach told me that Glenn had been in a serious car accident. The Virginia state police hadn't given Pat a whole lot of information, only that Glenn was in emergency at the University of Virginia Medical Center in Richmond. Glenn had fallen asleep behind the wheel of his Camaro and plowed into the back of an eighteen-wheeler parked on the side of the highway.

I phoned the hospital. Glenn was in serious condition with possible internal injuries and a compound fracture of his femur. The doctor suggested we come immediately.

The previous year, Glenn had transferred to Richmond, Virginia, to manage the office at ITT Financial Corporation. He'd been working with ITT since 1985 after an unsuccessful job hunt in Toronto. This move was a real treat for me and history repeated itself once again. We had access to two houses, but this time in the sunny south. On Dave's jaunts to Europe, Sammy and I would drive the two hours to Richmond and spend the weekend with Glenn. Mommy's visits sometimes interrupted his social life, but on the other hand, Mommy fulfilled Molly Maid duties.

Because we had taken our car on this trip, I had no choice but to fly from Ottawa. Dave drove. I thought I'd never get there, and when I finally landed in Washington, D.C., I phoned the hospital. Glenn was stable and waiting for surgery. A thousand thoughts went through my mind. I remembered Glenn when he was young. I could smell the baby powder. I remembered the summer evenings after his bath when he and his brother, both in their pyjamas, would jump up in their car seats and screech with delight as we headed for A&W for a small mug of root beer. I remembered the time when he picked a neighbour's prize roses to bring home to me. I remembered the needles he was mistakenly given that day in school. I also remembered times when I had no patience and would sometimes scold him for no reason. I couldn't stop the flashbacks as they raced through my head. I couldn't stop them. They scared me. I arrived in Richmond by early afternoon.

Glenn had been moved to a private room to await surgery. The Virginia Medical Center was an extremely busy hospital, and surgery was performed on a priority basis. Glenn's injury was listed as urgent but not a priority. To this day I fail to understand why a bone protruding from a thigh is not considered a priority.

When I walked into his room, I was stunned. Glenn's face looked like it had gone through a meat grinder. I couldn't count the number of stitches, there were so many. He was also hooked up to all kinds of tubes and bottles. A nurse was assigned to his room, but Glenn could not receive any pain medication because he was scheduled for surgery. She continually monitored his blood pressure, however, and when she changed the bandages on his leg, I had to leave the room. To hear a man, six-foot, five inches, and weighing 250 pounds scream in pain is heart-rending. It had been twelve hours since his accident.

Glenn told me that he had had a late night meeting in Virginia Beach, and instead of staying over, he had decided to drive back home to Richmond. He kept falling asleep at the wheel, but didn't pull over. I know I have done this at one time or another, and fortunately never suffered the consequences of getting hurt or hurting someone else. Something always snapped me back to reality. But nothing jolted Glenn that night. When he woke up, he was lying on a stretcher in the trauma unit at the University of Virginia Medical Center.

For nearly four hours I sat with Glenn waiting for the still unscheduled surgery. I had to do something. I couldn't stand to see Glenn in such pain. I practically ran to the nurses' station at the end of the hallway where everyone appeared unfazed.

Could they not hear my son scream in pain? At my wits' end, I demanded to speak with a doctor. He didn't know we were Canadian citizens, as Glenn had medical insurance from his job. Whether or not my nationality became an issue was difficult to tell. All I know is that wheels turned, and about five minutes later, I accompanied Glenn to the operating room entrance. Finally something was being done to help my son.

Dave arrived around midnight and joined me in the waiting room. Glenn was still in surgery. At 1:30 a.m., almost twenty-four hours after the accident, the surgeon informed us that all had gone well. He knew I had been concerned about a possible blood transfusion, which, thank heavens, hadn't been necessary. I had heard horror stories about tainted blood supplies, but wasn't calmed by the doctor's assurances that blood donations received at his hospital were screened—whatever that meant.

"In fact," he said, "I'd even give my own mother blood from this hospital." However, that still didn't make me feel any better. What if he didn't like his mother?

The surgeon told us that Glenn might have bled to death had the fractured femur punctured the arterial artery. Also, had the hospital not been equipped with a trauma centre, Glenn's condition might have been fatal. And still, he had had to wait for surgery.

The pin inserted into his leg measured eighteen inches and extended from his hip to his knee. We later learned that Glenn's surgeon had served two tours in Vietnam, patched up people, and saved limbs sometimes with little or no equipment. Glenn's injury was commonplace for him.

After viewing Glenn's Camaro, it amazed us how he had ever survived. There was nothing left of the driver's side. Even the investigating state trooper was astounded that he lived. He said he must have had a guardian angel protecting him.

When Glenn fell asleep, he veered off to the shoulder of the road where an eighteen-wheeler was waiting for him. The driver could see him coming in his rear-view mirror and had the forethought to move his truck. Because of the gravity involved when the truck was in motion, the impact had been lessened. At full impact, the flat-hooded Camaro would have gone under the truck.

Glenn was released from hospital two weeks later with no cast. Twice in Austria and once in Virginia his right leg had withstood a fracture. Who might have been Glenn's guardian angel that day—his grandmother, his grandfather? Someone was certainly hovering over his shoulder. Glenn was not wearing a seat belt.

When Glenn was well enough to return to work, I drove him to Richmond. Dave was in Europe again so I had the task of taking my first-born back home. Glenn relied on crutches to walk, as he could not bear any weight on his leg. However, when we arrived in Richmond that night, guess what we discovered had been forgotten?

After helping Glenn into the car, I had forgotten to put the crutches into the trunk. They were sitting on my driveway. However, without crutches, there was no means of support to get Glenn out of the car. I can't remember laughing so hard. We were both hysterical. Even Sammy sensed the nervous tension as she barked along with us. But we had to get serious. What were we to do? I had to get this six-foot-five guy out of my car and into his house. I wouldn't be able to do it alone.

We were two hours from Virginia Beach. It was late, and I wasn't in a mood to drive back home. We stopped at a few rescue centres and fire stations, but no one had crutches they could spare. Finally we decided to try the emergency department of the hospital where Glenn had initially been admitted a few weeks before. Perhaps a staff member might recognize him and show some sympathy.

After being helped to a wheelchair, we waited four hours to see the doctor. Only he was authorized to give out crutches.

The emergency room was hopping. Based on the injuries that came through the doors, we were definitely not top priority. It was scary. But, we were in Richmond, Virginia, the murder capital of the U.S.

Finally around five in the morning, the doctor appeared and issued Glenn crutches, but only after I handed over $200. Both Glenn and I hobbled out the door that morning, exhausted.

"Not a problem!" I said to Glenn. "I'll sell the spare set when I get back home."

A year later Glenn had the pin removed from his leg. Alan, our medical student, told him horror stories about how this procedure would be performed—something about an anvil and a hammer. Glenn wasn't interested in how the hammer pounded the pin from the leg, inch by inch. He didn't want to think about it. Glenn prayed that he'd get a double dose of ether.

When the nurse wheeled Glenn into the recovery room, she handed me the pin. Lord in Heaven, this had to be the biggest pin I'd ever seen. I expected it to be the size of a knitting needle, but this shiny, stainless-steel pin was the size of a rod for a coat rack— two inches around and eighteen inches long.

It must have done the job, however, for the following week Glenn played racquetball.

CHAPTER TWENTY-FIVE

The year 1989 was a momentous one for the Russells, for three reasons: our beloved pet, Samantha Athena Poseidon, developed cancer of her thyroid; Alan graduated from medical school and got married; and Dave retired from the Canadian Armed Forces.

Dave's retirement, April 9, 1989

We named Sammy our "squirrel dog," after the episode with the squirrels in our home in North Bay. She was a purebred Maltese and was registered with the Canadian Kennel Club. She had class.

Sammy loved Virginian squirrels. We were certain she would grow a furry tail before we came back home. She loved to chase them in our backyard as they ran along the top of the fence. The squirrels teased her from on high, knowing they were safe. She ran at a greyhound's speed, barking like crazy, but always with a crooked grin on her face and sparkles in her eye. Every day the squirrels waited for her to come out and play.

One day as Sammy sat on my lap, I felt a lump in her throat. A shiver went through my body and, immediately, I took her to our veterinarian. He felt the lump as well, but didn't feel it warranted a panic attack. We monitored the lump, and all that month, Sammy had choking spells. We went back and forth to Dr. Gordon, and he recommended we see a doggie specialist. He wasn't optimistic and felt that the growth was malignant

The specialist said that there was only a ten-percent chance that Sammy's lump wasn't malignant. A chance? Well, that's all we needed to hear. We had to try!

We subjected our dear little animal to a horrific operation. The malignant tumour was removed from her neck, but because the muscles and cartilage were damaged during the operation, she could barely hold up her little head. Chemotherapy treatments were recommended to ensure the growth wouldn't return.

We would have had to take her to Duke University Hospital in Durham, North Carolina. We didn't know what to do. Had we been guaranteed this treatment would be effective and not cause her any more sickness or pain, we would have opted for it, no matter what the cost. But, neither the specialist nor Dr. Gordon could promise it would work.

We didn't do it. We took Sammy home and looked after her ourselves.

There were good days and bad days—days Sammy could still chase the squirrels, and days she would topple over at her food dish. She had no appetite other than for KFC. She had loved that chicken from the time she was little. Mention the word "Kentucky," and she went wild. Dave and Sammy made regular trips to the KFC drive-through, where she leaned on his arm as they picked up her chicken nuggets.

We decided that Sammy needed a diversion from her illness—perhaps a canine companion. We felt she needed a different kind of comfort that only an animal could bring. We would find her a baby Maltese.

Muffin was six weeks old. At first Sammy was jealous of this trespasser and wanted nothing to do with her, but soon things changed and she began to mother her. They would lie down together and drink from the same dish. And no matter where Sammy went, Muffin trotted behind. Muffin consoled Sammy.

Sammy could hardly breathe. She slept with us, and when Muffin heard her panting, she would jump up on the bed and begin to lick her. Perhaps this was her way of trying to make Sammy feel better. This hopelessness went on for a couple of more weeks before we decided that we had to make the decision to put Sammy to sleep forever. It was inevitable; we couldn't be cruel to our little animal any longer.

Morning came too quickly that day. Glenn and I said goodbye to Sammy. Her small eyes were clouded, and she could hardly keep them open. We bent down and kissed her, and in all her weakness, she managed to give us both a lick. Dave picked her up and took her outside.

She wiggled to get down from Dave's arms. Sammy wanted one last chance to chase the squirrels that had taken over her neighbourhood. She made a valiant effort. When Dave picked her up, ever so gently, the squirrels stopped on the top of the fence and looked at her as if saying goodbye. It was very sad. The last time Glenn and I saw Sammy was in Dave's arms as he pulled out of the driveway. I had Muffin in my arms.

When Dave arrived at the veterinarian's office, Dr. Gordon was waiting for them. Dave held Sammy as the needle was given. She simply sighed, closed her tired little eyes, and then lay very content. Both the vet and Dave were weeping. Samantha had put up such a brave and courageous fight, but now it was finally, peacefully over. She died November 2 at the age of twelve, or eighty-four in human years.

Sammy was cremated and her ashes are now in a box, in our cupboard at home. We decided not to bury her alone.

Our theory is that Sammy developed cancer because of the insecticide used to kill the weeds on our lawn. We tried not to let her go outside until the lawn dried, but sometimes her bladder couldn't wait. When she'd come back into the house, her paws were always green, and if we didn't get to her first, she would lick them clean. Dave and I feel so guilty. It didn't have to happen.

Muffin became our pride and joy and wrapped both Dave and me around her little paw. She barked and we jumped. For nearly twelve years, she was our protector, our comforter, our playmate, our alarm clock, our child, our best friend.

It's silly to think you can hear silence, but this is what we hear. We'll listen for the sound of her kisses, the sound of her barking on Halloween night as she tried to lure the children indoors so she could steal their treats. We'll listen for the sound of the cushions tossed from the sofa as she snuggled her teddy bear. We'll listen to the sound of her glee when her leash was picked up. We'll listen while she sat quietly waiting for the squirrels to taunt her. We'll listen for that wee little growl she made when a piece of bread, with real butter, was offered. And we'll listen for that contented sigh as she snuggled into bed under our duvet, with only two small eyes peeking through. For how could we possibly have known that our beloved Maltese dog, Muffin, would be snatched up into the jaws of an attacker and killed?

It's been said that dogs offer unconditional love, but what is unconditional love and what are the conditions that produce and nurture it? Do people have stronger feelings for their animals than they do for other humans? It's hard to understand sometimes. But when the threat is to a dog, the resulting publicity is amazing. When Muffin died, we were astonished at the outpouring of sympathy we received.

A dog's love is very focused, as well as passionate, often unmeditated, and always reciprocated. A human's love is harder to explain. Our love is sometimes taken for granted. It's there, but often not expressed enough to our children, to the people we love. It's just easier to show love to a dog. It also brings out the best in us.

Muffin was born on August 7, 1989, in Chesapeake, Virginia. Two months later, the three of us travelled for a luxury weekend at the Washington Hilton in Washington D.C., a birthday gift to Dave from our son, Alan. Muffin was comfortably zipped in Dave's green windbreaker as we entered the hotel.

We registered and sneaked Muffin in past the concierge. We anticipated our two-month old would snooze in our room when we left for the evening. However, Muffin had other plans. We dined on take-out Kentucky Fried Chicken.

Later that evening we hustled off to the hotel bar with Muffin securely tucked into Dave's windbreaker again. We sat down, hoping and praying she wouldn't appear and show her furry face. Unfortunately for us, the bartender spied the black button eyes. "Sorry, folks," he said, "no dogs allowed. You'll have to leave."

"Dog? This isn't a dog." Dave replied as he retrieved Muffin from her hiding spot. "Look, she's so little," he crooned. "She won't bite. She's just a teddy bear."

The bartender, however, wasn't buying it, and with a shake of his head, we carried our nightcap and our "teddy bear" back to our room and climbed into bed. Muffin snored until morning.

The following day we went to Arlington Cemetery. A sign on the bus read "No animals." I have a habit of ignoring signs, so we hopped aboard. Surely no one would notice two small black eyes. The driver gave us a wink. "My lips are sealed," he said with a smile.

Muffin was allowed to breathe and poked her head through Dave's windbreaker. There was no barking at John F. Kennedy's gravesite. Muffin knew better.

We transferred to North Bay in 1990 and Muffin, now a year old, weighed seven pounds. Her coat was long, silky, and pure white in colour. It hung evenly down each side from a parting that extended along the centre of her back from her nose to the root of her tail.

Muffin's personality belied her fine looks. She was first and foremost a guard dog and inspected everyone who came to her front door, ready at all times to protect her mistress and master. We dubbed Muffin, "our military protector."

And, of course, Muffin did not eat dog food. She loved steak and pasta—flank steak and elbow macaroni were her favourites—and these two dishes became known in our neighbourhood as a "Muffie dinner."

Muffin was simply a spoiled dog. Well, maybe not just a dog. Everyone who knew her said she thought she was a person.

My friend Sheila would say, "When I die and am reincarnated, I want to come back as a dog. Dave's dog!"

February 20, 2001—that fateful day—will be forever engraved in our memory. The sun was brilliant in the clear blue sky, and the warm temperature hinted that spring was on its way. People, weary from the cold and fed up with the winter's heavy snowfall, headed outdoors to feel the sunshine's warmth. Mothers strolled with their children on the snowy paths and even lawn chairs appeared on some balconies and porches.

At 11:30 a.m., Dave wrestled with Muffin to get her coat on. She wore a doggie LaParka, fashioned from fabric samples collected from my boutique (LaParkas are unique coats created for women by the Canadian designer Linda Lundstrom). And, oh, what a coat it was! Made of soft wool, it had a patchwork pattern of dusty rose, azure blue, lavender, and dove grey with a dusty-rose synthetic fur collar. All that showed above the fabric was a furry white head, black nose, drooping ears, inquisitive eyes, short straight legs, and the graceful well-feathered tail that curled over her back.

What a picture Muffin portrayed that day. Dave had the camera, as he wanted to capture this charming look. Plus, Muffin loved to have her picture taken. She would pose and look straight into the lens. However, much to our annoyance, we had no film.

Muffin had a daily routine before her walk. She would lie on the floor, munch on her bone, and play with her leash. She did this for about ten minutes or until she became too warm wearing her wool coat. Dave waited patiently. Finally when she was ready, she'd look up at Dave and bark.

"Okay, it's time now. Let's go to the beach." And off they went, man and his faithful companion.

Sunset Beach was Muffin's favourite stomping ground during spring and summer, but in winter, she preferred Champlain Park. There was more to do there, more places to explore. She and Dave would cross the frozen lake and walk through the bush on the opposite side. Rabbit trails were Muffin's favourite sniffing ground.

Champlain Park was a bit further up the road from Sunset Beach, but on this day, with the sun shining and all, Dave decided to give Muffin a treat. He got such pleasure from watching her inhale those scents, her nose going fifty miles an hour. Even in her dreams at night, she whiffled little noises. Perhaps at imaginary rabbits?

Dave pulled into the parking lot, and he and Muffin stepped from the car. Dave then put on her leash and they headed for the frozen lake. As they made their way along the trail, Dave heard a car engine. He looked behind and saw a woman get out of a small car, accompanied by three huge dogs. Dave wondered just how the woman had room to drive. The dogs were not leashed and he noticed that one of them broke away from the pack to race through the parking lot. He cringed a little, but continued along the trail.

Muffin was having a ball. She hopped over the snow banks, exploring and sniffing both sides of the trail. Her small nose resembled a marshmallow it was so filled up with snow. Suddenly Dave heard a noise. It sounded as if someone was running through the bush, snapping branches from the trees. When he looked up, he couldn't believe what he saw. At first he thought it was a wolf, as he had never seen a dog so big. With enormous teeth bared, the shepherd made a deep, angry snarl.

Immediately Dave picked Muffin up in his arms and cradled her to his chest. A non-aggressive dog would have stopped at this point, but obviously Dave was no threat to him. He charged Dave, knocking him to the ground. Dave is six-foot-three and weighs 210 pounds, yet he fell to the ground like a puppet. And, as hard as he tried, he couldn't hang on to Muffin. She flew from his grasp, looking at Dave, bewildered. She had that ever-trusting gaze in her eyes.

Muffin hadn't yet hit the ground when she was snatched up into the jaws of this crazed animal. She dangled from his mouth, suspended in the air, and he shook her like a rag doll. Muffin managed to nip the attacking dog's nose. The shepherd killed her instantly by sinking his teeth into her spleen. Dave stood by horrified. He could not help her. He could not help his poor defenceless Muffin.

The shepherd would not release Muffin. Blood splattered everywhere as his teeth destroyed her little body. Her pastel coat was covered with her blood. Dave shouted, "Let her go, let her go!" and kicked him. He pounded the shepherd's head with his fists, but he still wouldn't let her go. Although Dave was now physically and mentally exhausted, somehow he found the energy to pry open the strong, powerful, and bloody jaws of this predator. Muffin finally fell to the ground.

Dave, his strength now zapped, fell to his knees. He grabbed Muffin and put her behind him, but the shepherd would not go away. He wasn't finished with Muffin and he was determined to attack again. His teeth tore at Dave's hands, then ripped into his heavy parka. Dave could hardly defend himself. But, little did this predator know that my husband was a military man, and there was no way, come hell or high water, that an animal was going to outwit him. This crazed predator would no longer do a dishonour to his beloved pet. Dave was willing to die, to defend his pet.

Finally, Dave saw the owner. She was running down the hill screaming, "Oh, my God, oh, my God." She was horrified. Two other shepherds were by her side, also unleashed.

Dave yelled at her, "Get your dog off me, get your god-damned dog off me!" Dave didn't fear the other two shepherds charging towards him.

The owner tried to get her dog to stop. She grabbed him around the neck, she tugged at him, she kicked him, she screamed at him. Finally, the shepherd just let go. He gave up and walked away.

Dave grabbed Muffin, a limp little rag in his hands, and ran. He put her on the front seat of the car and raced out of the parking lot, his tires slipping on the packed snow. He talked to Muffin as he sped down the highway.

"Hang on little girl, you're going to be okay. Hang on. Please hang on."

Dave was certain he could see Muffin's eyes blink. Hope battled with despair as he travelled the five miles to the veterinary hospital, praying every second of the journey that the vet could breathe life back into her. Muffin just had to be saved.

However, there was nothing the vet or anyone else could do.

How was Dave going to fill the gaping hole in his heart?

Do animals have souls like ours, and will they be with us in an afterlife? Dave wasn't prepared for the quickness of Muffin's death. He would have loved to have had a minute or two before she died. To say one more goodbye. To apologize for bringing her to her death.

It has been said that dogs do not fear death as men do. I just know Muffin didn't suffer. It was over before she could even remember smelling the scent of rabbits.

The dogs in our lives, the dogs we come to love and who love us in return, offer more than consolation, companionship, and fidelity. They offer comedy, irony, wit, and a wealth of anecdotes—the shaggy-dog stories and stupid pet tricks that are the commonplace pleasures in life. They offer a model for what it means to give your heart with little thought of anything in return. Dogs act as mirrors for our own beliefs about what would constitute a truly humane society. Perhaps it's not too late for them to teach us some new tricks.

Although Muffin was not human, she brought out our humanity—sometimes in ways other people couldn't. Each day she taught us little lessons in trust and steadfast affection.

Like Sammy, Muffin was cremated, and her ashes are in a box, in our cupboard. We decided not to bury her alone, either. Muffin has touched our lives in her own special ways and she will remain forever in the warmest corners of our hearts.

There just has to be a heaven for the animal friends we love.

Future plans for Air Force life were once again upon us. Would we simply carry on with military life and retire gracefully at the age of fifty-five, the compulsory retirement age, or try something new. Dave was pushing fifty-one.*

We had a choice of two transfers—Truro, Nova Scotia, or Ottawa, Ontario. The postings were prime ones. In Truro, Dave would command the NATO Satellite Ground Terminal and in Ottawa he would be the career manager for his trade.

Meanwhile, two civilian NATO positions became available in Virginia for which Dave could apply. So, it became a toss-up. What should we do? Should we leave the sunny south and go to Truro for four years, a posting I wasn't enthusiastic about? Should we go to Ottawa and take a position where Dave would be on the road all the time? Or, should we stay put and retire in Virginia?

The NATO jobs tempted Dave. He was confident he would get one of them. His current position would not be refilled by a military person but would be categorized as NATO Civilian. Salary, an important element, could not be overlooked.

We decided to retire from the Canadian Armed Forces and stay put in Virginia.

After a career that had lasted thirty-one years, from October 1958 to April 1989, Dave was to enter the next phase of his life and the dress code would not be Air Force blues.

How many retirement parties have we attended over the years? I can't begin to count. And yes, they were all boring! The traditional roast beef dinner with apple pie and ice cream for dessert made me feel archaic. I would have preferred to munch on tacos or hamburgers or something new in the culinary world. As a retiree, I would want to feel young again. And the finale to a retirement evening always got to me. A handshake for a job well done. The prize? A gold wristwatch. Is that all there is after thirty-some years?

Dave's farewell on April 9, 1989, overcame my skepticism. Alexander's on the Bay, an exclusive restaurant in Virginia Beach, was the scene for Dave's retirement party. More

---

* It has since been recommended that the military adjust their retirement age from age fifty-five to sixty.

than 200 people attended, both military and civilian personnel. I was presented with a gorgeous bouquet of red roses, with too many flowers to count. A bagpiper led Dave and me to the reception area and to our guests. Those who organized our party knew we hailed from the East Coast of Canada where bagpipes were as commonplace as guitars in Nashville. We both felt very special and were taken aback at the presence of so many people.

Crowded into this room were Navy, Army, Air Force, Marine, and civilian personnel from the U.S., Canada, Britain, Portugal, and Belgium. The commander of ROCLANT (Regional Operations Center Atlantic), Captain Hagan, was master of ceremonies. It was an honour to have a high-ranking official of the U.S. Navy take on this responsibility and then to speak so highly of Dave. He had the room in stitches recalling times he was in Dave's company on various trips throughout Europe and Canada. The stories he told confirmed my suspicions of Dave being a practical joker at work.

On a more serious note, he spoke of Dave's involvement at ROCLANT HQ and his no-nonsense approach at all the commander's conferences overseas and at home. He also mentioned that, although Dave had been offered his commission many times during his career, he remained loyal to the rank of a non-commissioned officer and had climbed to the top of that ladder. Dave retired as chief warrant officer.

During Dave's tour in Virginia and his travels to Belgium, England, Portugal, and Iceland, he made friends with many people from NATO countries. Numerous messages affirmed the high esteem in which his colleagues regarded him. He was the personification of an airman. I believe Dave's head began to swell when these telegrams were read.

In every one of the good wishes, Dave's stogie was mentioned. So, I suppose Dave won't only be remembered for his good looks and military bearing, but also for his presence in a room clenching that everlasting, stinky cigar in the corner of his mouth. To this day when I mention the perils of smoking, Dave reminds me that George Burns lived to be ninety-nine, drank five or six martinis, and smoked fifteen cigars each and every day. Need he say more?

As I listened to the many stories being told about Dave and watched his colleagues laughing and clapping, I was filled with a sense of pride for a husband and father who was not only loved and revered by his family, but by his peers as well.

How many times have we attended a funeral and listened to the eulogy? Why people wait until the end of one's life to say something nice about him or her has always eluded me.

So, after this spectacular day, Dave retired his uniform, boots, and Air Force wedge.

For the remainder of that summer, Dave played golf and lazed around on his boat in the Chesapeake Bay. I continued to slave away at R. J. Reynolds.

It's hard to imagine that retirement in itself can become a career. I'm sure I would have reservations after thirty-one years.

But Dave didn't miss his wedgie.

During the last year we spent in Virginia we had the opportunity to reflect on our future. Unfortunately for NATO, Dave was not selected for the NATO job. However, in government postings, politics play an important part in a selection procedure. The position was awarded to a young British soldier with half of Dave's knowledge and experience. Interestingly, the selection committee comprised four British civilian and military personnel, one U.S. commander, and one Canadian officer. Need I say more?

All of our friends were totally flabbergasted that Dave wasn't chosen for the exact same position he had vacated only a few months before and a position he had held for more than five years.

News of this rejection came as a great shock and disappointment, but because Dave had retired and was no longer an employee of NATO, the grievance papers he filed could not be admitted. However, he couldn't let this unfairness go by without comment, and in a brief accounting he wrote:

> I feel I have been misjudged as a Chief Warrant Officer in the Canadian Forces. My qualifications and intelligence for the position of Chief Technician TMSO have been made a mockery of. You have informed me that because I am no longer a member of NATO a grievance procedure will not be accepted. In my opinion I have been discriminated against, not only for my qualifications and experience in the electronics field, but for my nationality and quite possibly, in this case, my age. I would not wish to revel in the thought that the selection process and decision had been influenced by individual personal factors.

We learned later that Dave could have grieved this decision despite what the committee told him. We also discovered that nationality played a key role in the selection process; the British committee had been prejudiced. A personality conflict had developed between Dave and another committee member. Did that make us feel any better?

It's ironic that a month later another position with NATO became available, and this time, one for which I qualified. I had the perfect qualifications for a job at Williamsburg, Virginia.

When a NATO position surfaces for civilian personnel, the job description is listed throughout the various administrative offices of the NATO countries. Anyone working with NATO may apply and, if qualified, may have an edge over a civilian applicant. I was the civilian applicant. This particular job in Williamsburg, one of the most picturesque towns in the south, was definitely attractive for people working outside the U.S.

A selection process began before anyone was contacted for the interview. I was chosen along with three other candidates: a woman from Brussels who already worked at NATO HQ, another from Birmingham, Alabama, and a gentleman from London. We were placed in a room together to await our interviews.

We made friendly chatter, and I was baffled as to how these people were selected for an interview in the first place. From what they told me, I gathered that none of them had experience in the secretarial field. It appeared they applied for any job that became available in NATO, whether it was secretarial, housekeeper, nanny, interpreter, or maintenance worker.

The young girl from Brussels could barely speak English, and it was obvious that she desperately wanted to live in America. The girl from Alabama worked as a cashier in the commissary at a military base in Birmingham. The gentleman from London, a former aide to a British general, now worked in a church in England.

In my estimation I had no competition.

More confident than ever now, my heart rate steadied. Power dressed from head to toe in a business suit of royal blue silk, white blouse and matching accessories, I entered the interview room with an assured air. I took my seat at the end of a long table, around which were six men and two women, many of whom I recognized. Three of them had sat on the selection committee that intentionally discounted my husband's skill and knowledge when he applied for the job he had mastered for five years. My good feeling began to sink.

It came as no surprise that the panel appeared uncomfortable and hesitant to interview me. By this time the committee had already received Dave's reaction to its decision. Initially, I don't think they knew that Dave was my husband, but during the interview they made the connection. Some of the questions posed were virtually unrelated to my experience, and I was equally sure they were unrelated to the job itself.

Stop beating around the bush, you bunch of idiots. If you think you can intimidate me, think again!

"If you have any reservations over my candidacy for this position," I began, "I'd appreciate hearing about it. You haven't asked me one question about my qualifications or my past job experiences."

Most of them had the grace to blush. They stammered and stuttered. They cleared their throats, but they didn't answer me. They sat there like a bunch of dim-wits. One of them mumbled something. It became obvious that another Russell was about to be rejected.

What is it with NATO positions? Do they not want to hire the best? Did this committee read the résumés from the other candidates? Did they read mine? Beats me!

Once this so-called interview was over, I reluctantly but graciously shook hands with my tormentors and closed the door. I overheard a whisper, "Do we really want to hire Dave Russell's wife?"

Can you guess? I didn't get the job. I couldn't believe it. Not once in thirty years of employment had I come off second best. I reread the job description, and sure enough, it required a focused, articulate, well-organized, experienced, and never-before-rejected secretary. The British aide won the competition. It took a great deal of fortitude for me not to put in a grievance. I knew it would be a total waste of time.

CHAPTER TWENTY-SIX

Alan brought Dave, Glenn, and me to Newfoundland twice in 1989—first for his graduation from medical school and then for his wedding.

A visible bond was prevalent among all the graduates that night. I suspect that when you work with one another day and night for six years, you become very close—helping each other study, helping each other stay awake, consoling each other in times of need, and pushing each other to reach your goals.

Alan graduated from medical school at Memorial University in St. John's on May 27, 1989. There were fifty-four graduates in all, of which twenty-three were women.

Watching the convocation I was thrilled by the pomp and circumstance. The faculty, doctors, and graduating class filed across the stage all dressed in their robes. Over that sea of robes, towering above most of his classmates, was our son. When he mounted the stage in cap and gown and accepted his scroll, I felt this moment was the jewel in my crown.

The Russell and Shetler clans came to praise our golden boy. A special pride and admiration could not be erased from our faces. His grandfather's wise words remain with Alan to this day: "Be your own person and never conform to what you don't believe in."

At the graduation dinner, the valedictorian related a story to the parents and families in attendance. The day was November 22, and she asked one of her classmates if he remembered what he was doing on that day in 1963. Practically the whole world remembered that day when President Kennedy was assassinated. The student replied, "In 1963? Sorry, I can't answer that question because I didn't come into this world until the following year."

Pointing at Alan, she said, "There he is, ladies and gentlemen, our baby, sitting right there. Take a bow, Alan." The whole room broke up with laughter.

Alan was one of the youngest men to graduate from the university as a doctor.

SHINGLES NIGHT

Class of 1989
Faculty of Medicine
25 May 1989

Memorial
University of Newfoundland

Dr. Alan Russell, St. John's, Newfoundland, May 27, 1989

The night was a mixture of joy and sadness, joy because each and every one of the students had successfully completed their studies and sadness because the group would split up and go their separate ways. Would they keep in touch?

It was a bittersweet feeling for Dave and me when Alan informed us that he and his fiancée, Patti, would marry in August. We felt it was too soon in his career to make this commitment. He had a year of internship to get through and then he had to find a job.

We prayed that Patti's diamond would keep her finger warm for at least a year, but plans were being prepared at a quick pace in Newfoundland. They would marry three months after Alan's graduation.

We raised our children and guided them towards the right path throughout the years, and because of that, Dave and I took it for granted that we might have a stake in their future. But actually, we didn't. Children live their lives the way they want to, especially when they meet a young woman and fall in love.

We were no longer the major influence in Alan's life. We now had to share his love. Alan had been gone for six years, and Dave, Glenn, and I wanted so much to recapture his presence. However, those years were not ours to bring back.

When Alan left for university at age eighteen, he left behind a family he was very close to. It was a major transition for everyone, and I could see change happening. That transformation was natural, I suppose. He was becoming a man and growing up without us. Hindsight keeps popping up throughout my story—should we have, could we have, would we have. These are three words we are accustomed to using in the English language. Perhaps we should not have taken the transfer to Virginia. Had we done this, would we have retained our closeness? Our military strategy failed us this time.

Alan didn't experience the loneliness that most kids do when they leave the roost and head for university. Alan's grandfather, aunts, and uncles were there at his beck and call. On the other hand, Glenn, who came to Virginia with us, missed out on this extended family relationship. One son reaped a certain benefit, the other, a different kind. So, what could we do? There is only one answer. You do the best you can.

Alan met Patti Hawkins at university; their lockers were side by side. They made a handsome couple, and wherever they walked, heads turned.

During the years Alan spent in Newfoundland, he became very close to the Hawkins family. I imagine that you count your blessings when your daughter brings home someone like Alan. He was well-raised, intelligent, kind, and good-looking. But the most important factor of all was that his future was assured. Now what parent wouldn't want those qualities in their child's partner? On the other hand, Patti possessed those same qualities, and we counted our blessings that Alan met her. Unfortunately, we never achieved the closeness to Patti that his future-in-laws got to have with our son. The Hawkinses assumed a surrogate parental role with Alan and practically adopted him into their family. They developed an intimate relationship with our son.

The closeness we once had was slipping through our fingers. Alan came home to Virginia at Christmas and for a short time during the summer months, but as the six years flew by, his visits became less frequent. We'd see Alan for a few weeks during the year, while Patti and her family were in close contact with him on a regular basis. We missed him so much.

Blood pressure checks, ear checks, throat checks, and any other checks Alan practised throughout his medical studies would have thrilled me to no end had I been a participant. I would be the perfect guinea pig. But I wasn't there. I couldn't comfort him during his down times nor praise him for his accomplishments.

Missed out? I can't think of a more appropriate expression. But, that's life.

So, how would I feel about my baby being cared for by someone else? "If there is anyone here who has a reason why this couple should not be joined together in holy matrimony, please speak up." Would I be silent?

After I accepted the reality of a wedding in August, I was determined to be helpful in any way I could. A designer in St. John's created the pattern for Patti's wedding gown and her bridesmaids' dresses, but because she couldn't find a suitable fabric for the bridesmaids' dresses, Patti asked me to try and find something appropriate in Virginia Beach. She was very specific. It had to be pink cotton with a pastel floral design. My friend Jan and I hunted high and low across the state. Swatches were mailed to Newfoundland. Finally, one swatch was a "go." I shipped the fabric. The dresses were underway, but the designer needed one more bolt of material. Luckily, the fabric shop had one left and had it wrapped when I arrived to pick it up. We brought the bolt with us when we drove to Newfoundland for Alan's graduation, but talk about surprise when we opened the package. It was the same fabric, but a different colour. The clerk wrapped up the wrong material! What a way to establish a relationship with my future daughter-in-law. Panic City that day! I phoned Jan and told her of the dilemma, and being the good friend that she is, guaranteed the problem would be solved. And it was.

When Alan informed Patti's parents that his dad would wear his Air Force dress kit and not the traditional tuxedo the rest of the wedding party would be dressed in, they were apprehensive. Unfamiliar with the military, we speculated that the Hawkins family might be concerned that Dave would wear his blue military uniform with perhaps a rifle slung over his shoulder. Discreetly he was asked to please, please rent the traditional garb. Dave was proud of a uniform that he had worn while helping to make our country safe and free, and he would wear it for this special occasion. He would not hear any ifs, ands, or buts.

When we arrived at the church those who had doubted stood in awe. The dress kit is a military tuxedo in navy serge, complete with silk cummerbund. He was a hit. Although Alan looked more handsome than I ever remembered, his dad outranked him.

On August 18, 1989, the bridesmaids, to my great relief, led the wedding party dressed in matching pink pastel. Patti and her father walked slowly down the aisle of Cochrane United Church in St. John's, her beauty captivating everyone there. Alan, his eyes shining, stood next to Glenn, his best man. How handsome they both looked. I was filled with pride for my two sons. Where had time gone? It seemed like yesterday when these two mischievous brothers frolicked together.

Mr. Russell took his seat in the church and beamed with pride when his grandson walked to the front. Alan was the first grandchild to become a doctor and the first to be married. He affectionately referred to Patti as his little beauty. He was more than pleased with the union.

When husband and wife signed the register they stood in a direct path of light that shone through stained-glass windows. The light sparkled from the necklace Patti wore, creating a halo around her. I sat mesmerized. Was this a sign that the marriage was made in heaven? I hoped so.

Three people there in spirit were Alan's two grandmothers and his grandfather Shetler. My mother had a saying: "I'll be there with bells on." And that clear August day, I'm positive I heard a tinkling. And when I looked over at Mr. Russell, I sensed he was not alone.

CHAPTER TWENTY-SEVEN

Until we moved to Virginia Beach, I eagerly looked forward to relocating every few years. The anticipation of living somewhere new and the research into a community always gave me a shiver of excitement. But not this time! My outlook had changed. I didn't want to leave Virginia.

The Canadian Forces asked that Dave resume his military career. Although he had retired from the regular force in Virginia, he was now offered a position with the Air Force Reserves in North Bay. The Canadian Forces didn't want to lose this man just yet, and he had five years to go before the compulsory retirement age of fifty-five. This extension would be a great opportunity for him to continue with his career and in a place where he would be content.

What a dilemma! I didn't want to leave Virginia and move back to North Bay. I was content to stay put. I had found my paradise. But I had to be realistic. Unless Dave worked and earned U.S. dollars, the exchange rate on his pension would kill us. It seemed foolish to fritter away all that money. Also, the U.S. medical care system didn't compare with the Canadian one, and in the event of an illness, the cost would be prohibitive. We really had no choice but to return to Canada.

Well, it all began in North Bay, and yes, it still sounded cold. How would I spend the long winters? Someone told me my blood thinned in the hot weather and now I might freeze to death.

I hated snowmobiles, ice fishing, and any other activity associated with snow. Maybe I'd sit by the fireplace and drink wine all winter long. That sounded like a good plan. But I'd probably tire of that. I was too young in spirit to retire.

I was forty-nine years old and too old to start a career in a new environment. Where did I hear those words before? Overqualified would not be the excuse this time. I'd become my own boss.

However, shortly before we moved back to North Bay, we received a phone call that Dave's father had died in Newfoundland. We were devastated. When I married Dave at the tender age of twenty I needed a father, so I adopted my husband's. He was much like my own in terms of creativity and intelligence. My father was in the newspaper business and so was Mr. Russell. My father was an avid reader, as was Mr. Russell. And my father was a loving, caring, witty and compassionate man, as was Mr. Russell.

I never had the pleasure of sharing my father's memories, nor the delight of having him take part in life's major events. Mr. Russell filled that void for me over the thirty years I knew him. I believe he regarded me as much a daughter as his own. He confided in me and I always looked to him for sound advice. He called me Jennie.

David Russell was the patriarch of the Russell clan, revered by his family and friends. Everyone who came to Bay Roberts always dropped by D. B. Russell Printing to chat and to catch up on the happenings in the area. He was the community's historian.

Although Mr. Russell was knowledgeable about almost everything, Hollywood's news, however, was not top priority. He may have heard of John Wayne and Gary Cooper, but his expertise and knowledge on who's who in the movies was practically non-existent.

Take the time the movie based on Farley Mowat's book, *A Whale for the Killing*, was being produced in St. John's, and Mr. Russell unabashedly treated two movie stars to his culinary skills and his historical knowledge. The cast and crew ate every day at a restaurant owned by Dave's sister-in-law. A classic historic home in the heart of the old city had been restored and converted into a gourmet restaurant, the first of its kind in St. John's. The specialty of the day was always a fresh catch from a local fisherman and handpicked at the dock each morning.

Dave's brother, Wilson, mentioned to the cast one day that his father was a renowned cook and reputed expert in the preparation of corned beef and cabbage, peas pudding, and blueberry duff. But his culinary skills had been perfected in the cooking of seal flippers—a Newfoundland must on any menu. The stars were intrigued and begged for a down-home invitation. Peter Strauss and Richard Widmark received an invitation for Sunday dinner in Bay Roberts.

They arrived around noon on Sunday. Within a short time, it became apparent that no two movie stars had ever been treated so normally and with so little fuss. Mr. Russell wasn't quite up to scratch on the Hollywood scene since John Wayne died, and he had never heard of the two actors he entertained. But that remained his secret.

The two men shared a day and evening they'll always remember. They were mesmerized over some of the tales the Bay Roberts historian related and sat around the dining room table until well past midnight. Peter and Richard were ecstatic about their seal flippers, but what they enjoyed most of all was the simplicity and sincerity of this wonderfully intelligent man. Mr. Russell was invited to be their guest in Hollywood anytime he chose.

Dave and I phoned the next day, unaware of this dinner party. "You had who there?" I asked. "Did you say Peter Strauss, the movie star? He had dinner at your house. Oh, my God, he's my favourite! Please, please, whatever you do, don't wash the glass he drank from. Save it for me."

Who will believe this? Why wasn't someone there with a camera? Where was the *National Enquirer*?

Glenn and I did not attend Mr. Russell's funeral. However, we were not upset. We both hated to say goodbye.

Time had stopped. A loving father and grandfather was now but a memory.

CHAPTER TWENTY-EIGHT

Leather 'N Silk Boutique—a dream come true!

I have told many during the past few years that when all of this is over and I retire, I want a monument erected showing a happy face on a price tag with the inscription, "No thanks, just looking!"

Leather 'N Silk Boutique, North Bay, Ontario, September 1990–March 2002

On the other hand, I'll probably be remembered as that lady with the red hair and designer clothing who checked into the psychiatric hospital—frequently.

In August 1990, the movers arrived in Virginia Beach and found their way to our home, much to my chagrin. Sadly, we left behind Glenn, my brother Pat, our friends, the golf courses, our favourite restaurants and department stores, and the wonderfully warm weather. Lake Nipissing would have to substitute for the Atlantic Ocean.

Dave was happy to be back at work. Retirement wasn't what he had imagined it to be at fifty. He missed the Canadian Armed Forces. Now, he could serve six more years with the Air Force Reserves, enjoy the same rank, and wear the same uniform.

I opened Leather 'N Silk Boutique on September 13, 1990 (luckily the thirteenth fell on a Thursday). Thus began the vocation of a true entrepreneur. I hoped and prayed that this newfound venture would make us rich and famous.

While you'd think that a name like Leather 'N Silk Boutique would tell people exactly what you sold, you'd be surprised. Sometimes people simply don't think. Boutique to me indicates a designer shop that sells fashionable merchandise. So, if I walked past a storefront with a sign that said Leather 'N Silk Boutique, I would say, "What a unique name. I bet they have some special leather and silk merchandise in there. I must pop in."

I'd been in business for more than a decade, and continued to receive questionable phone calls. "Do you sell edible underwear? Do you sell crotchless panties? Do you sell motorcycle jackets with lots and lots of zippers? Do you sell feathers?"

"Feathers? What kind of feathers?"

"Ostrich!"

After one particularly frustrating day, I came home, put my aching feet up, and ordered my military man to fetch me a glass of white wine. "Dave, should I change the name of the store? How about, 'No thanks! Just looking!'"

Dave relished being back in the military. He loved the life. In retrospect I feel guilty that I didn't support him more in Virginia Beach. I knew he wanted to take the job in Truro. He said it would have been the job of a lifetime, but I didn't listen. I didn't want to go back to Nova Scotia and live in a small community. I simply didn't want to leave Virginia Beach. Pure and simple selfishness! Never in a million years had I thought Dave's civilian life wouldn't have taken place. I had counted on him winning the NATO job.

What if? What if? Story of my life!

CHAPTER TWENTY-NINE

October 12, 1994. Dave had no choice this time. Mandatory retirement age for the Canadian Forces is fifty-five years, and in Dave's case, an exception had been made and he received a one-year extension.

Our rambles with the Canadian Forces had the ingredients for a pot of military stew. I had revelled in the constant moving around, making new friends, working at different jobs, and getting into and out of scrapes. I suppose I was a magnet for trouble, but not everything was a roller coaster of laughter.

Being a military wife was a fun job, and many of my friends envied my nomadic lifestyle. And as a military wife, I never lacked good company. I travelled and came to know a lot of my country from the Atlantic to the Pacific, as well as the United States and Europe. Everywhere I found myself in exciting company, but to taste life is not to be confused with understanding what life is really all about.

I am struck now about how simple and calm our lives were. However, with all the uneasiness in the world today, I often think about the military wives out there. But for a gallant spirit there can never be defeat.

Where did the time go? My birth certificate is starting to send me a message. It seems I was just forty and a year later I was sixty-two. When I look in the mirror with a straight face, it doesn't appear as if I have wrinkles, but when I smile, the Grand Canyon seems to be etched across my cheeks. Even so, I can't stop smiling. I love life and I can't imagine getting up in the morning and not being able to look forward to the day. I must have a purpose. I can never retire. So if I should reap the benefits of living a long and healthy life, bigger and better things are in store for me. The closing of one door is only a challenge to open another; the death of one hope leads but to the birth of a new one.

Of course my favourite person is Dave. We still like to eat escargots and drink wine. Dave continues to enjoy his stogie.

What is my greatest hope and fear for the future? Well, my greatest hope is that my grandchildren continue to live in a free and safe world and that they experience love and joy as I have. What am I afraid of? Well, maybe of dying before I feel I'm ready.

Any woman who has been loved as I have been loved, and who also has loved as I have loved, has experienced life in its fullness. I have known the joy of being raised by devoted parents, and I have known the joy of rearing loving children. I feel my life has been blessed.

A woman's life can be a succession of lives each revolving around some experience, emotion, or joy. I have had a full share, and at this moment the paths of my life have led me to contentment.

But I cannot imagine life without my husband! Spring, summer, fall, or winter! If I ever lost him, I don't believe I could ever make another life for myself. Dave and I have a deep love for each other, but a love we don't show openly. It's just there, and four decades together proves it. He is still my best friend, lover, and precious partner. We're each other's support in everything we do, and we share a great rapport whether it's social, personal, or business. We are a team. How many people can say they can look someone straight in the eye and know exactly what the other is thinking? That's Dave and me, and we're still going strong.

More than four decades have passed since Glenn was born that hot, humid day in July 1962 at the General Hospital in Sydney, Nova Scotia. He resides in Virginia, still a bachelor. Perhaps he should return to his hometown on Cape Breton Island to find his true love. His father did! Glenn remains a devoted and loyal son and has developed a wit, much like his two grandfathers. We visit him on a regular basis.

Dave and I have three adorable granddaughters. Lauren was born on March 29, 1995, Natalie on June 5, 1996, and Elise on April 12, 2001. Alan and Patti reside in Leamington, Ontario, where Alan practises medicine, participates in triathlons, and shares in the raising of three daughters. Their days are extremely busy entertaining three children. Sometimes nights are sleepless.

Because Dave and I are long-distance grandparents, lots of pictures keep us in tune with their growing-up years. A picture is worth a thousand words.

But let's face it, parents can only write so many letters, take so many pictures, and afford so many phone calls. Dave and I thought that we could resolve the situation by moving closer. However our relocation was never encouraged.

How we would have loved to see our granddaughters get their first tooth, take their first step, and say their first word, or see them with chocolate pudding smeared on their little faces.

Throughout time, parents and children have been separated because of career choices. Many grandchildren grow up without grandparents living next door. But because of this, our granddaughters will miss out on that special love only grandparents can give. A grandparent's love is the most precious gift we can bestow.

Children believe that grandparents know everything, and the fact is, grandparents know things that parents may have forgotten. They know all the old nursery rhymes, fairytales, superstitions, and proverbs. They keep the whole family connected. How sad it must be for children to grow up and not know their grandparents.

It has been said that mothers shape most women's lives like no one else, but I also believe they shape most men's lives as well. Who was it that said, "Behind every successful man stands a woman"? I believe that woman is the mother.

Whether you model your choice on her path or cringe at the very thought, your mother is your North Star, and while she lights your way, she also links you to the past—bedtime books, heirloom china, and in my case, the story of a military wife and mother.

There are moments when we're all drawn to reminiscing about yesteryears and all that they mean. To share a small corner of my life with you was a way to recapture memories that were slipping away all too quickly.

I believe the most important legacy a person like me can give future generations is her memories. I also believe that the most appreciated gift a mature person can present to her friends and relatives is a written record of the most interesting events of her life.

My memories are my personal gifts. I don't want to be just a name and date on a family tree. I want to be known as the person I am. I want my grandchildren to know what transpired in their parents' lives and feel the unique events that shaped theirs.

From the earliest days of warring tribes, the women of warriors were viewed as chattels who followed their men from camp to camp. They gathered food, raised children, and remained loyal. Basically, these women performed sexual and unpaid domestic services for the men. They had no recognized status in military camps, and when the commander decided that their presence was counterproductive, they were evicted.

Over the years, some things have changed. Most military wives have come to be a part of the makeup of the military structure. During recent wars, military wives were welcomed into the predominately male workforce to fill vacancies caused by the war. When the soldiers returned, however, the women were sent back to their kitchen and child-rearing duties. Fortunately, this perception has since changed and rules have relaxed.

After reviewing my years as a military wife and despite the formalized structure of the military, I was able to have a normal, civilian-type life working and connecting with people in the communities where I lived. I was able to direct my own life, simply because I refused to conform. I lived my life the way I wanted to, but was able to carry on as a valued partner in my husband's career while he contributed to keeping the world safe for democracy.

My nonconformity did not prevent my husband's advancement through the ranks to become a chief warrant officer. In fact, that was a rank we achieved together.

If I had it to do over again, would I change anything? Would I marry the military or the man?

I'd marry both again, and love it more.

ABOUT THE AUTHOR

Jeanette Russell was born in Halifax and raised on beautiful Cape Breton Island. In 1962 at RCAF Station Sydney, she married David Russell from Newfoundland. Jeanette has said that she has had to pinch herself many times to convince herself that the opportunities she and her family had to travel the world were real. And, everything was made possible by the largesse of the Canadian Forces.

Jeanette and Dave still travel the world, visiting family and keeping in touch with military and civilian friends they made during their career.

Photo Album

Dave and me, 2003

Alan and Patti, 2003

Dave's 65th Birthday,
October 12th, 2003

Dave and me with our
grandchildren, Lauren, Natalie
and Elise, 2003

Glenn and me, 2003